Economic Crises and Electoral Responses in Latin America

Fabián Echegaray

UNIVERSITY PRESS OF AMERICA,® INC.
Lanham • Boulder • New York • Toronto • Oxford

University Press of America,® Inc.
4501 Forbes Boulevard
Suite 200
Lanham, Maryland 20706
UPA Acquisitions Department (301) 459-3366

PO Box 317
Oxford
OX2 9RU, UK

Printed in the United States of America
British Library Cataloging in Publication Information Available

Library of Congress Control Number: 2005931621
ISBN 0-7618-3274-2 (paperback : alk. ppr.)

∞™ The paper used in this publication meets the minimum requirements of American National Standard for Information Sciences—Permanence of Paper for Printed Library Materials, ANSI Z39.48—1992

To my mother

Contents

List of Tables

Preface

Throughout the last decades, explanations centered in the pivotal role of economic calculations have exerted a tremendous influence in the way social scientists think and advise about democratic governance. Critical issues such as oscillations in political support, the dynamics of government accountability, and the nature of citizens' behavior in the public sphere have been understood mainly as reactions to financial conditions or perceptions about material gains and losses. Indeed, for all the intrinsic complexity of human behavior in the realm of politics, the simplification of the forces shaping how millions of voters across time and nations feel and decide look like a small heaven.

Among those many scholars devoted to the understanding of the sudden emergence and maintenance of democratic experiences in Latin America, the parsimony and intuitiveness of economic voting models constituted not only an elegant argument but also a wonderful intellectual ally in dealing with all the particulars and perplexities that surround events in the region. Moreover, the emphasis on an economic rationality, even if focused on processes of decision of individuals, resulted in a moderate discontinuity with traditional narratives of Latin American politics based on the persuasions of personalities, the actions and omissions of interest groups, or the State.

Ironically though, fascination may have rapidly turned into puzzlement with every instance that arguments of economic voting were transported to some electoral experiences of the region. Let me illustrate this point better. In May 1989, Argentineans were electing a president for the second time. The relevance of such an event was out of question since it symbolized a critical step forward to democracy consolidation, away from the days of authoritarianism. The election took place under the worst possible scenario: four months of uninterrupted hyperinflation; a plummeting economy with negative growth rates; and almost half of the population sliding into poverty. Everything would have suggested that the incumbent party was bound not just to lose the election, but to do it miserably. In actuality, the Radical Party was defeated but its ability to retain four out of every ten valid votes puzzles anyone who assumes that citizens go to the polls to vote for their pocketbooks and act as a ruthless "god of vengeance" in front of financial adversity.

A few months later, Brazil also held presidential elections. Although inflation had been running continuously high, the situation was far from replicating the abrupt economic collapse and lack of governance in Argentina. Nonetheless, Brazilians went to the polls and not only threw the "ins" out, but did it angrily: only five percent of the valid votes went to the forces of the ruling coalition. Naturally, the economy was key in both occasions; yet what was it that caused such a difference compared to what economic voting models would have predicted? What else was influencing Argentinean and Brazilian voters that kept the former from humiliating the "ins" and that motivated the latter to punish them so mercilessly?

These questions contain the puzzle that inspired this book. Naturally, they unfold a much larger and ambitious sequence of interrogation, and of crucial resonance to a region characterized by economic instability and material discontent. When and how does political support rest on economic success? How economically intensive is voters' rationality at the polls? Do voters hold leaders accountable for material benefits as much as for symbolic payoffs? Do voters seek for extra-economic forms of representation?

My intention is to provide some possible answers to these questions by looking at the individual and collective behavioral patterns of Latin Americans when they go to the polls. Following this strategy are details about the factors which nurture mass political decisions in highly volatile and uncertain contexts, such as those featuring transitions from dictatorship to democracy. Moreover, this shall also offer a window to explore the way citizens-in-the-making articulate their condition as voters, the standards through which they reason before making a political choice, and the nature (even if tacit) of their embedded notion of political representation and government accountability.

Fabián Echegaray
Florianópolis, SC
March 19, 2005

Acknowledgments

This book is founded on a large scale of empirical study. Such an enterprise took many years and resulted from the cooperation and assistance of many people. The years were long and have now becomc the past, but the memory of the intense involvement with so many people remains vivid, and that is what I would like to remember.

First, it is my debt of gratitude to the late Everett C. Ladd and The Roper Center for Public Opinion Research that made it possible to undertake my doctoral degree at the University of Connecticut. It was there that my first ideas for dissertation matured and evolved into the preliminary content of this study. At the Center, I benefited from exchanging ideas, receiving suggestions and criticisms, and getting support and advice from friends, colleagues and mentors who were concerned with the course and peculiarities of the democratic process taking place around the world, particularly Latin America. In addition to Everett Ladd, then the director of the Center, I would like to thank Carlos Elordi, Elizabeth Mahan, Francisco Abundis, Frederick C. Turner, Gerardo Adrogué, and Gustavo Gurrieri for their help, comments and patience when discussing findings. Other friends and colleagues outside the Center are Jorge Buendía Laredo, Julio Carrión, Mara Kolesas and William Keech, who read specific chapters and provided insightful observations.

The project was born out of informal conversations with Michael Lewis-Beck in the summer of 1994 and Karen Remmer during the winter of 1995, whose works inspired this study. The cooperation of data and insights of pollsters across all major Latin American countries made the project possible. Special thanks to Agustín Canzani, Alfredo Torres Guzmán, Ana Cristina Covarrubias, Carlos Denton, Enrique Zuleta Puceiro, Graciela Romer, Miguel Basáñez, Orjan Olsen, Polibio Córdova, and Ricardo de la Peña. Discussions with other Latin American scholars represented valuable contributions to the early incarnations of this project as well, among these I would like to remember Juan Carlos Torre of Universidad Di Tella, Federico Estévez of ITAM, Leonardo Valdés Zurita of UAM, Rachel Meneguello of CESOP/Unicamp, and Raúl Jorrat of CEDOP/UBA.

As this is a study about how people make political decisions and how continuous elections have offered that chance for citizens, I benefited from further conversations with other Latin American friends such as Marcello Baquero of UFRGS and Rodolfo Sarsfield of Instituto Mora (Mexico), before completing this book. For the final version, Eliza Marciniak edited with great care and competence.

Finally, this book exists because of the love of three people: my mother, Massumi and Kendra. In different ways, at different moments, all three shared my anxiety and my absence in the years that this work migrated from a simple idea to final book format. I could not have done it without them.

Chapter One

Introduction

"When you think economics, think elections; when you think elections, think economics." (Tufte, 1978: 65)

"The fact that economic conditions influence voters is a leading commonplace of conversation in election years. The question is: is this fact in fact a fact?" (Stigler, 1973: 160)

"[T]hose politicians or political commentators who concentrate on the president's ability to provide economic prosperity may be underestimating the dramaturgical element in politics. The public wants both bread and circuses, and it wants each equally badly." (MacKuen, 1983: 191)

The conventional wisdom that economic conditions and popular satisfaction with the economy drive people's decisions at the ballot box might have found no better test than in Latin America from the 1980s through the mid-1990s. After all, if governments are expected to gain support in good times and lose it in bad times, the regional economic crisis of the 1980s and the strong recovery in the 1990s should have provided plenty of room to evaluate both sides of that proposition.

Yet, between 1982 and 1989, as most economies in the region recorded negative growth rates and double- and triple-digit inflation, as well as a regression to the standards of living of the 1970s, about a third of the incumbent parties managed to win a plurality of votes large enough to stay in office. Between 1990 and 1995, on the other hand, as inflation was drastically cut, consumption recouped and production grew, over half of the parties-in-government ended up being voted out of office. Why did the most severe collapse of postwar Latin American economies not result in a more extended pattern of incumbent turnover? And why did electoral gratitude reveal itself only half-heartedly once prosperity arrived?

Answering such questions involves first examining the issue of voter rationality and the assumptions that underlie electoral choice. But before these can be addressed, a more fundamental question must be answered: Do elections matter? While many scholars conceive of voters as the sole king-makers of democratic politics and ballots as the effective instrument of popular control (e.g., King 1981), others contend that elections are symbolic rituals that legitimize structural inequalities and the political grip of a power elite (Ginsberg and Stone 1991). Some point out that elections do not change the fundamental structure of power in Latin America, which is dominated by business and landed elites, the Catholic Church, the military, and foreign governments (Drake and Silva 1986: 1–7; Petras and Morley 1992: Chapter 1). Others argue that elections rarely modify the presence of clientelistic networks, powerful rural and urban structures and machine-type party organizations who, ultimately, define who will rule (Özbudun 1987: 394). Likewise, as the policies of elected governments are perceived in greater consonance with the demands of elites than with the needs and wants of the masses, elections are sometimes deemed not as an instrument for the advancement of popular sovereignty but as an asset of conservative forces (Weffort 1989). Finally, some scholars dismiss elections because of the insincere nature of electoral politics, crafted mainly as "demonstration elections" (Herman and Brodhead 1984).

More obvious, empirical reasons for downplaying the role of elections in Latin America have been the regularity of fraud-ridden elections (e.g., in México til year 2000), military vetoes against unwelcome victors (e.g., in Argentina, Perú and Ecuador in the 1960s, and in Guatemala and Panamá throughout the 1970s and 1980s), and the use of elections and plebiscites by authoritarian regimes for self-legitimating purposes (e.g., in Dominican Republic, Nicaragua and Paraguay since the 1960s, Guatemala and El Salvador since the late 1970s, Chile and Uruguay in 1980). Yet it is clear that the region is characterized by a massive turnout in election after election (Nohlen 1993) and a high rate of incumbency turnover (Dix 1984), two occurrences that among advanced democracies indicate a deep-seated predisposition to participate and to hold governments accountable. As well, as Seligson and Booth (1995) point out, elections have finally become the accepted mechanism of democratic legitimation.

Despite the limitations of the electoral method and the outcomes of many Latin American elections over the past twenty-five years, it is my firm belief—and a central assumption of this work—that elections in the region do indeed matter. As Eulau and Lewis-Beck argue (1985: 3), elections "make a difference [because] at periodic intervals they set the limits or constraints within which capitalist as well as anticapitalist elites pursue their economic and political goals." Thus, the question of the determinants of electoral outcomes remains central, if only to know "how and why popular electorates respond as they do to more or less elite-managed economies," and "how and why elites in turn take account of or are responsive to whatever messages they may receive from the electorate" (Eulau and Lewis-Beck 1985: 3). What drives voters' decisions, what substantive mandate underlies electoral majorities, and how changes in the incumbents' electoral fortunes should be understood are issues crucial to the understanding of Latin American politics and society.

Presidential elections have become a central feature of Latin American politics since the early 1980s, as most countries traveled the road from authoritarianism to democracy. In contrast to the political past of the region, free and competitive contests for the highest office have come to represent the main occasion for regular collective action and selection of political authorities by citizens. The current predominance of electoral procedures to perform these functions stands in contrast to the traditional plurality of "praetorian" means such as military coups, revolutions, guerrillas activism, etc. (see Anderson 1992; Huntington 1968). Accordingly, as is the case for the group of advanced industrial democracies, Latin Americans expect to find in elections a significant form of popular input, an opportunity for demanding political accountability from elected authorities, and a crucial means of political equalization of economically unequal citizens. As Butler, Penniman and Ranner (1981: 1) state, "the electoral process lies at the heart of democratic government, and the critical difference between democratic and non-democratic regimes is to be found in whether or not they hold elections."

The general tendency to dismiss elections as significant political events has directly affected our knowledge of the voting behavior of Latin Americans. The nature of citizens' voting rationality, the impact exerted by different conditions over voters' calculations, and the determinants of political continuity in the electoral arena have received little attention. As a result, many questions have gone unanswered. For example, what are the forces that shape electoral results in Latin America? Do incumbents' electoral fortunes in the region hinge exclusively on the state of the economy and their citizens' financial satisfaction, or do they depend more on accomplishments in the political domain? Do Latin American voters look only after their own economic satisfaction, or are psycho-social considerations, such as partisan attachments, candidates' attributes, or the president's popularity, also a part of their decision process? Which are the dimensions of the economy that matter the most to the average voter: inflation, unemployment, or growth? How do economic and political factors interact in the voting decision, and how do their effects vary by social class? Does institutional development and the type of party system make a difference in how economic and non-economic forces shape the vote? Do periods of economic decline and crisis motivate voters to rely on sources of decision that are different from those on which they rely during periods of prosperity?

These questions are anything but original; for decades, students of advanced democracies in North America and Western Europe perused electoral results and voters' decisions and estimated the extent to which they were functions of economic conditions, political events, psychological tendencies or sociological forces. However, the relative novelty of electoral politics after decades of authoritarian rule and the brutality of macro-economic transformations undergone since the early 1980s initially suggest a peculiar pattern of responses for the Latin American experience with voting. Thus, a complementary question to those already stated is how does the average Latin American voter behave compared to his or her fellow citizen in the advanced democracies.

In addressing these questions, I will be directly tackling the issues of the political rationality of Latin American citizens and the bases upon which support for political continuity is built in situations of democratization—two topics that have been generally limited either to impressionistic or historical accounts of the "national character" of the region, or to single-country empirical tests of the correlates of support for democracy. It is one of my contentions that Latin American voters rely on certain decisional clues when going to the polls, and that the choice boils down to a binary decision of supporting the incumbent or voting for change. An investigation of the decisional clues that determine voter behavior is at the heart of this study. It is my firm belief that by knowing why voters systematically rely on certain determinants, we can gain deeper insight into the substance that nurtures individual decision-making in the political arena, the extent to which voters may actually become victims of politicians' manipulations of the economic environment and/or authoritarian drives in the face of public dissent, and—indirectly—the degree to which effective political support becomes contingent upon economic success.

This last questions brings us back to the main topic of this study. As the quotations opening this chapter illustrate, there exists a common assumption that it is satisfaction or dissatisfaction with the existing economic conditions that drives the citizens' decisions at the ballot box. Yet, as mentioned at the outset, Latin American reality often contradicts this theory. Approaching the complex process of voters' decision-making from a view that emphasizes the economic underpinnings of individual voting rationality does not provide a realistic response to the conundrum of electoral choice. What, then, lies at the heart of electoral choice in Latin America?

A thorough examination of data from forty-one competitive presidential elections held in Latin America between 1982 and 1995 reveals that the results of elections depend on certain key factors—both economic and political—that vary with the context and milieu in which these elections take place. The patterns that can be observed both at the macro (aggregate) and micro (individual) levels can shed light on the results of past and future elections in Latin America, as well as provide insights into elections elsewhere. Indeed, the very same peculiarities that distinguish Latin America from the group of advanced democracies—such as its profound economic crisis amidst a process of political democratization—make the investigation of Latin American elections likely to offer valuable contributions to the study of other regions undergoing somewhat similar experiences, such as Eastern Europe, Southeast Asia and Africa. In this regard, the Latin American voting experience of the 1980s and 1990s constitutes an unparalleled laboratory in which to check the extent to which, under adversarial conditions, political support builds itself upon economic or extra-economic motivations.

OVERVIEW

I begin this study by presenting common theories of electoral choice developed in the context of advanced industrial democracies. I then summarize the empirical research done to date on Latin American elections, pointing out gaps and erroneous assumptions and highlighting the tension between the emphasis on economic factors and non-economic factors. Then, in Chapter 3, I examine the assumptions that undergird the model of economic voting and the extent to which these match the available evidence of how the average Latin American voter approaches the voting decision. I challenge some of these assumptions and sketch the premises upon which a discussion of voting rationality in Latin America should be developed. I go on to survey the conditions that structure the environment of electoral choice, arguing that given cognitive limitations, ordinary citizens in Latin America rely heavily on certain decisional clues that guide their choice. In addressing this issue, I scrutinize the opportunities and circumstances that favor or diminish the effective influence of diverse sources of decisions over the individual's process of political learning and decision-making.

In Chapter 4, I emphasize the complementary nature of macro and micro perspectives and the importance of context. I then build on the preceding discussion to introduce six models of choice: affirmative voting, party voting, economic voting, democratic preference voting, political referendum voting, and candidate voting. These models are then used as the basis of analysis at both the macro and micro levels.

I begin Chapter 5 by explaining the methodology used to analyze data from forty-one competitive presidential elections held in Latin America between 1982 and 1995. Then I inspect those features of the economic sphere that are more influential in shaping the electoral outcomes, that is, whether voters react mostly to inflation, recession or unemployment, and the time-frame of these reactions, that is, whether voters behave in a myopic fashion reacting to short-term changes, or are more sensitive to long-term patterns. I also explore the impact of economic variables after controlling for the effect of non-economic factors such as party identification, candidates' attributes, government performance on democratic issues, etc. This discussion provides an initial view of the relative weight of each major model of voting and offers clues as to which variable best repre sents the argument embedded in each particular model. Finally, I introduce a variable tapping the public evaluations of presidential performance in non-economic matters to assess the relative importance of the political referendum model.

Chapter 6 is a follow-up to the previous discussion. Here I estimate the extent to which those factors modelling the vote behave differently under dissimilar contextual scenarios in terms of levels of political institutionalization, types of party systems, and macro-economic profiles. The underlying belief is that contextual differences provide dissimilar stimuli and opportunities for the familiarization of individuals with the factors shaping the vote. I contrast electoral scenario characterized by a high level of institutional development against one characterized by a poor level, one characterized by a two-party system against one with a multiparty system, and one characterized by a recent past of economic prosperity against one of economic collapse.

In Chapter 7, I shift to a level of analysis centered on individuals' behavior, focusing on survey data of voters' reactions to the economic situation for three particular presidential elections: the election in Uruguay in November 1994, the election in Perú in April 1995, and the election in Argentina in May 1995. I argue that these three scenarios reproduce on a smaller scale the variation in contextual conditions previously reviewed. The micro focus offers a closer look at the process of economic reasoning that supposedly underlies most voting decisions, thus addressing elementary questions such as how dependent voting choice is on economic promises, whether voters follow their pocketbooks or not, and whether individuals with different social backgrounds pay attention to the same economic cues. Thus, this new analytical perspective based on micro-level data complements the aggregate-level discussion by offering a window through which analyze the way individuals organize their choice at the ballot box.

Finally, in Chapter 8, I summarize the major findings of this study and discuss the lessons one might infer from the theory, data and findings presented in this work.

Chapter Two

Theories of Electoral Choice and Empirical Research on Elections in Latin America

Latin Americanists have not placed the study of electoral phenomena at the top of their agendas. Nonetheless, the questions of what moves the decisions of voters and what shapes the results of presidential elections in the region have not passed unnoticed. Hunches and rationalizations were voiced after democratic institutions were reestablished through elections.

Politicians generally attempted to appeal to the voters by emphasizing liberal values of pluralism and tolerance, invoking pocketbook concerns, raising issues of public morality, or underscoring the need for tough leadership. Such variation in the focus of elections is illustrated by president Raúl Alfonsín's call for a vote for democracy in the 1989 Argentinean elections, candidate Ernesto Zedillo's motto promising Mexicans "well-being for everyone" ("*bienestar para todos*") in 1994, candidate Fernando Collor's pledge to become the "hunter of privilege" ("*caçador de marajás*") in the public administration of Brazil, candidate Alberto Fujimori's slogan emphasizing "work, honesty and technology" in 1990s Perú, and the pleas to voters by former president Efrain Ríos Montt in Guatemala and incumbent president Joaquín Balaguer in Dominican Republic to bless a strong, authoritative leadership in the 1990 elections of each country, respectively.

Newsmakers have made their own contributions to the examination of elections, explaining the electoral public mood variously as resulting from economic conservatism and material satisfaction, fascination with the political will of strongmen, divisions anchored in societal cleavages such as race or class or region, and divisions based on group loyalties and ideological conceptions. For example, in the Brazilian election of 1994, the media agreed on the diagnosis that "Brazilians . . . voted for stability and continuity rather than the uncertainties offered by the opposition candidates".[1] In the case of Perú in

1995, it was stated in the press that "Fujimori's success is a consequence of his determination in coping with terrorism and the boldness and courage to put in motion a liberal program that stabilized the economy." [2] In contrast, in the 1994 Dominican elections, "candidates have spent the greater part of the time trading insults and accusations, touching on personalities, religious beliefs, age, race and ethnicity"[3], this underscores the saliency of candidates' attributes before the eyes of the media.

Analysts and observers presented their own insights, pointing from economic grievances to personal qualities of the candidates and from longstanding partisan attachments to overt exchanges of support for particularistic benefits in classical patron–client molds. For example, Mexican pollsters Ana Cristina Covarrubias and Ricardo de la Peña explained the 1988 results in México by citing economic grievances, the 1994 elections in terms of partisanship and political leadership reasons, as well as personal benefits from pork-barrels politics, and the 2000 outcomes as a result of all the above, plus the allegiance to renewed democratic feelings.[4] A similar emphasis on the economy nurtured the views of most pollsters of Argentina for the 1989 and 1995 elections[5], though new factors such as claims for public morality entered the equation in the interpretation of 1999 results. In contrast, after years of political consulting experience in the Andean region, U.S. pollster Joseph Napolitan stated that "the single most important determinant of voting behavior is party affiliation". [6]

All these postulates have enriched the landscape of possible answers in regard to the question of the forces driving the vote in Latin America. Yet, however provocative and insightful many of these educated guesses may have been, they could hardly serve as a valuable substitute for systematic research on the subject. Rather than leading to the creation of an orderly source of knowledge and debate, they have left the topic looking like an anarchical patchwork of responses and interpretations where everything is likely to fit depending on which election, which country, or which contending party one is focusing upon.

To make sense of presidential elections in Latin America, a more systematic and theoretically sound approach is needed. Thus, before analyzing the available election data for possible patterns, it is necessary to understand how elections can be explained theoretically, so that theoretically significant parameters for analysis can be set.

Approaches to Electoral Choice Modelled on Western Democracies

As discussed above, the process of electoral choice has received relatively little attention in Latin America. Its theoretical underpinnings have been particularly neglected, as Latin Americanists tended to follow mainstream conceptual approaches based on the study of Western democracies. These approaches can in fact be useful tools for analyzing elections in Latin America, if they are adapted to suit the Latin American milieu. But before examining why and how such adaptations can be made, it is necessary to understand the theoretical debates on electoral choice that have emerged from the North American and Western European experiences with elections.

A Historical View of the Sociological and Socio-psychological Approaches

Three major disciplinary paths—sociological, socio-psychological, and economic—have defined the evolution of electoral behavior research in Western literature, each one basing its conclusions upon a specific set of assumptions, methods and empirical evidence. Detailed accounts of each one of these paths have been developed elsewhere (see Beck 1986; Dalton and Wattenberg 1993), and it makes no sense to reproduce them in capsule form here. Rather, a summary review of the major approaches, as modelled after each path, can provide a functional overview whose aim is to introduce the Latin American polemic on the topic and put in perspective the methodological decisions made in this study.

Focusing on the social cleavages cutting across society and on the social origins of party policy profiles, the sociological perspective, predominant in the 1940s, started from the notion that voters make choices depending on their social standing. Political behavior was said to reflect social group-based identities (Berelson et al. 1954), which in aggregate terms meant that voting alignments represented the ongoing demographic divisions of the social structure. Class cleavages emerged as the primordial force explaining voting patterns, along with other structural forces such as religious divisions and regional origins (Lipset and Rokkan 1967).

However, as this perspective was taking roots in the academic community, challenging evidence mounted. To begin with, the vote-share of political parties varied from one election to the next beyond what could be reasonably attributed to changes in the social structure. In addition, the very phenomenon of social mobility conspired against the premise of stable group-based identities. Furthermore, parties approached contests increasingly as organizations aiming at "catching" all sorts of interests and themes, seeking to represent a space of political convergence rather than a class-specific interest (Kirschheimer 1966). Finally, cross-national data made explicit the decline in class-voting (see Franklin et al. 1992).

Significantly, the sociological approach revealed an important degree of heterogeneity in the way social forces shape the vote. Admittedly, the development of group consciousness and an explicit cognitive connection between the group's social interests and its political preferences shaped many voters' decisions, but others constructed their political choices upon a simple, often unpoliticized, linkage between group and party. Thus, while situations of class identity, described in the first place, presupposed the vote to be a consequential tool of ongoing social divisions, the latter situation presented a model of a voter whose social position was devoid of explicit political content and who merely reacted to habitual ties with specific groups in the society. If this plurality in sociological profiles of voters helped to make this argument more flexible and comprehensive, it also disappointed those scholars seeking to build upon the social background of individuals a parsimonious explanation of why people voted the way they did.

A socio-psychological perspective on voting gained support when sample surveys superseded aggregate statistics as the main source of evidence about electoral behavior, around the early 1960s. The focus now shifted from the group to the individual. Still, this change did not mean that the voter was going to become a self-oriented decision-maker or that long-term forces were bound to be discarded for more immediate and contingent reasons. In actuality, the emphasis on partisanship conveyed by this new perspective did not attempt to establish a theoretical discontinuity with the social group-based approach. Rather, it meant to qualify the order by which different long-term forces shape the vote. Accordingly, since party loyalties entailed a more explicit political meaning than social class or religious groupings, they were considered as more proximate to the voting decision and, therefore, more salient to its analysis. Implicit in this approach, party attachments were viewed as political expressions of the major social cleavages structuring the society; it naturally followed that class divisions would be translated into contrasting party ties of the different social categories.

Assuming that political preferences originate in an individual's lifetime process of socialization, partisanship became the archetypical answer of the literature during the 1960s and 1970s (Campbell et al. 1960). Because political attitudes developed in response to the individual's exposure to parental values and other personal learning experiences related to politics, as much as to group considerations and policy orientations, partisanship stood out as an enduring and long-term force structuring people's electoral decisions. Even if conceived as part of a series of factors sequentially affecting the vote, as wonderfully captured by the notion of a "funnel of causality" (Campbell et al. 1960), the effects of partisan attachments remained largely responsible for directly molding individuals' choice, as well as for an indirect impact through short-term forces like candidates' appeal and assessments of government performance.

However, even as the explanatory leverage of party identification became established, empirical evidence began to challenge this picture. To begin with, cross-national data showed that publics could rapidly become unattached to parties and prefer independence rather than remaining even weakly identified (Dalton 1988). Partisan dealignments followed these trends, and under presidential systems they sometimes inclined voters to turn elections into presidential plebiscites (Ladd 1981), where voting was based on retrospective evaluations of presidential performance whenever an incumbent stood for reelection. Likewise, multiparty systems could mean a public more willing to define their political identity according to specific issue standings or ideological schemas rather than allegiance to a particular political organization (Dalton 1988). On the other hand, short-term forces were both increasingly detached from the effect of partisanship and more independently molding the electoral results (Jackson 1975; Page and Jones 1978). Some scholars even preferred to reverse the causal order, or at least consider reciprocal effects, and assume party identification as equally likely to become a consequence of short-term forces (Fiorina 1981).

In a similar vein, as candidates became independent of modal party positions and rallied around extreme interpretations of some key issues (e.g., Wallace and Goldwater on civil rights, McGovern on the Vietnam war, Reagan on traditional moralism), with the subsequent effect of heightening issue voting and mobilizing issue publics, or as candidates rallied in defense of topics excluded from the traditional partisan agenda (e.g., environmentalism, nuclear policy, gay rights), partisanship receded to a second-order position. Candidates and issues were now placed as primary motivations of the electorates.

Utility, Candidates' Attributes, Accountability Models and the Economic Voting Approach

All these changes brought under fire the premise that political socialization based upon parental transmission of values could still generate the basic impulse for voting behavior. For some scholars, however, such criticisms offered an opportunity to broaden the notion of political socialization rather than to get rid of it. These scholars saw the need to include in it larger-scale experiential forces politicizing the individual, such as those associated with the levels of material and physical security contextualizing the individual's political learning process. Concomitantly, this revised notion of political socialization demanded acknowledgement of the presence of generational effects as age cohorts overlapped different lifetime experiences (Inglehart 1990). In accordance, scholars postulated that different socialization experiences raise different issues priorities. Also, some argued that in view of the rising standards of material well-being and education, the absence of war and the lassitude of collective experiences of physical insecurity, together with the opportunities for self-actualization provided by a democratic state and market-based economy, fundamental changes in the process of political learning were set in motion that ultimately enabled larger portions of the electorate to become autonomous decision-makers (Dalton 1988).

As a result, partisanship has lost considerable ascendancy as the single determinant of the political behavior of the individuals. The generally accepted picture of the voter is now one in which citizens build their own choices autonomously from one election to the next, remaining sensitive to candidates' profiles, the issues of the day, and the ways in which government handle economic and non-economic matters while in office.

An alternative explanation to a somewhat similar diagnosis is conveyed by those challenging the principle of political socialization and assuming that the exclusive rule followed by voters in every election is what their natural drive toward utility maximization dictates. Usually, that notion of utility is ultimately defined by the individual's income or material interest (see Simon 1957; Downs 1957). For this economically oriented path, voters are rational agents acting upon costs-benefit calculations. In procedural terms, this behavior may take different contours. For example, voters may seek to optimize the distance between their own issue positions and the candidates' and/or parties' standings, and choose the one that on average gets closer to their views. This picture represents the standard model of spatial voting, which holds voters as attentive scrutinizers of politics driven by the goal of maximizing utility contained in issues and policies, and assumes a partisan world clearly differentiated in policy terms (see Enelow and Hinich 1982). According to another version, voters may strive for a less demanding process of pondering the pros and cons of former and current administrations before coming up with a decision and—occasionally—project this analysis to the future and take it into account as well when voting. This view represents the classic interpretation of the retrospective-prospective voter, which holds voters as reacting to varying levels of satisfaction with the government outputs without paying much attention to policy instruments or to non-economic results (Key 1966; Downs 1957). One final variant is captured by the notion of policy voting, which contends that voters define their party choice considering the policy standings of each party and the ideological implications of each position. Obviously, this view presupposes that voters are able to make sense of politics in ideological terms and that parties have stuck to a number of policy proposals that clearly differentiates one from another (Downs 1957; see also Kiewiet 1983).

At the center of these arguments lies the concept of utility. Scholars have seen utility as defined by values relevant to the individual's experience and information; thus utility can vary over time and is amenable to both instrumental and symbolic objectives (Lau and Sears 1986). At one point, individuals may find utility in pursuing values more closely associated with their class status. At some other point, they may find utility by reacting to party traditional standings on specific topics. On occasion, they may feel that basing their choices upon the candidates' attributes and positions (independent of what party he or she is running for and whatever the party's traditional standing might have been) is the more satisfactory route to fulfill their utility. Some other times, they may seek to fulfill utility by voting upon their impressions of government's handling of its public responsibilities, however diffusively or specifically that may be summarized by the state of the economy, their sense of how the nation has fared socially and politically in recent times, or the way the administration managed scandals or critical events.

The multiplicity of factors defining what moves the voter beyond social origins and partisan attachments has taken the scholarly discussion on this topic into two different directions. One emphasizes the value of accountability, where electorates' decisions are seen as reactions to recent occurrences (or expectations for future ones) according to the level of utility maximization achieved—or, as the literature has conceded in a more realistic manner, according to the level of relative satisfaction attained (see Bennet and Salisbury 1987). The other places the political leadership of actual and would-be authorities (that is, candidates' personal and political attributes) at the center of the stage. Naturally, the acknowledgment of individuals' emotional and cognitive approaches to the political world and the moderate cognitive demands posed by candidates and presidents as sources of decision in information-gathering terms make of candidates' and presidents' qualities a natural object of study (see Sigelman 1990; Kelley 1995).

Considering the closeness between the central role of candidates and the way voting operates in practice, and also taking into account the way the media and most politicians deal with campaign topics during elections (Patterson 1984), a focus on personalized sources of decision such as the president's or the candidates' attributes has become a parsimonious way of understanding electoral choice. Among many scholars, it has been "partisanship and reactions to the candidates' personas [that] generally have more influence than perceptions of the candidates' stands on the issues" (Luskin 1990: 353). Candidate voting thus represents the relevance of personal characteristics (Campbell et al. 1960), but this is not to say that cosmetic traits or physical attractiveness are what makes candidates matter (see Rosenberg et al. 1987). Candidates' attributes become relevant sources of the voting decision in view of the candidates' personal values and the political implications of holding such qualifications: such sources are composed of the public perceptions of their degree of competence, integrity, leadership, and empathy (Kelley 1995).

In contrast, other scholars have tended to de-emphasize the role of candidates, since they run under specific party labels, market themselves upon single issues or policy commitments, or ride upon the president's coat-tails. In this view, candidates' effects are a subproduct of the individual's politicization experience and of his or her approval of the instrumental and symbolic goods delivered during the incumbent party's tenure (see, for example, Markus and Converse 1979). Based on these assumptions, accountability models of voting choice make government performance their focus of analysis.

In the view of many scholars today, although ruling parties and contending forces often seek to underline achievements (and proposals) in matters of social policy, foreign policy, moralization of public life, or civil rights, what usually captures the voters' attention is what they have done (or promised to do) for the economic well-being of the nation and its members. The seminal work of Kramer (1971) on the impact of economic conditions at the national level on U.S. electoral outcomes landmarked this new approach from an aggregate level perspective and served to formalize the argument of economic voting, which has become so prevalent.

The basic contention of the economic voting approach is that citizens react to their material environment, supporting the incumbent's reelection when conditions are good and endorsing the opposition in bad times. For some authors, this economic sensitivity has set the basis for a view of electors as "responsibly" responding to their past experiences (Key 1966). Some scholars have further refined this idea by presenting voters as rational agents able to elaborate on these retrospective outcomes and project them into the future (Downs 1957), while others, more skeptical of the voters' abilities and power, have seen them as easy prey of politicians' ruses to ensure office-holding through the recreation of political business cycles (Tufte 1978; Keech 1995). In any case, the fundamental questions of whether voters respond to past or future conditions and whether they care for their own well-being or for that of their society have constituted the major stimulus behind the controversy on economic voting (see Kinder and Kiewiet 1981; Nannestadt and Paldam 1994).

After over twenty-five years of research, this economic voting hypothesis has proven generalizable across time (Hibbs 1987; Markus 1988) and across nations (Eulau and Lewis-Beck 1985; Lewis-Beck 1988; Clarke et al. 1992). On the other hand, it has also unveiled a need for theoretical revision and constant respecification (Paldam 1991). Thus, the corroboration of a model of the economic voter at the national and cross-national levels depends of the form of measuring variables (see Clarke et al. 1992), the level of analysis chosen (Paldam 1991), the relaxation of key assumptions of the rational choice tenets underlying each model (Bennet and Salisbury 1987), and/or the non-economic information that needs to be incorporated in order to portray a realistic and unbiased image of the electoral decision process (see Lewis-Beck 1988).

Interestingly enough, the very same discussion of economic voting at the individual level has called attention to the non-economic underpinnings of the economic models. For example, whenever voters are found to be guided mostly by sociotropic considerations rather than by their pocketbooks, cultural reasons are rapidly brought to the table (Kinder and Kieweit 1981; Nannestadt and Paldam 1994; but see also Miller and Listhaug 1985). Whenever voters rely on forward-looking orientations toward the economy instead of retrospective ones in order to reelect the incumbents, candidate's attributes and ideological inclinations emerge as "usual suspects" (Joslyn 1991; Lewis-Beck 1988). Whenever signals of macro-economic hardship get positively—and thus counter-intuitively—correlated with support for the ruling party rather than for the opposition, scholars end up turning to the political and cultural bases of the social fabric and admit that clientelism and personalism may organize electoral choice even more strongly than pure economic considerations can (Belluci 1985; 1991), or they assume high levels of economic tolerance (Mancha Navarro 1995).[7]

Similarly, whenever the effects of economic grievances on voting are blurred by the incorporation of information on the president's popularity, there is a need to broaden the concept of competence in performance to include notions of political command and dramaturgical skills in the public arena (MacKuen 1983). Whenever comparable economic complaints do not translate into similar electoral responses across the board, class and education may offer better explanations (Fiorina 1981; Sniderman et al. 1991). Whenever party choice remains stable over time in spite of incumbent economic misperformance and voters' acknowledgment of it, party images and partisan leanings are pointed out as likely reasons (Kieweit 1983; Hibbs 1987). And last but not least, whenever the background of vote-driving economic expectations is explored, partisan leanings are usually discovered (Weatherford 1983).

A final caveat is posed by the question on the degree to which voters explicitly connect their impressions of the economic environment with the worthiness of reelecting the incumbent. In all likelihood, such a linkage depends of the intensity of the assignment of responsibility to the government for the state of the economy. Unless voters hold the authorities liable for their current situation, it makes no sense for them to rely on economic data to decide whether or not to support political continuity at the ballot box (see Kramer 1983; Peffley 1985).

All these considerations serve as cautions about embracing the economic voting approach without reservations. More importantly, they make clear the desirability of adding to the heuristic and empirical strengths of the model other, non-economic forces present in the process of political choice, either to evaluate competing theories or to improve the specification of the political and institutional circumstances under which economic conditions come more decisively to shape electoral support (Powell and Whitten 1993). It is obvious that the economic voting model cannot by itself account for the wide range of electoral results in various contexts. Other major explanations of choice must be considered, and their impact on the effect of the economic variables should be controlled for if a complete, accurate picture of electoral choice is to emerge.

The corollary is that explanations centered on performance are not exhausted by instrumental considerations of financial contentment or policy accomplishment. Non-economic issues also critically define the management aptitudes of the party-in-office and thus shape its electoral chances. According to the empirical evidence, electorates have been anything but indifferent to domestic issues, political scandals, levels of corruption, or foreign policy events when deciding for whom to vote (RePass 1971; Fiorina 1981; Budge and Farlie 1983; Lewis-Beck 1988; Norpoth et al. 1991; Fackler and Lin 1995). In the case of nations undergoing a process of democratic consolidation, electorates are supposed to be anything but indifferent to the quality of the democratic conduct of their rulers and to mold their vote accordingly (see Crewe 1994).

By the same token, judgment of government's achievements may involve a broader assessment of political leadership and the nation's quality of life under the administration. As authority gets inevitably personalized, especially in presidential systems, an appraisal of its successes and failures can often be made based on the president's popularity. How much this assessment of the chief of government's performance is uniquely instrumental or symbolic in nature is an empirical question, one that involves finding out whether the president's popularity is defined by his or her efficacy on specific grounds that are materially consequential to the individuals or by his or her ability to provide an overall sense of psychic and collective security through displays of command over public affairs (see MacKuen 1983; Sigelman 1990; Edwards III 1995).

The current plurality of contentions explaining voting choice has proven adequate to understand the longstanding electoral practices of voters in advanced democracies. But how well does each argument fit the experience of Latin American voters during the last decade and half of electoral politics?

EMPIRICAL ELECTORAL RESEARCH ON LATIN AMERICA

Overall, there is plenty of heterogeneity in the responses substantiated in analyses of aggregate and individual-level data available for Latin America. Regrettably, this variety is neither a byproduct of empirical tests seeking to build upon previous findings or looking for answers beyond simple bivariate correlations, nor the result of cross-national and longitudinal studies. In fact, most Latin Americanists simply investigated what data permitted and common sense suggested. Thus, as economic volatility struck the region during the 1980s and 1990s, a model of economic voting prevailed. Such a choice tacitly incorporated all the underlying tenets of that model; what has remained unclear is whether those assumptions actually fit the empirical evidence about the way voters approach elections.

The reasons for the popularity of the economic voting model are manifold. Most importantly, beginning in the 1980s, Latin America experienced a massive financial upheaval and extensive socio-economic changes. Between 1981 and 1990, the accumulated decline in GDP per capita amounted to −7.9 percent, followed by an upturn between 1991 and 1994 of +6.1 percent. On average, this yielded a weighted accumulated decrease rate of −3.9 percent for the whole period (CEPAL 1994). The consequences of such a negative trend are not hard to imagine. Mainstream literature tended to emphasize rational expectations, and the commonplace accounts of elections by local politicians, pundits and journalists who put a premium on economic explanations helped to place economic concerns in the spotlight. As a result of these trends, economic arguments gained a pivotal position among those studying the region (see Méndez 1983; Dietz, 1987; Nelson 1990; Panzer and Paredes 1991; Anderson 1994). Some scholars have even gone so far as to suggest that no other factor could offer as compelling an account as economics could for a particular election under observation (Catterberg and Braun 1989; Meneguello 1995). Generalizing, Trindade claimed that in Latin America, "the economic situation is increasingly tending to affect the lives of the population to such an extent that it is becoming the central variable which determines attitudes in elections" (1991: 308).

Yet other scholars have followed exactly the opposite path, emphasizing the role of non-economic forces to the extent of positing an almost complete obliteration of economic reasons (Domínguez and McCann 1992, 1995; Canzani 1995). Still others conjectured that electoral choice makes more sense if understood from a class perspective (Mora y Araujo 1986; Dix 1989; Petras and Morley 1992; Cameron 1994; Dugan and Dietz 1995), from the consideration of partisan structures and traditions (Seligson 1987; Catterberg 1991; Remmer 1991; Ames 1994; Coppedge 1994; Domínguez and McCann 1995), or from a focus on the role of ideologies and broader conceptualizations of politics (von Mettenheim 1995). On one hand, such a divergence is intellectually stimulating. On the other, given the absence of a core line of argumentation against which new evidence and different interpretations could be compared, this diversity of contentions has contributed little to an orderly discussion of the subject and the possibility of cumulative knowledge.

Not surprisingly, an examination of the empirical evidence, even when focusing on same country-studies, shows mixed results. Take Brazil, for example. In discussing the 1994 presidential elections, Meneguello (1995) echoes the widespread belief in economic considerations as critical molders of people's options; other factors such as partisan loyalties are overtly effaced from the scene. And yet, following Ames's (1994) account of the previous 1989 elections, one gains a sense that, even if not equally critical, the role of party-related influences should not be dismissed.

For the researcher looking for a coherent answer, the difficulty resides in two distinct problems. One is the qualitative difference in information provided by individual-level and aggregate-level data. The other involves explanations that fail to control the favorite variable's effect that one author champions for the impact of the contending variable that another scholar advocates. Missing control variables or overlooking counter-intuitive factors is a common error made by analysts of elections in the region. All too often, it also implies adding (if not resting whole arguments upon) irrelevant information. Emphasis on demographics is one instance that illustrates this point. Anderson's (1994) examination of the 1990 Sandinista defeat, for example, contains page after page of cross-tabulations of votes and occupational categories of a sample of Nicaraguan respondents without ever making a strong point on the vitality of such connection. In contrast, Seligson's (1987) analysis of Costa Rican electoral outcomes is explicit in dismissing demographics as a causal factor and putting the accent on partisan ties.

Many single-country studies are fraught with problems. Studies of Mexican elections, for example, are illuminating for the heterogeneity of explanations they provide as much as for the types of methodological controversies they foment. For example, after studying the series of 1952 to 1988 presidential contests, Brophy-Baerman (1994) concludes that preelectoral economic conditions have played no role in explaining the incumbents' vote-share, although these have greatly contributed to the fluctuations of the vote garnered by the left. If intuitively sound, this conclusion raises other doubts. For example, can one expect electorates voting in non-competitive elections such as those in pre-1988 México to be likely to use elections as opportunities to pass judgment on the economy? In other words, if electoral outcomes are pre-determined, does it make sense to voters to hold governments accountable for their performance in the voting booth? Brophy-Baerman's findings are only partially consonant with previous evidence linking support for the right-wing opposition with economic advancement, and showing no association with support for leftist forces (Ames 1970). Nor are they consistent with discussions of the recent 1988, 1991 and 1994 elections, which revealed a marginal role for economic grievances in general (Arroyo and Morris 1993; Moreno and Yanner 1995).

On the other hand, Domínguez and McCann's (1995) analysis of the 1988 and 1991 Mexican elections has been quite consistent with Brophy-Baerman's basic point in relation to support for the PRI. Testing most of the classical arguments about determinants of the voting choice, these authors conclude that economic orientations were peripheral in comparison to the effect of party-related considerations. Rather than voting their pocketbooks or submitting the economic leadership of the government at the national level to a sort of electoral referendum, the majority of Mexicans chose the party that had better prospects as a national force. If these contentions are useful in the context of the lively controversy between economics and party-based arguments, they suffer the risk of conceptual tautology. In other words, the dependent variable (party choice) and the independent variable (perceptions of party future) are too close to comfort, tapping very much the same phenomenon.

Perplexed by the contrast between their findings and what most studies conducted elsewhere have revealed, Domínguez and McCann stressed the need to take into account the degree of institutional competition as a crucial variable in determining the salience of economics in appraising the ruling party's electoral fortunes. To some other scholars, however, the lack of statistical significance of the economic measures is not so much a byproduct of institutional practices or the absence of instrumental motivations shaping the choice of Mexicans but of the poor validity of the measures used (Buendía 2001).[8] Thus, where standard measures of retrospective and prospective evaluations of the economy are used, stronger indications of economic voting surface.

On top of this, Mexicanists as well as Latin Americanists in general have recognized the importance of candidate voting. Indeed, the more the election involves a step forward in the democratization of the country, the more significance candidates seem to have. This phenomenon is a result of weak party systems and undeveloped opportunities for partisan socialization, both of which dominate the Latin American scene, but it may also occur when highly institutionalized systems open up to competition. The Mexican elections of 1988 and 1994 seem to fit the pattern in which a more pluralistic juncture, immersed in a situation of economic decline, is accompanied by processes of partisan dealignment/realignment.[9] Whatever the process that underlies the detachment of big portions of the electorates from their longstanding party identities, one consequence has been the increasing salience of candidates' attributes: as of the 1994 Mexican election, candidates' images ranked immediately after party-related effects in determining the vote. The extent to which the contender exhibited political leadership qualities, namely a "personality to govern," was particularly important (see Moreno and Yanner 1995: 18).

In the case of Perú, Cameron's (1994) ecological analyses illustrate the complex relationship between class and vote by revealing high correlations among the right and left forces but poor correlations with the ruling parties. In discussing the 1995 election, Dugan and Dietz's (1995) aggregate-level study suggests that a poor correlation may be the result of misspecifying a nonlinear relationship between class and vote as a linear one, rather than of the inexistence of any relationship at all. Having won reelection with the support of lower and upper classes, a linear bivariate estimation of that connection underlying Fujimori's support will simply miss the point. But is class-analysis the appropriate tool to understand electoral politics in a society like Perú's, where all cleavages—class, ethnic, linguistic, racial, and educational—overlap dramatically, and where radical changes in the conditions of living have taken place since the return of democracy? Early work conducted by Dietz (1987) hinted at such a connection and focused on the sources of electoral choice among the lower strata and impoverished residents of Lima. His conclusions posited that the most economically disadvantaged sectors of the electorate chose based upon a variety of stimuli, pocketbook concerns being a priority but leadership factors having a considerable relevance as well.

If confusion surrounds the findings for single-country studies, it reigns when one attempts to perform cross-national comparisons. Panzer and Paredes's (1991) discussion of the 1988 Chilean plebiscite suggests that only macro-economics molded the electorate's choice, something that represents quite a contrast with the seemingly economic insensitivity of Costa Rican voters, as depicted by Seligson and Gómez (1989). In a like manner, Canache et al.'s (1994) study of the electoral behavior of Hondureans leads to the conclusion that ideological orientations permeate the calculus of decision, something that strongly defies traditional views of Hondurean politics and voters as clientelistic and poorly sophisticated (see Rosenberg 1989). More surprisingly, it also radically opposes the findings for electorates with higher levels of political mobilization and cognitive capability, such as in the case of Argentina, characterized by a highly inconsistent ideological view (Catterberg and Braun 1989).

The record of studies focusing on individual elections and individual countries opens the door to accommodate almost any contention. Unfortunately, given the methodological and model specification features of most of this research, this also means that what in one study looks like solid evidence may vanish in the next. Time-series, multivariate, and better specified studies of the determinants of choice are the natural paths to follow. Yet data unavailability or the paucity of electoral contests themselves have prompted only a handful of truly comprehensive analyses.

Remmer's (1991) examination of twenty-one Latin American competitive elections between 1982 and 1990 stands out as the single exceptional piece complying with most of these requirements. Unfortunately, for reasons of data unavailability and the restrictions imposed to the statistical power of the author's design, this work does not take into account all major approaches present in the literature. Interestingly enough, when the author submits the notion of economic voting to the empirical test, her data reveal that macroeconomic indicators trail behind political conditions in explaining the electoral support gathered by the incumbent party. Controlling for aggregate measures of the nature of the party system, inflationary pressures—which stood out among the economic factors—play a secondary role in undermining electoral support for political continuity (as assessed by the proportion of votes gathered by the incumbents' candidates). According to these findings, one can expect aggregate-level measures of partisan influences and other noneconomic forces to exert a substantive influence in the context of Latin American electoral politics, thus relativizing the incidence of economic-oriented decisions at the ballot box.

Remmer's study also points to the salience of institutional factors in accounting for the impact of economic forces. She concludes by saying that the "relationship between economic conditions and aggregate electoral results was mediated principally by party system structure, which insulated two-party democracies from the volatility experienced by their more politically fragmented counterparts" (1991: 794). This conclusion suggests that variations in degrees of political development constitute an important intervening variable when specifying the relative effect of different determinants of electoral choice.

Despite the gains made by such studies, serious limitations still cut across the topic of electoral choice in Latin America. Replication and validity tests of previous findings have been absent. What is more, fundamental theoretical assumptions have often been ignored or developed spuriously. In fact, scholars have barely undertaken the job of making explicit the postulates of what they consider to be the nature of voters' decision-making process and rationality—a topic that lies at the heart of the study of electoral choice. When faced with such a vacuum, one can assume that for the advocates of economic voting, all voters behave as self-interested utility maximizers, whereas for the advocates of class voting, all voters hold conscious class-based identity links, and for those advocating party voting, all voters move according to their socio-psychological backgrounds.

In reality, many scholars have preferred either to avoid inquiries into the essentials of how and why predictors of choice perform as they do, or to presuppose that these essentials are so universalistic and context-free that they can be automatically inferred from the standard literature developed for Western Europe and North America. To be sure, data unavaibility, non-standardized measurements, and the singularity of the political process in Latin America conspired against such convergence.

How realistic and accurate are the universal assumptions of voting rationality based on the principle of utility maximization when applied to Latin American voters? Should one assume that despite the recent experience of authoritarian politics and highly volatile economics, the average voter of the region[10] follows the same standards that orient Western publics, characterized by decades of democratic experience, predominant market economies, and moderate levels of social inequality?

It is my strong conviction that voters in Latin America cannot be assumed to make voting decisions in the same way as do publics who learned to vote under conditions of political and economic stability. Given the gulf of different experiences and opportunities, one can hardly assume that Latin American electorates will behave like their counterparts in established Western democracies. The question that remains is how differently these electorates approach elections and what implications those differences have for a comprehensive view of voting behavior.

In the next chapter, I turn to the basic assumptions that have been made about voters, their rationality and the ways in which they approach voting, out of a firm conviction that an accurate picture of the voters' decision-making processes will permit a better grasp of electoral choice in the region and provide meaningful theoretical underpinnings to the analysis of data.

NOTES

1. Editorial, "Cardoso Heads for First-Round Victory as Lula Clings to Hope of a Run-off," *Latin American Weekly Report*, 13 October 1994, 457.
2. Editorial, *Expreso*, 10 April 1995, 2
3. Editorial, "Trouble Whatever the Election Result," *Caribbean & Central America*, 19 May 1994, 3
4. Seminar for the Analysis of National Surveys on Political Culture and Citizen Practices, Secretaría de Gobernación, México, DF, 14 August 2001
5. Editorial, *El Cronista Comercial*, 19 May 1995, 14

6. Joseph Napolitan, Personal communication, 10 March 1995

7. Stokes refers to the phenomenon of publics reacting in a supportive manner to environments of economic deterioration as "intertemporal politics," which involves a variant of rational expectations making of current grievances the "proof" that good times will be met around the corner. Naturally, this takes form against a context of economic ungovernability which makes people to put a premium on the political will of rulers to cope with the crisis no matter how. Thus, temporal inflation upsurges, transient recessions, or persistent unemployment rates may constitute not only some of the costs people would circumstantially tolerate but even the signs that the political will to restore economic governability is in motion (see Stokes 2001).

8. Buendía argues that given the authoritarian nature of the Mexican government til the end of 1990s, legitimacy could only be appraised through assessments of economic performance achievements rather than through regular tests of electoral support. Furthermore, after 60 years of single-party rule, whether citizens were able to hold the incumbent responsible for outcomes was no longer an issue; that is, for most people it should have been clear that good or bad news could only be attributed to the PRI rule. In my view, these points do not necessarily invalidate but rather qualify Domínguez and McCann's contention that the type of institutional development matters.

9. Interestingly enough, while party-related attitudes remained the most important consideration of the Mexican voter, diachronical evidence revealed a substantial degree of preference volatility and rising partisan independency, which indicated that voters relied their future options on non-partisan clues such as candidates' appeals (see Basañez 1990: 248–50, 277; Molinar Horcasitas and Weldon 1994: 66–67; Domínguez and McCann 1995).

10. By average Latin American voter, I mean those individuals that concentrate at the typical median value of the attitudes and conducts reviewed, and that, by extension, constitute the majoritarian central tendency in terms of behaviors.

Chapter Three

Electoral Choice and Decisional Clues

CONFRONTING THE COMMON ASSUMPTIONS ABOUT VOTERS

In theory, all individuals seek to maximize utility in the electoral arena following a cost-benefit analysis of the consequences of their choices. Typically, such utility is defined in economic or material terms, or by the economic consequences of holding specific values or issue positions. The voters' reasoning may take the form of a careful weighing of the payoffs received in for past decisions and a projection of conclusions and implications thereby developed with regards to eventual trade-offs involved in future choices (Downs 1957; Grofman 1987). Downs, for example, assumes that voters perform these calculations as a conscientious evaluation of candidates' and/or parties' platforms, thus getting involved in complex estimations of issue proximity between platforms and their own positions, as well as an assessment of the likelihood of a program's fulfillment in office. Having weighted these elements, they vote for the candidate or party whose expected policies are appraised, on balance, as the most desirable. As utility optimizers, voters seek a perfect theoretical equilibrium between costs and benefits, according to which their most critical demands are met.

This view implies that citizens are highly sophisticated actors who enjoy close to perfect information on the parties' achievements, candidates' philosophical beliefs, and policy promises. Moreover, it also assumes that they are able to hold clear-cut preferences on every issue of relevance and a reasoned judgment of the secondary effects implicated in different issue priorities becoming public policies. As a prerequisite, they therefore must exhibit a high level of political engagement and exposure to political news, to enable the issues to acquire public saliency and elicit opinion intensity. A further implication is that individuals perceive high payoffs for becoming fully informed agents. Based on this picture, it would be logical to expect minimal levels of political cynicism among voters, a monolithically high valorization of electoral mechanisms, and a sizable belief in the autonomy of the electoral sphere from non-electorally accountable actors.

Moreover, the idea of fully informed citizens presumes party policy profiles that are unequivocally defined, publicly recognizable, and stable across time. This presupposes two things: one, that parties, and candidates as well, have enjoyed the opportunity to develop a policy identity and diffuse this across the public, and two, that not even the most volatile and pressing economic conditions are able to subvert this policy expertise by forcing upon leaders a policy direction radically different from the one traditionally associated with that political organization. Finally, the underlying assumption is that citizens' electoral preferences are authentic and not merely subproducts of rationalizations from group considerations or projections of previous political commitments.

Is this picture a realistic one? Does it accurately reflect the situation and characteristics of voters in Latin America? It is clear that most of these presuppositions hardly match anything experienced by most voters *anywhere*—and particularly in Latin America. Let us tackle the major components of this theoretical view of voters one by one and attempt to provide a better description to serve as the basis for tracking voters' electoral behavior.

Voters Are Not Encyclopedic

To begin with, perfect information is rarely found among the publics of most advanced democracies, and this is the case even more in Latin America (see Converse 1964; Neuman 1986). Evidence collected by pollsters and scholars in different countries of the region shows that knowledge of candidates, awareness of policy proposals, and even acquaintance with the electoral schedule in electoral years is rather poor.[1]

For example, the issue of economic liberalization embodied one of the major policy cleavages among parties of the region since the mid-late 1980s, so familiarity with this topic should have provided a valid measure of levels of information. As of June 1993, however, only half of respondents in a study of eleven countries in the region were aware of economic liberalization. In percentages, lack of knowledge ranged from 24 percent in Colombia to 71 percent in Bolivia.[2] In a similar vein, if TV news viewership tells us something about levels of information and attentiveness, it is instructive to know that, on average, 46 percent of urban residents in eight major Latin American nations did not follow any political news at all, or admitted to pay almost no attention to them.[3] An indication of even lower political inputs received by the average voter in the region is reflected in the level of newspaper readership: less than four in every ten followed the news in the paper.[4] Political indifference is the other side of the coin. Cross-national evidence collected around the 1994–95 wave of presidential contests revealed that, on average, political interest was a virtue for less than four in every ten citizens.[5]

Moreover, political intelligence is a commodity tremendously skewed in its distribution among electors. Being a function of education and educational opportunities, as well as of news exposure (Sniderman et al. 1991), cognitive sophistication is limited by structural restrictions on mass access to higher levels of formal schooling in the region and the increasing deterioration of the educational system (see IADB 1995), as well as by the poor level of news attentiveness displayed by the electorates.

These contentions support the claim that poor levels of information are not merely the voters' fault. After all, choosing political ignorance may be a rational strategy in a situation characterized by institutional weakness and policy fluidity. For various reasons, candidates' issue positions have been increasingly aimed at establishing closer rapport with special-interest groups rather than with broader constituencies so as to warrant some minimum degree of governability (O'Donnell 1992). Often, elected officials simply bury their campaign promises and choose radically opposed policies in the hope that by the next electoral round citizens' annoyance over incumbents' unresponsiveness will recede, the burden of policy choices will dissipate, and the positive consequences of those policies could pave the road to a favorable business cycle (see Geddes 1995; Stokes 1995, 2001). As a result, parties' policy profiles remain pretty much unsettled, adding more confusion to voters' poor informational basis and thwarting policy-based voting. All this makes the costs of being politically cognizant quite high and depresses the prospects of identifying textbook versions of rational voters (that is, able to comply with the requirement of scrutinizing the policy positions of candidates and parties, striving to maintain issue consistency and ideological coherence in their choices over time and closely monitoring party policy commitments and accomplishments across elections).

Voters Are Satisfaction-Oriented

If most voters remain unaware of the political situation, doubts mount about their ability to strive for an optimum electoral outcome in utility maximization terms. In principle, such voting rationality would require surveying each alternative's potential benefits, assessing its corresponding costs and then coming up with a choice that optimizes the difference between expected benefits and costs. Given a backdrop of faulty informational endowment and low interest, can one still grant voters the capacity to engage in fully maximizing behaviors?

Cognitive limitations necessarily qualify the assumption that voters seek to maximize utility. A more realistic view is that voters in Latin America react to the relative degree of satisfaction derived from those pieces of information that *are* available regarding the major electoral options. We should therefore think of voters as data scanners, likely to only skim through the issues. Voters do indeed value results and react to the material or symbolic gratification that these convey, but they simply skip policy considerations and instead put emphasis on the instrumental and/or symbolic value of their leaders' actions. They choose on the basis of the relative satisfaction provided by government outputs and symbolic bonds with parties and leaders of the polity, which makes pragmatism the essence of their approach to the electoral arena (see Fiorina 1981).

Voters' pragmatism is not merely an endogenous subproduct. It is also a natural response to the conditions of institutional uncertainty surrounding each contest. In this sense, a second supposition of the standard rational theory presumes that individuals can effectively pursue maximizing strategies in the electoral arena, that is, that non-electorally accountable forces would barely have any influence over electoral outcomes and the way electoral support translates into policy outputs. Admittedly, this is not the case in Latin America, where the influence of non-elected forces such as the military, business corporations, and international agencies over the new civilian governments is explicit. As in most of the developing world, elected leaders seem more sensitive to special interests than to "the whims of the voting majority" (Remmer 1991: 355). These factors limit the autonomy of electoral politics and introduce constraints on the political responsiveness of elected officials. In turn, such constraints can only stimulate cynicism among voters and thus pose reasonable doubts about the value of voting as a technique conducive to reaching an optimum equilibrium.

A standard way of tapping this concern through survey research is asking people about their perceptions of the fairness and responsiveness to be expected from the electoral process. Asked in first place within a battery of questions about confidence in political institutions in twelve Latin American nations, trust in the presidential elections elicited an average of 48 percent of negative responses. Aligned in a rather intuitive pattern, the highest confidence was found in Uruguay and Chile, while the lowest confidence was found in Dominican Republic and México.[6] A question with slightly changed wording about confidence in the system "to elect authorities" asked four months later to a somewhat similar pool of countries yielded an average of distrust of 54 percent. Again, Uruguayans displayed the highest level of confidence while Venezuelans and Colombians showed the lowest trust feelings.[7] Questions about electoral fairness asked to national samples from eight countries revealed that half of the respondents view elections as fraud-ridden (the figure reached 58 percent when no answers and no responses were included). Cross-national variability could not be sharper, with Chileans, Uruguayans and Argentines at one end, and Paraguayans and Mexicans at the other end, these firmly viewing their elections as fraud-ridden.[8]

A widespread perception of the usefulness of voting and the conviction that voting embodies an assertive action of positive consequences are two ubiquitous requirements for those who hold that voters maximize their individual utility through the vote. If both rules are poorly substantiated, one can hardly think that voters could believe the electoral process to be one permitting the achievement of an optimum equilibrium of benefits and costs.

In a similar vein, if voters are cynical about elections and pessimistic about electoral responsiveness, it would make no sense for them to spend their time learning about the issues and voting accordingly. The panorama in Latin America clearly points to these flaws, considering that 34 percent of the public, on average, approach elections with skepticism.[9] Turning to electoral responsiveness, the landscape looks even less optimistic for the prospects of voters as utility optimizers, considering that, on average, 70 percent of voters agree that representatives do not care much about the public interest.[10] Even if the question does not refer to how elected presidents are perceived in terms of responsiveness, it still communicates a sense of the existing perceptual obstacles to the development of the conventional model of rational voter. Accordingly, since the conditions to reap future benefits as a result of specific choices are deemed to be grim in Latin America, an approach to voting founded in a rationality of expected utilities is untenable.

Given this picture of individual voter capacities and the decision-making environment, how then can we approach the voting decision? Is the notion of utility useless? Are voters not rational? We need not go as far. The logical solution is to relax the requirements governing the process of electoral choice and assume that citizens seek to achieve a "satisficing" (rather than optimizing) equilibrium in terms of cost-benefit thinking before the voting booths (see Bennett and Salisbury 1987). That is, voters limit themselves to choices that seem to be "good enough" or satisfactory in view of their global objectives. Accordingly, they stick with the status quo if it satisfies them, disregarding (at least to a certain degree) the possibility that they could do better by changing; on the other hand, they tend to make changes when they are dissatisfied, even if the existing situation is the least of all evils. This supposition is consistent not only with broader patterns of political behavior under conditions of uncertainty characterized as risk-aversive, but also with the very nature of the electoral choice as voters face it. (This point will be discussed in more detail later on.)

In sum, individuals react to changes in their immediate environment and its effects on their contingent notions of satisfaction; that is, they react to relative levels of contentment with outputs and symbolic assets displayed by the incumbent force. Voters behave, therefore, as specific value satisfiers rather than as maximizers of some hypothetical, abstract, and universal notion of utility. In a milieu of institutional and economic uncertainty, predominant feelings of political skepticism and unresponsiveness, and meager political engagement, the act of voting by means of developing a carefully weighted assessment of past payoffs and future trade-offs that each electoral option might represent (as the standard version of voting rationality would have it) is hardly an option available for the majority of Latin American voters. Not just that, it is not even a rational option.

Voters Hold an Economic and Non-economic Notion of Utility

Utility has usually been defined in economic terms, with voters being seen as guided only by their material concerns. Yet cross-national survey data show that this view of utility is overly restrictive and does not take into account other important factors. First, instrumental definitions of utility are not exhausted by goals of economic performance; rather, achievements in the domain of collective security and public order also count. On average, in the early to mid-1990s, about 40 to 46 percent defined a principle of utility in terms of economic performance (by putting economic stability, growth and inflation control at the top of the list of government priorities).[11] Conversely, those doing so in non-economic terms amounted to 18 to 19 percent (by giving priority to national defense, internal order and crime control). In a similar vein, the evidence shows also the vitality of non-instrumental goals; those defining utility in expressive and symbolically oriented terms amounted to 32 to 35 percent (by claiming as main concerns political participation and civil liberties, as well as environmental issues).

These findings point to the need for a multidimensional notion of utility, one that lays the foundation for the individual decision by encompassing not only a search for material values but for emotional and symbolic goods as well (see Sears et al. 1981). Therefore the array of available sources an individual uses to arrive at a decision about whom to support needs to be broadened when studying voting behavior. These additional sources must be ones that do not demand high levels of information or rational sophistication and that, on the other hand, do allow resorting to instrumental (e.g., material) as well as symbolic (e.g., emotional and identity-related) incentives in the process of decision-making.

Studies of voting publics in Latin America substantiate this point. Exploring the basis of lower-class political preferences and activities in México and Venezuela, Davis and Speer (1991: 335) conclude that "workers . . . do not engage in politics simply because of economic needs. Expressive orientations to politics also shape their political evaluations and behavior in significant ways." For these authors, expressive orientations involve ideological and value dimensions of political conflict, attributes that may be relevant in relative terms but are far from becoming major sources of behavior when considered in absolute terms. Other researchers claim that among weakly ideological and issue-inconsistent publics, other symbolic goods come forth as contents of people's notion of utility. Some scholars view leadership qualities and the political ability exhibited on the eve of dramatic events as crucial (MacKuen 1983); others contend that it is partisan attachments as providers of political identity that count (Fiorina 1981). Government outputs in general constitute an important source of reference, but many voters can be motivated by a sense of utility fulfillment molded after the opportunities for political self-expression and identification. Whatever the symbolic content, it is important to recall that political behavior does not result solely from instrumental goals.

Voters Exercise Incumbent Voting

The relaxation of the notion of utility, when seen in the context of actual cognitive and environmental limitations imposed upon voters, demands a simplified view of the nature of individual choice at the voting booth. Such simplified view entails centering the decision over the destiny of incumbents. Reducing the scope of the decision to the incumbent odds dialogue well with two other core predispositions of general publics: avoiding risks and the prevalent cultural pattern to frame (and cope with) political options in plebiscitarian terms. It is my contention that, to the average voter, electoral choice presents itself as essentially a binary resolution: whether to support or repudiate the incumbent government.

The reason is simple: incumbency provides more visible and ready information to the average voter than any other option. It represents the status quo, something that can be easily grasped by voters whatever the type of outcomes they pick for guidelines. Any other option represents change. Therefore, the basic frame of electoral choice faced by individuals is one of continuity or change. For this very reason, incumbent rulers are usually regarded as less risky than the challengers, who are often unknown and whose policies could drastically alter the current trends, for better or for worse (see Quattrone and Tversky 1988: 724). From a perspective of voting rationality structured by levels of relative satisfaction, however, the advantage of the incumbent becomes contingent upon how positively or negatively his or her tenure is perceived.

In a situation characterized by high volatility in the economic and political spheres, uncertainty about the application of procedures and officials' policy intentions, and individuals' own poor level of information, one should expect this "satisficing" rationality to "train" voters not just to side automatically with the option that offers a less radical alteration with everyday rules, but to develop a two-fold attitude towards risk. To wit, people should be expected to become risk-averse in the domain of gains and risk-seeking in the domain of losses (Quattrone and Tversky 1988: 723). This view presupposes that voters judge their levels of utility satisfaction in relative, not absolute terms. It is relative not to suspicions or extrapolations of how outcomes might have looked under a different administration, but relative to a subjective threshold determining where discontent with outcomes translates into risk-seeking orientations at the polls, that is, into repudiation of the incumbent party.

Analysis of public opinion data endorses these contentions. Regressing support for gradual versus accelerated changes against measures of economic performance (e.g., inflation and per capita income) reveals a clear pattern which shows that as the material scenario preceding the interviews entails progress, support for gradualism becomes stronger, while the opposite trend takes place if conditions involve retrogression.[12] This shows that risk-seeking and risk-aversion attitudes are conditioned by specific circumstances. Of course, how automatically this polarity implies a withdrawal of votes from the incumbent is something empirically determined by the position of that subjective threshold. Until that threshold is surpassed, it holds true that "if people are risk-averse for gains and risk-seeking for losses, the less risky incumbent should fare better when conditions are good than when they are bad" (Quattrone and Tversky 1988: 724).

This pro-incumbent bias contained in attitudes toward risk is further supported by the data. As the standardized coefficient of inflation for predicting "gradual" changes is somewhat larger than the one for "accelerated" changes (−.67 versus .63), it seems reasonable to assume that publics are more sensitized by contextual conditions to avert potential losses than to pursue uncertain gains, thus reacting more strongly in favor of gradualism than of radicalism. This evidence further urges in favour of a perspective centered on the fortunes of the incumbents. Given that Latin American voters reveal themselves as proportionally more conservative in the face of acquired gains than audacious before the opportunity of reversing current losses, the incumbent takes the natural lead.

The basic implication of such approach to the world of political choice is clear-cut: voters go to the polls to make a decision which is fashioned as involving two "risks"—the risk of suffering eventual losses and the risk of harvesting uncertain gains—and each "risk" is contained not in particular policies or issues but in the dichotomy between siding with continuity or opting for change. The bottom line is, therefore, that elections embody a binary choice: they are about continuity or change, that is, supporting or repudiating the incumbent. For the average voter, the valid choice is to keep the "ins" in or throw them out.

A binary perspective on elections is also reinforced by the interplay between the characteristics of the presidential office, cultural orientations toward leadership, the ways in which leaders and the media frame the contests, and the way electoral outcomes are ultimately interpreted by most analysts. For example, politicians and media analysts tend to describe contests and results as matters of either conforming to the status quo or contesting it; as a consequence, voters get used to thinking of them in similar terms.[13] Institutional features such as strong presidentialism also offer key incentives for the development of plebiscitarian orientations at the time of electing a president. The presidential office, characterized by its independence of power and direct mandate from the people, gives the incumbent a "sense of being the elected representative of the whole people" and teaches him or her to rule accordingly (Linz 1994: 25, see also 19–20). In turn, this sense of non-mediated identity between leader and people can only nurture a plebiscitarian use and understanding of presidential authority and the stakes involved in a presidential election.

In some countries, a plebiscitarian approach to national contests derives from the way people have been practicing electoral politics previously, as well as from popular conceptions of electoral choice. For example, survey data suggest that during the political liberalization period, Brazilians conceptualized partisan support in terms of their sympathy towards the regime (Lamounier 1980; von Mettenheim 1995: Chapter 6). In the case of México, the longstanding rule of the PRI has been interpreted as conditioning voters to approach elections through a two-step process, starting with the decisive question of whether they will continue to support the ruling party or not. As survey data gathered for the 1988 presidential elections confirm, "[f]irst and foremost, [voters] asked themselves, Am I for or against the party of the state and its leader?" (Domínguez and McCann 1995: 45). Similarly, electoral politics in post-Pinochet Chile seems to follow the political divisions of the Pinochet era, with the electoral alignments of the 1990s correlating more strongly with the distribution of votes derived from the 1988 plebiscite (which separated the political waters between those in favor and against military rule) than with anything else (see Scully and Valenzuela 1993: 13, 23–24).

In addition, popular notions of what elections are about critically configure the call for voting as an occasion for expressing political alignment with or against the incumbent. Thus, individuals construct an electoral choice in very much the same way as they may "cheer for a soccer team" (Reis 1988: 35). Of course, such notions derive from the structure of opportunities presented to individuals. For example, among Brazilians, the "forced bipartism" of the post-1974 authoritarian period motivated "the[ir] political views . . . to coalesce around new issues either in opposition to or in support of the military government" (von Mettenheim 1995: 166). Among Peruvians, political choice is contingent on the direct link forged between the mass and the leader, with the incumbent authority structuring people's reference set as the natural depository of the collective destiny, the one able to impart a sense of justice and the source of patronage benefits for everyone (Parodi and Twanama 1993).

Under democratic conditions, these plebiscitarian orientations hold the particular effect of cutting across the different factors that shape the vote, each one bringing about a particular electoral consequence in terms of the likelihood of supporting or dampening the "in" party at the ballot box. Considerations at play in the electoral scene pose themselves in dichotomous terms. Thus, economic conditions become better or worse, the command over the political agenda is perceived as strong or weak, the government helps "the rich" or "the poor", the ruling party is "ours" or "theirs," one's own class interests are favored or hurt. This means that voters may rely on different sources but, in practical terms, their response is uniquely defined as voting in favor or against the incumbent. Incumbency-oriented voting becomes the common ground upon which everyone works out his or her own electoral decision.

Given the Latin American voters' limited knowledge of and interest in political issues, their tendency toward pragmatic "satisficing" based on a notion of utility that encompasses both economic and non-economic factors, and their attitude toward elections as involving a binary choice, how exactly are electoral decisions made? If voters do not spend countless hours weighing the pros and cons of proposed policies and hoping to maximize material utility through their decisions—as many theorists would have us believe—and if they see elections as, to a large degree, contests involving voting for or against the incumbents, how exactly do they make up their minds at the voting booths? What processes do they follow to come to their decision, given the limited informational resources at their disposal and the rather low willingness to engage with the issues? And are they, in fact, capable of making meaningful choices?

Decisional Clues to Electoral Choice

Voting does not occur in a vacuum. Nor does it reflect a random process of influences chaotically dispersed by the socio-economic forces and political trends of society. Every individual is engaged in some minimal consideration and follows some sort of rationale in making up his or her mind at the voting booth. As we have already seen, Latin American voters hardly ever choose based solely on individual will or cognitive capabilities. Rather, the electoral decision is constrained and fed by the presence of short-term and long-term forces, economic and non-economic stimuli, and structural as well as idiosyncratic factors. But even if voters are poorly informed and inattentive, they should not be dismissed as incapable of making meaningful choices and acting cogently at the polls. After all, electoral outcomes are easily explained by many conditions preceding the contests, in spite of citizens' political ignorance. However, the fact that one can interpret the electoral choice of the average voter in Latin America does not turn her choice comparable to the way a fully informed elector would make it. The question that remains is how the average voter, who is loosely connected with the political reality, becomes capable of making consequential decisions. How could it be possible that voters arrive at a meaningful decision if they remain unaware and uninterested in politics? On what basis are their choices made?

The response provided by most political psychologists is quite simple: since most voters are minimally motivated to overcome—and actually can comfortably live with—their status of cognitive misers before making electoral decisions, they can simply resort to the intensive use of "decisional clues." In due course, they may rely upon the guidance these supply and thus articulate valid choices at the ballot box. By decisional clues scholars mean a series of practical devices encompassing electorally consequential stimuli that a) work as information shortcuts, b) help voters reduce the complexity of developing choices by making use of "judgmental heuristics"[14], and c) represent sources of motivation and guidance for political action.

The idea is as useful as it is simple, and many scholars have utilized it. However, certain assumptions about how decisional clues function must first be examined—and potential misunderstandings clarified—if this notion is to offer a useful, accurate way of examining voter behavior. In narrowing the notion of information shortcuts, Lupia (1994), for example, includes influential personal acquaintances of the voter and highly credible sources from the world of political experts she may be exposed to (see also Brady and Sniderman 1985). This characterisation certainly suggests a parsimonious solution to the problem of how voters come up with meaningful choices despite cognitive limitations, but it is flawed as fellow citizens (however influential they might be) are rarely any more politically enlightened than the typical voter. Moreover, the individual's own political inattentiveness conspires against enabling political experts to become influential cuegivers at a mass level.

Sniderman and his colleagues (1991) emphasize the notion of "judgmental heuristics," which are information cost-saving mechanisms contained in likability sources and group identities through which voters can rapidly grasp the implications of choosing a particular candidate or party. Yet in newly democratized regimes such cues are rarely available, since, as a rule, political alignments of the elites and the masses are characterized by fluidity.[15] Furthermore, the rationality animating political parties' standings on the eve of elections typically entails a tactical propensity to seek centrist positions in order to enhance each party's likelihood of getting elected, a strategy that can only dilute any potential identity (see O'Donnell et al., 1986).

From a different perspective, Popkin (1991) traces information shortcuts to daily life experiences of individuals, assuming that individuals make decisions exclusively upon matters of personal relevance. The problem here is two-fold. On the one hand, this understanding of information shortcuts makes matters of personal relevance contingent upon particularistic and circumstantial forces, many of which are hardly politicized and only loosely connected to the public sphere, where elections occur. On the other hand, Popkin's assertion presupposes that voters' sensitivity to specific topics or dimensions solely defines the direction of their choices, discarding the possibility that politicians and the media may manipulate the agenda—a factor leading the public to choose, occasionally, on matters beyond personal relevance.

In light of such shortcomings, there is a need to specify in more contextual terms how ill-informed voters tend to be guided in their choice-making by decisional clues. This task is to map the types of conditions surrounding the act of voting and review empirically the extent to which decisional clues are effectively available as well as the circumstances that condition such availability. Focus should be directed to the interplay of cultural, institutional and economic conditions, and the way they structure the opportunities for political socialization and heighten the eventual effect held by contextual and short-term events.

Background Conditions and Decisional Clues

If decisional clues are to provide the key to understanding voter behavior, one of the key questions to answer is: How do generally inattentive voters find clues that are politically consequential and that serve to compensate for information shortfalls? At this point, the focus of attention switches from the individual's attributes to his or her broader context and background. In other words, the answer lies not so much in asking how voters personally overcome their cognitive limitations but what conditions and motivations make some clues more easily and readily accessible to them than others. Put succinctly, to the extent that the availability of these decisional clues depends on the cultural, institutional and economic backgrounds of voters, as well as on the political contingencies surrounding the elections, the examination of these backgrounds and contingencies will yield knowledge about the opportunities and channels through which voters elaborate their choices.

In determining which clues might become electorally salient, a few key principles should be borne in mind. To begin with, clues must have the chance to develop and become a visible component of the political context. Unless some minimum prerequisites of development and stability are satisfied, a clue cannot have any considerable effect upon voters. For example, since partisanship takes time to evolve, this clue tends to be underdeveloped in post-authoritarian settings. Likewise, the more highly visible a clue becomes because of some inherent drama in its content, the more likely it is to become a reference for voters. For example, the hyperinflation upsurges of the mid and late 1980s with its major disordering of people's everyday lifes, facilitated the salience of economic conditions as a principal clue contouring electoral processes.

Second, the correspondence with longstanding cultural or institutional characteristics of the region is likely to help a clue become more relevant at election time. Thus, *caudillismo* and the strong personification of presidentialism, described as central components of political behavior and the political systems in Latin America (Dealy 1991; Linz 1994), can enhance the electoral conspicuousness of clues such as presidential leadership and the candidates' appeal. Conversely, the corporatist and antipluralistic ethos associated with the Latin American character (Wiarda 1992), along with the weak institutionalization of most party systems (McDonald and Ruhl 1989; Mainwaring and Scully 1995), suggest very little room for the emergence of partisan clues.

Third, the more explicitly political the content of the decisional clue, the more likely it is to become a source of guidance for voters. In other words, those forces providing cues to voters should intrinsically carry an understanding of the political responsibilities involved. Inflation might have been cut or unemployment might have swollen, but only after identifying a clear attribution of responsibility to the government's policies for both can that economic performance become politically salient. Thus, if voters cannot automatically attribute political meaning to the available clues in terms of prescribing responsibilities for the levels of satisfaction attained, these clues can hardly become electorally consequential.

Finally, if it is true that to become a relevant guideline for electoral behavior a clue should be closer in meaning and consequence to the realm of the electoral scene, it should not be too distant from the voter's own experience either. As personal experience is a more material yardstick than abstract speculation, conditions that affect personal life—assuming that this effect has a political meaning—are more likely to help articulate voters' choice. In this sense, pocketbook drives may become salient clues only if government actions are seen as at least partly responsible for variations in a voter's personal finances.

Following these principles, let us now review the conditions surrounding elections and examine how these raise or lower the probability that different decisional clues will shape the electoral choice of the average Latin American voter. I distinguish and comment six types of available and politically mobilizing clues: ideological, class-based, partisan, performance related, leadership connected, and candidate sources. The identification of these clues resume the shortcuts elicited by both the post-authoritarian environment and/or the literature on electoral choice, which seem appropriate for discussion within the Latin American context.

Ideological Clues

Ideological thinking has been traditionally conceived as the individual's capacity to think of political objects, policies and philosophical orientations in terms of an overarching continuum going from left to right, or from liberal to conservative. This conceptual continuum summarizes the abstract principles structuring people's positions in the political world and, as such, represents a judgmental shortcut likely to guide individuals' decisions (see Converse 1964). The question at stake, then, is: How readily do Latin American voters rely on these clues?

Ideological battles between left and right that animated the region's electoral and extra-electoral politics in the past tempted analysts to place ideology among the most influential factors in voters' choice. For some, the rhetorical clashes of the interrupted electoral experiences of the 1970s signified the power of ideology to shape electoral cleavages (see Valenzuela and Constable 1992). In the post-authoritarian decades of the 1980s and 1990s, some observers pinpointed ideological disputes as the ones nurturing people's decisions at the polls, as in the cases of Perú in 1985 and 1990, Brazil in 1989 and 1998, and Uruguay and Venezuela in 2000 (see Cameron 1994; Dugan and

Dietz 1995). However, these references to ideology came more as supplementary observations than as core explanations of the voting decision.

The assessment of ideology as a salient electoral clue necessarily raises the question of how central ideological thinking is to the average Latin American voter and how familiar he or she is with those particular ideological labels that may convey decisional clues. Scattered public opinion data show that, on average, standard ideological clues do not motivate voters in the region. Concepts such as "left" or "right" do not ring any bell for one out of three of them (i.e., 32 percent). As expected, there are significant variations in responses depending on the country: labels are more meaningful among Chileans and Uruguayans, while Venezuelans and Paraguayans seem more unable to make sense of them.[16]

Moreover, if ideological self-placement is a pre-condition for using ideological labels in selecting a political choice, the fact that an average of 41 percent of respondents that face electoral tests fail to identify those labels or to locate themselves along the continuum points out the limited relevance of ideology as an information shortcut.[17] Besides, the ability to identify ideological labels does not necessarily mean that the individual makes a consistent use of them. In Argentina, for example, there is a notable mismatch between the individuals' self-placement on a left–right scale and the position attributed to their party of choice (see Catterberg and Braun 1989).

Another approach to the topic is Converse's (1964) levels of political conceptualization, but the meager number of cases examined under this lens does not leave much hope for ideological clues either. The breadth of the public's political conceptualization capabilities in the context of the 1989 and 1994 Brazilian elections, for example, reveals a fraction of "ideologues" as tiny as the one Converse found among Americans in the late 1950s (see von Mettenheim 1995).

All this suggests that Latin American mass publics make limited use of ideological labels and only a marginal portion of them may find ideological concepts instrumental to compensate for low levels of information and attentiveness. The notion of elections as serving as the scenario of a combat between alternative ideologies, and voters constructing their choices based on their appeal, can hardly be sustained.

Class-Based Clues

The irrelevance of ideology as sources of guidance means that other factors must have the explanatory upper hand. Two "usual suspects" are class position and partisanship, the first through the orientational function of class interests—as developed through personal experience or as transmitted generationally—and the second through the work of party labels—as comprehended through parental socialization and governmental and campaign-related experiences. To be sure, one cannot be seen as totally independent of the other, since the electoral relevance of party attachments is critically linked to the persistence of basic social cleavages (Lipset and Rokkan 1967).

Class-based clues in Latin America face many of the same challenges that led analysts of most advanced democracies to disregard them as critical determinants of the vote. Social mobility, an economy increasingly based on the service sector, and rising structural unemployment all suggest a less salient role for class positions in elections. On top of this, the Latin American economic crisis of the 1980s shifted the political consequences likely to be expected from class alignments.

Since the early 1980s, there has been a wave of changes in the social composition of Latin America. In 1991, all but one country holding competitive elections revealed a per capita income level below that of 1980. The picture of negative growth was not a mild one: the slump reached almost ten percent, affecting dramatically the overall well-being of voters and deepening poverty (see CEPAL 1994). As a result, class positions were drastically redefined.

Along with vast alterations in the well-being of citizens, the demographic reduction of the industrial belt of most countries also had repercussions for the class composition of the society. Compared to twenty years ago, a conservative calculation of changes in the structure of production in Latin America yielded an increase in the share of the services sector of about 6 percent, most of which happened at the expense of the manufacturing sector (see World Development Report 1993). Between 1981 and 1990, a shift of almost 8 percentage points (from 51.5 to 59.3 percent) occurred in the proportion of people employed in the services sector within the largest electorate of the region, Brazil's, while the proportion of workers in agricultural activities shrank almost 6 points (see Urani 1995: 17). The national outlooks on these developments and their consequences for the characteristics of the social class structure (as well as for the potential demobilization of class-based clues by labor unions) is already well recorded (see Schatan et al. 1991; Rakowsky 1994).

The evolution of income inequality and poverty levels are two other indicators that illustrate the limited effectiveness of social class as source of information. As conditions deteriorated in steady and massive numbers, social class lines eroded.[18] One result of this deterioration was income concentration at the top. For example, in Argentina, between 1980 and 1989, the distribution of family income for the highest quintile went up from 45.4 to 57.6 percent, while the joint share of the three lower quintiles of the population decreased from 32.3 to 23.2 percent (see LoVuolo 1995: 49). This income concentration was complemented by an experience of massive pauperization between 1980 and 1989. If the statistics for poverty and extreme poverty are added, the following increases in the percentage of the population living in poverty can be observed: in Argentina, from 3.2 to 8 percent; in Bolivia, from 73.6 to 77.2 percent; in Brazil, from 46.3 to 59.6 percent; in Honduras, from 70.3 to 77.1 percent; in México, from 19.1 to 29.9 percent; in Perú, from 34.4 to 50.6 percent; and in Venezuela, from 4.7 to 16 percent (Edwards 1995: 258). Stunned by the brutality of these changes, one observer asserted that "during the 1980s . . . Latin America generated twice as many poor people as it procreated Latin Americans" (Vilas 1995: 326).

Naturally, such exceptional experience could not pass lightly noticed by individuals themselves. Even after the strong recovery of the 1990s, survey respondents in a 1995 multi-country study still perceived increased pauperization as a major reality in their recent lives. On average, 55 percent of the respondents perceived that poverty has gotten much worse in the last half decade. Adding those deeming poverty as having increased a little, the average proportion reached 75 percent.[19]

Objectively, the social landscape of Latin America has been dramatically affected by severe transformations in the overall levels of well-being, the structure of production, the degree of income inequality, and the proportion of population slipping into poverty. The consequences for the instability of class status and the corresponding downplaying of social class as an effective decisional clue are not hard to deduce.

Finally, if class-based clues were to exert any influence as information shortcuts, a relatively clear picture of collective interests and identity would need to be present. A critical consequence of the economic reshuffle in the region was precisely the formidable atomization of the individuals and, consequently, the pulverization of any class consciousness or structurally rooted group identity (Zermeño 1989). Changes in the economy gave way to social fragmentation and weakened the social basis of electoral behavior. Many scholars agreed that a sequence of "anomic individualism" and "defensive survivalism" emerged as substitutes that inspired short-term interests and pocketbook considerations at times of elections (Zermeño 1989: 137; Weffort 1991: 10–20).

Partisan Clues

One of the conventions commonly accepted by political scientists is that voting choice reflects mainly the individual's party allegiances. This belief takes for granted a prior history of stable partisan politics, where there are opportunities for parties to "socialize" individuals and for the individuals to make first-hand acquaintance with the pros and cons of each major political force during a reasonable period of time. It also assumes a relatively smooth intergenerational transmission of partisan allegiances, a gradual (if any) transformation of partisan policy expertise and identity, and a set of clearly defined partisan myths and rituals easily retrieved by candidates and national leaders during the campaigns. Furthermore, it presupposes a relatively strong and stable party system; otherwise, the acceptance of parties as legitimate institutions of representation and government is challenged, party organizations become exclusively subordinated to transient personal leadership and the distribution of patronage, and party rooting in society is hard to accomplish (Mainswaring and Scully 1995). Finally, this conventional view presumes the absence of strong de-socializing forces counteracting the partisan education of citizens, such as those conveyed by an antiparty sentiment or a widespread lack of credibility of such institutions.

The Latin American experience with party politics contradicts these assumptions. First, skepticism with the level of partisan institutionalization still predominates (McDonald and Ruhl 1989; but see Dix 1992). Under poorly developed party systems, many politicians have more incentives to play personal politics rather than partisan politics. When exacerbated, this situation leads to a practice of party-switching by congressmen, candidates and even presidents—a practice known as *camisetazo* or *fisiologismo*. The personalization of political loyalties and a reliance on an exchange of favors between leader and follower become the rule.

Secondly, the erosion of the class basis of politics, as previously reviewed, tends to dilute the very same sources of long-term partisan support (see Dix 1989).

Moreover, democratic breakdowns interrupted the work of partisan socialization, in cases where they did not openly reverse it. To be sure, many authoritarian experiments preceding the period under consideration sought to "re-socialize" the political identities of individuals (see Brockman Machado 1978; Valenzuela and Constable 1991). Even if not fully successful, dictatorships were very effective in diluting previous identities and legitimizing an antiparty rhetoric.

In addition to the newness of democratic politics in most countries, political parties have to overcome a series of challenges coming from the economic pressures that followed democratization, the scant antecedents of institutional robustness, and the anti-institutional mores of the modal political culture of the region. The extent to which economic hardship during the 1980s and the effective implementation of policy reforms throughout the 1990s constituted a challenge to politicians' survival has been documented at length (Nelson 1990; Conaghan 1992; Smith et al. 1994). Quite often, when reaching office, parties chose to adopt a path of economic policies radically different from campaign promises or their policy traditions, which only added more confusion and, occasionally, shifted the balance of party loyalties (see Stokes 1995).

Finally, a measure of confidence in political parties provides another indication of the institutional robustness of party systems and the likelihood of political forces to become sources of mass electoral orientation. On average, 61 percent of the publics judged political parties as essential to democracy, with Venezuelans and Brazilians exposing the lowest degree of agreement with that vision and Uruguayans displaying the highest.[20] This means that over a third of the electorates had reservations about the role of parties in electoral politics.

This assertion is further reinforced by the poor credibility of political parties in pre-electoral times. An average estimate of 26 percent signaled "a lot" and "some" confidence in parties in thirty-one cases. (For percentages for individual countries, see Table 3.1.) This negative view of parties is consistent with features of the political culture of the region such as the tendency to develop notions of political solidarity based upon organicistic arrangements or clientelistic compromises, and people's fascination with individual personalities rather than with institutions.[21]

These findings point to a limited proportion of "partisans" among the public and, in consequence, a limited effect of partisan ties as information shortcuts. Table 3.1 offers a glance at the potential electoral leverage exerted by partisan clues. On average, 37.7 percent of Latin American voters surveyed at different occasions prior to electoral rounds refused to pick a party label as a significant source of attachment or identification.[22] Moreover, a comparison of the degree of non-partisanship (that is, the percentage that lacks partisan allegiances) across countries with different levels of party institutionalization reveals that partisan independence follows systematic lines. The average value of non-partisanship for Costa Rica, Uruguay and Venezuela (countries characterized in the mid-1990s as holding a high degree of party institutionalization) was 20.3 percent; in contrast, the average value for Brazil, Ecuador and Perú (all of them charcaterized as holding a low degree of party institutionalization) was 53.8 percent. This speaks of a 33.5 percentage points difference which demonstrates the degree to which partisanship is constrained by the institutional context.

On the whole, a review of the conditions contextualizing the relationship between electorates and political parties in the region shows limited opportunities for the emergence of partisan attachments and the crystallization of party labels as important decisional clues at electoral times. This situation is a byproduct not merely of the structural or political weakness of partisan ef-

Table 3.1. Public Opinion Indicators of Partisanship and Confidence in Political Parties

Country	*Partisanship*			
(Election Month/Year)	*Non partisans*	*Incumbent*	*Opposition*	*Confidence in Parties*
Argentina (5/1989)	48	19	27	63
Argentina (5/1995)	68	12	7	26
Bolivia (7/1985)	N/A	N/A	N/A	N/A
Bolivia (5/1989)	N/A	N/A	N/A	33
Bolivia (6/1993)	51	15	30	15
Brazil (11/1989)	37	10	16	34
Brazil (10/1994)	49	10	14	22
Chile (12/1993)	20	55	12	32
Colombia (5/1982)	42	36	19	51
Colombia (5/1986)	39	24	38	N/A
Colombia (5/1990)	13	47	22	51
Colombia (5/1994)	40	33	13	14
Costa Rica (2/1982)	21	18	54	N/A
Costa Rica (2/1986)	14	45	41	23
Costa Rica (2/1990)	15	43	42	13
Costa Rica (2/1994)	16	39	45	27
Domin.Rep.(5/1982)	N/A	N/A	N/A	N/A
Domin. Rep.(5/1986)	N/A	N/A	N/A	N/A
Domin. Rep.(5/1990)	N/A	N/A	N/A	N/A
Domin.Rep.(5/1994)	32	24	29	33
Ecuador (6/1984)	47	11	4	N/A
Ecuador (1/1988)	71	N/A	N/A	N/A
Ecuador (5/1992)	57	5	14	36
El Salvador (3/1989)	34	39	14	11
El Salvador (3/1994)	45	27	15	23
Guatemala (11/1990)	63	5	1	45
Honduras (11/1985)	15	42	37	10
Honduras (11/1989)	11	39	46	5
Honduras (11/1993)	8	44	45	6
Mexico (7/1988)	65	36	14	N/A
Mexico (8/1994)	26	43	19	23
Nicaragua (2/1990)	50	26	29	20
Panama (5/1994)	20	14	26	14
Peru (4/1985)	57	2	26	N/A
Peru (4/1990)	73	6	2	17
Peru (4/1995)	80	9	1	20
Uruguay (11/1989)	*14*	*21*	*30*	*57*
Uruguay (11/1994)	*9*	*29*	*29*	*36*
Venezuela (12/1983)	*39*	*12*	*22*	*24*
Venezuela (12/1988)	*42*	*36*	*17*	*N/A*
Venezuela (12/1993)	23	17	36	11

Domin.Rep.: Dominican Republic
N/A: not available
Sources: See Appendix G.

fects, but also of the way partisan ties themselves have been forged. In this sense, their heavy reliance on the exchange of material benefits and strong personalities has been of extreme importance. Thus, as parties themselves become less reliable clues, voters are ready to turn to other sources of information, such as performance evaluations and leadership appeals.

Performance Clues

In the worst of all worlds, voters may arrive at the polls without a clear notion of class positions, having developed no partisan ties, too ignorant of the issues to choose on a policy basis, and too unsophisticated to choose according to ideological worldviews. Still, as Fiorina (1981: 5) reminds us, citizens "typically have one comparatively hard bit of data [at hand]: they know what life has been like during the incumbent's administration." Performance clues, either economic or political in content, constitute the most widely available source of information. In a context of weak partisanship, weak class consciousness and weak ideological commitments, performance may represent the most efficient source of decision.

Performance considerations are connected to the vote in three basic ways. First, they take the lead in shaping the priority lists of individuals. As preoccupations with broader economic and social issues rank high in the public's list of national concerns, one may expect an important degree of voters' sensitivity to what the government is able to accomplish in those areas. Second, performance clues surface in the context of the quality of the environment and the type of conjunctural challenges faced by the incumbents. If electoral decisions take place in times of unusual economic and political hazards, voters tend to articulate their choices around topics of government performance; in particular, two topics of performance have stood out across the past twenty-five years: the need to advance and consolidate democracy and the need to make the economy governable. Third, performance considerations depend on the extent to which the government is perceived as responsible for economic and non-economic outcomes. Naturally, unless individuals can establish an explicit connection between results and the administration's actions and omissions, performance considerations will rarely play any role as electoral clues.

Priority Lists and Performance Clues

Priority lists measure the most salient or problematic contemporary themes facing the nation, as perceived by the public. They are compiled using open-ended questions related to people's current concerns (see RePass 1971). They provide an overall view of the types of contents and decisional clues most likely to shape people's choice, such as, for example, inflation, poverty, corruption, law-and-order considerations, etc.

In twenty-five out of thirty-two contests under examination and for which pre-electoral survey data are available, the public's major concerns relate to the domain of economic performance (see Table 3.2).[23] Mentions of unemployment-related concerns rank first in forty-one percent of these contests. References to inflation or the rising cost of living follow closely in 34 percent of the elections. Remarkably, electorates show themselves concerned about unemployment two and half times more frequently than about anything else.[24] On the other hand, elections that meet inflation at the top of the agenda are as frequent as those that do not (a ratio of one to one to non-inflation matters). Altogether, unemployment, inflation, wages, or other more general economic matters (such as recession, lack of growth, shortages, external debt, etc.) critically shape 44.5 percent of the elections. References related to economic performance matters represent 62 percent of the total number of mentions.

While economic issues are of great importance, they do not exhaust the list of voters' pre-electoral concerns, nor do they absorb all considerations about government performance. Social issues such as poverty, education, health, and housing elicit important reactions from voters in different elections. Twelve percent of the electoral contests are conditioned by these issues. If one adds drug-related issues to this dimension, the ratio becomes one mention of social topics out of every five mentions. Voters do also react to issues of physical insecurity (e.g., crime and urban violence) and system survival (e.g., civil or external war, terrorism, and guerrillas). In relative terms, twenty percent of the elections are preceded by publics placing these issues at the top of the national agenda. Likewise, electorates have been sensitive to the impact of corruption, capable of rallying the public's attention in five contests out of thirty-two.

The message conveyed by these figures is that voters may be open to follow performance assessments as decisional clues in relation to what they deem to be national priorities. A heightened concern for economic matters translates into decisions shaped by voters' impressions of government's management of the economy. Still, since priority lists also convey a verdict on extra-economic areas of performance, a performance-centered voting may evoke the use of other clues, such as presidential leadership. Likewise, if concerns with corruption occupy a central position, other decisional clues, such as candidates' image and past record, are likely to be influential.

Table 3.2. Ranking on Priority Lists of the Electorates in Latin America[25]

Country	Economy Issues				Non-Economy Issues			
(Election Month/Year)	*Inflation*	*Unemployment*	*Wages*	*Crisis*	*Poverty*	*Crime*	*Social Policy*	*Corruption*
Argentina (5/1989)	1	0	2	0	0	3	0	0
Argentina (5/1995)	0	1	0	0	0	0	2	0
Bolivia (7/1985)	N/A	N/A	N/A	N/A	N/A	N/A	N/A	N/A
Bolivia (5/1989)	N/A	N/A	N/A	N/A	N/A	N/A	N/A	N/A
Bolivia (6/1993)	0	1	2	0	0	0	3	0
Brazil (11/1989)	1	0	2	0	0	0	3	0
Brazil (10/1994)	3	1	0	0	2	0	0	0
Chile (12/1993)	0	0	0	0	3	1	0	0
Colombia (5/1982)	N/A	N/A	N/A	N/A	N/A	N/A	N/A	N/A
Colombia (5/1986)	0	1	0	2	0	3	0	0
Colombia (5/1990)	0	1	0	2	0	3	0	0
Colombia (5/1994)	0	3	0	0	0	2	0	1
Costa Rica (2/1982)	1	2	0	0	0	0	3	0
Costa Rica (2/1986)	1	3	0	0	0	0	2	0
Costa Rica (2/1990)	N/A	N/A	N/A	N/A	N/A	N/A	N/A	N/A
Costa Rica (2/1994)	1	0	0	0	0	0	2	0
Domin.Rep.(5/1982)	N/A	N/A	N/A	N/A	N/A	N/A	N/A	N/A
Domin.Rep.(5/1986)	N/A	N/A	N/A	N/A	N/A	N/A	N/A	N/A
Domin.Rep.(5/1990)	N/A	N/A	N/A	N/A	N/A	N/A	N/A	N/A
Domin.Rep.(5/1994)	1	0	0	0	0	0	2	0
Ecuador (6/1984)	N/A	N/A	N/A	N/A	N/A	N/A	N/A	N/A
Ecuador (1/1988)	N/A	N/A	N/A	N/A	N/A	N/A	N/A	N/A
Ecuador (5/1992)	1	3	0	2	0	0	0	0
El Salvador (3/1989)	0	3	0	2	0	1	0	0
El Salvador (3/1994)	2	3	0	2	2	1	0	0
Guatemala (11/1990)	2	1	0	0	0	3	0	0

Honduras (11/1985)	0	1	0	2	0	0	0	3
Honduras (11/1989)	2	1	0	0	0	0	0	3
Honduras (11/1993)	1	3	0	0	0	0	2	0
Mexico (7/1988)	1	0	0	0	3	0	0	0
Mexico (8/1994)	0	1	2	0	3	3	0	0
Nicaragua (2/1990)	0	0	0	1	0	2	0	0
Panama (5/1994)	0	1	0	0	0	0	3	2
Peru (4/1985)	1	2	0	0	0	3	0	0
Peru (4/1990)	2	3	0	0	0	1	0	0
Peru (4/1995)	0	1	2	0	2	0	3	0
Uruguay (11/1989)	0	1	3	0	0	0	2	0
Uruguay (11/1994)	0	3	0	2	0	0	1	0
Venezuela (12/1983)	3	1	0	2	0	1	0	0
Venezuela (12/1988)	1	3	2	0	0	2	0	0
Venezuela (12/1993)	0	0	0	0	0	2	0	1

Domin.Rep.: Dominican Republic
N/A: not available
Sources: See Appendix G.

Economic Performance Clues

The habituation of Latin American publics to the routines of electoral politics took place in extraordinary economic times. Throughout the 1980s, the region experienced the most devastating depression in the postwar era. Output growth per capita fell almost ten percent (CEPAL 1994); in 1990, the level of income per capita was placed below the 1975 standard. In 1994, the per capita income was still below the 1980 one, at about $2,200 (IADB 1995). From an economic point of view, the decade was "lost."

Reports from international agencies described the economic landscape with dismay, as characterized by "an absolute reduction in investment levels and [as a result] a setback of living standards not experienced by the region's population for half a century" (CEPAL 1991: 1). Latin America experienced more and deeper recessions than advanced industrial economies, and as a result suffered "lower economic growth, reduced educational progress, a worsened distribution of income and more poverty" (Hausmann and Gavin 1995: 1). Even if some national differences remained in other dimensions, the general economic background unified the region in decay. As one leading scholar pointed out, "[Latin] America is unified by crisis, foreign debt, economic stagnation, inflation, rising unemployment and growing inequalities" (Weffort 1989: 93).

Recessions during the 1980s did not come alone. Their material impact was immensely magnified by all-time high inflation levels, deterioration of real wages, rising unemployment, and the exhaustion of monetary resources, which heavily constrained public investment and social spending (CEPAL 1991; 1994). For example, between 1986 and 1989, a weighted average rate of inflation for the six largest electorates of the region reached the figure of 1,494.3 percent. During the same period, mean real wages equalled, on average, 84 percent of the 1980 remunerations, and urban unemployment levels rose to 7.7 percent of the economically active population. Furthermore, between 1982 and 1990, the region suffered an all-time negative net transference of resources, which amounted close to $220 billions (CEPAL 1995). It is hard to overemphasize the potential of such a crisis to disorganize the economic life of Latin American societies and turn electoral tests into referenda on the coping abilities and rhetoric of governments confronting such critical conditions.

In a like manner, the strong economic stabilization and recovery of the 1990s, based on massive spending cuts, orthodox anti-inflationary policies, radical changes in the property structure, and the consolidation of high unemployment levels (see CEPAL 1995; Edwards 1995), could only tend to keep electorates highly sensitive to performance clues of a financial nature. Sudden rises in per capita income and mean real wages followed during the

1990s. Between 1991 and 1994, an average accumulation of eight percentage points in per capita income reversed the downward trend in material well-being and social mobility. In five of the seventeen countries under study, the output growth per person surpassed the single-digit figure. Exhibiting a similar effect, mean real wages in most of the largest electoral markets inverted the negative trend and overtook the 1980 baseline, reaching an average value of 103 (1991–94). This change represented an amelioration of about 25 percent in the paychecks of the wage-earning public *vis-à-vis* the 1986–89 situation (CEPAL 1994).

The dramatic and radical nature of economic developments in Latin America during the 1980s through to the mid-1990s constituted a unique setting for the flourishing of economic performance clues. Scholars such as Calvert and Calvert (1989: Chapter 7), for example, have interpreted the tendency on the part of voters to look for state economic protection, combined with irresponsible economic individualism, as likely to grant natural primacy to economic performance in defining political choices.

What is important to remember here is that electoral responsiveness to government's economic leadership is not solely a product of extraordinary economic circumstances; cultural factors also play a key part. It is important to pay attention to the way the interplay between economic situations and cultural legacies predisposes voters to identify office holders as politically liable for any amelioration or misfortunes undergone under their administration, a linkage that is critical in validating the role of economic performance as decisional clue. As well, the content of economic clues must not be limited to those of national scope, since proximity is likely to make personal financial conditions an important information shortcut. To the extent that individuals' attitudes toward national economics and their own personal fortunes are based on deep-seated notions of the role of the state and the government's responsibility, electoral reactions to pocketbook situations are as likely to occur as reactions to larger societal realities.

On average, 61.2 percent of voters hold the incumbent accountable for the country's financial situation. This figure is based on eleven observations for which data are available, with a range between 48 (Perú in 1985) to 79 percent (Uruguay in 1994).[26] Alternative sources of attribution, such as the opposition, fellow citizens, or external actors, constitute, on average, less than a third of the responses. Attribution of responsibility for personal financial conditions is also directed to the government. Data available for only five observations render an average of 71.5 percent of the public holding the incumbents liable for personal fortunes (see Appendix G for sources of data). Altogether, surveys reveal a public sensitive to and likely to rely on certain economic clues in order to pass judgments on the merits of the administration in power.

Non-Economic and Democratic Performance Clues

A lasting situation of economic disarray, with the disorganization of everyday life it carries, also influences the extra-economic dimensions of government performance. As galloping price increases rapidly drain budget allocations, fiscal revenues of the state collapse with recession, and monetary reserves evaporate with rising debt payments, the government is left with minimal resources with which to govern. At the same time, high inflation, recession and unemployment represent a direct threat to people's own material well-being, making their dependence upon the social intervention of the state more critical (see Nelson 1990). As high inflation speeds up the devaluation of money, it also depreciates power among rulers and political confidence among voters (Portantiero 1985). Accordingly, under extraordinary economic conditions, the quality of government performance in extra-economic domains, such as social policy-making and the consolidation of the political order, becomes highly constrained.

This does not mean, however, that extra-economic concerns are mere projections of what occurs in the realm of personal or national financial states, or that they become peripheral to voters' concerns. Rather, heightened by the economic crisis, they may become even more central to voters, since they may now appear closer to the practical notion of what effective government is. If due to macro-economic constraints social policy cannot be effective, voters may choose to react electorally to such incapacity rather than to the original structural limitations, since the ineffectiveness of social policy is closer to the perceptions and actual needs of individuals and therefore more likely to be translated into key decisional clues. Similarly, if economic adversity becomes so critical that takes the form of citizens waking up to news of looting, food riots, wildcat strikes, and urban violence, the ability of the incumbent to create order out of chaos and thus ensure social and political stability is bound to take precedence as a decisional clue *vis-à-vis* the more distant macro-economic antecedents of those problems.

Government performance presents as many opportunities for the creation of decisional clues as there are roles inherent in public office and standards for judging administrations. In the non-economic domain, social policy and political stability are two critical dimensions. The first concerns ordinary matters related to government's management of non-economic issues. The second dimension relates to matters that involve a test of the governance capabilities of those in office, in light of events connected to the existence and survivability of the socio-political order (e.g., violence, wars, democratic consolidation) or events that can serve as an opportunity to dramatize the incumbent's political commitment to maintaining the order (e.g., corruption, crime, foreign events). Both matters are interlocked in the notion of political leadership, which constitutes another critical decisional clue that voters are able to rely upon.

There is another aspect of government performance that, although in permanent dialogue with the notion of political leadership, entails a specific dimension of management: the extent to which the administration promoted democratization. The results obtained in this area are relevant in light of the original post-authoritarian agenda. On the other hand, the very event of re-democratization in the region under inauspicious structural conditions has generalized the belief among scholars that political choices involved a change in political values, with new priorities focused on the advancement of political rights and civil liberties (see Flisfisch 1983; Mainwaring and Viola 1984). Thus, privileging democratic performance as a decisional clue, Remmer concludes that "democratic goods may factor heavily into the calculus of voters, allowing elected leaders, particularly those emerging from a background of dictatorship, to maintain popular support despite acute economic crisis" (1991: 779).

While this argument suggests that voters' notion of utility may include an interest in deepening the democratic quality of the political system, it cannot rule out the fact that cumulative expressions of socio-economic disorder have usually gave way to demands for strong-handed responses by the government. This balance was illustrated by cross-national data that placed both democratic deepening preferences such as expanded freedom of speech and people's involvement in public affairs, and authority consolidating leanings interpreted as order maintainance, within close range of each other as the top public preference across time.[27]

As a result, one has to admit the unfolding of a trade-off of priorities in the public mind between the promotion of political rights and freedoms and the imperative of governability and maintenance of the public order. This last tendency takes on a particular connotation when set against the broad picture of the political culture of Latin Americans. If it is true that democratic transitions were paralleled by growing mass conformity with the idea of a democratic order, this commitment has revealed itself both greater at the abstract level than in regards to specific principles and situations, and conditional to the practical challenges faced by the public order.[28]

A tension raises between the inclination to put a premium on democratic deepening and a willingness to reward strong political authority when confronting public turbulence, which usually takes the actual form of a confrontation between a style of popular leadership based on democratic-spiritedness and another one based on the goal of order preservation. Conciling both highly demanded qualities yields the ideal notion of political leadership; however the region history too often demonstrated that the goal of strengthening political authority substracted, rather than co-existed with, opportunities to deepening democratic guidance (Torre 1993). Consequently, the issue is not whether Latin Americans endorse democratic or authoritarian regimes, but rather whether their notion of democracy encompasses a claim for liberties and freedoms as great as that for order and authority. Whether democratic performance becomes a relevant decisional clue, as a result of either progress in a pluralistic and liberal direction or against this to accomplish goals of law-and-order by authoritarian means, remains an empirical matter needing investigation.

Leadership Clues

Leadership considerations have always been granted a privileged place with regards to the political behavior of Latin Americans, with both cultural and institutional factors pointing to its significance. Morse suggests that under the circumstances such as those found in Latin America in the 1980s, "given conditions of political inexperience and social disorder, only strong *personalist* leadership could institutionalize government" (1992: 89; italics in original). This formula has consolidated itself around a leader-centered rule and highly personalistic politics, taking the form of a strong presidential system. Rooted in the *caudillista* legacy of post-independence times and the blessing of hierarchical authority by Catholicism, personalized leadership remains a key element to understanding mass political behavior in the region (see Dealy 1991). The president's management of non-economic matters is, in fact, the most visible shortcut to inform individuals about existing leadership qualities.

The pragmatic use of leadership clues in voting is far from being solely the product of cultural legacies and institutional formulas. Nor is it merely the result of the president's actions or omissions when confronting the challenge of economic uncertainty and instability. Even though it was stressed earlier that extraordinary economic times rapidly raise demands for strong leadership, this does not mean that voters turn only to this clue in the face of turmoil. Since leadership qualities involve a plurality of expressions, such as policy initiatives, audacious projects, law-and-order accomplishments, and approval-boosting events by the president—all, of course, conducive to the belief that power is being exercised and governability is being forcefully sought—presidential popularity should be seen as a variable construct based in multiple sources.

An initial look at survey data[29] reveals that, regardless how much economic disorganization and socio-political instability beset society, there has been a tendency to put a premium on strong leadership. Measured in net scores, those privileging a heavy-handed rule outpaced those opposed to it in most countries. In 1988 in Argentina, there were almost two people in favor of heavy-handed government for each person against it; in 1995, the ratio was tied, and pretty much the same happened in México in that same year. In Brazil in 1988, the ratio for tough government was sixteen in favor for each one opposed, but in 1995, the ratio shrunk to less than two to one. In Chile and Uruguay in 1988, there were fewer people in favor of strong leadership than otherwise, something like six for every ten opposed. By 1995, the situation reversed: among Chileans, more than two were supportive of a heavy-handed government for every one who was not; among Uruguayans, both positions were tied. Among Peruvians and Venezuelans in 1995, the preference was clearly pro strong leadership: about six and four were favorable to strong rule for each individual who was not, respectively.[30]

As the data suggest, there is nothing like a linear relationship between popular leadership and democratic leadership. Trade-offs are always present. Popular leadership may result from problem-solving abilities of the incumbent or progress accomplished towards political stability, but it may also result from mere theatrical displays of authority by the president. The logic followed by the public in assessing the popularity of their presidents resembles the one depicted by Huntington about the dilemma of societies in transition: leadership is endorsed not so much for its quality as it is for its quantity. What matters, especially after the experience of economic chaos and socio-political instability, is how much governability and ability to rule the incumbent is able to impose.

Carrión's (1998) empirical analysis of the basis of presidential popularity in Perú clearly suggests this is the case for people's reaction to Fujimori's leadership. While the economy was still in dire straits, poverty was on the rise, and terrorism remained active, the president's approval rating started to rise steadily. The appreciation of his leadership did not derive from performance records but from matters exogenous to the management of the ordinary policy-making process, namely, Fujimori's furious attack on highly discredited institutions such as the Congress and the judiciary, both of which he accused of being a hindrance to the development of the country and the source of political iniquity (see Carrión 1998: 10–12). This example brings attention to the extra-economic nature of presidential popularity. In fact, it is very telling that the handful quantitative studies of popularity functions conducted for Latin American countries have all been puzzled by the same paradox: why the president's approval increased (or decreased) if economic improvements (or failures) did not take place (see Canzani 1995: 8–9; Carrión 1998: 11). The answer is simple: presidential leadership does not depend solely on economic performance. And in actuality, this extra-economic dimension of the president's popularity has always been there to be detected whenever exploring sources of public approval other than merely economic outcomes (see Rius 1992; Stokes 2001).

In the case of Perú, Carrión (1998: Table 2) shows that between late 1980 and mid-1993, the largest partial effect on popularity is due to "honeymoon" influences involving considerations of political legitimacy and trust. Stokes (2001), who studies Fujimori's first administration (1990–95), concludes that political events such as the self-coup holds the largest impact on explaining mass approval. Analyzing presidential approval in Uruguay between 1986 through mid-1992, Rius (1992: 30–31) concludes that "honeymoon" cycles as well as the partisan origin of the government account better than economic indicators for the fluctuations in public support.

In conclusion, one can say that leadership clues are likely to articulate people's choice as a result of cultural predispositions, enhanced by the personalistic features embedded in the strong presidential system that characterizes the region. Voting by following such clues involves a "political referendum" on the leadership abilities of the incumbent. At the heart of that referendum is not a decision between policies or economic performances. Instead, the referendum is based on the ruling abilities of the incumbent force as personified in the president, abilities that are extra-economic in nature, since they are about making decisions and providing a sense of control and initiative. How efficient the incumbent has been in providing this general feeling of public reassurance is what reinforces the popularity of the president and identifies his or her political leadership, which, in turn, is what shapes the electors' decisions at the polls.

Candidate Clues

Whatever information shortcut that long-term forces (such as class positions and parties) or short-term ones (such as performance and leadership) fail to provide may be compensated by the personal and political attributes of the contending candidates. To begin with, candidates are more easily identifiable than parties, which helps in the process of developing empathy or aversion. In the period under study here, while verbalizations of party identification (with either the incumbent or its major opposition) rendered a median value of 26.5 percent, those embodying positive views of the top two rivaling candidates (the incumbent and his or her major contender) prompted a median response by 38 percent.[31] Contrasting the median proportions of survey respondents identifying themselves with the incumbent party (24 percent) and expressing supporting views of the incumbent candidate (45 percent) points in the same direction.

Indeed, since candidates remain untouched by longer structural trends, show a limited dependency on socialization processes (only to the extent that some of their attributes could acquire political meaning), and are capable of weathering the changes in performance, they represent one of the less cognitively demanding and more readily available clues upon which voters may orient their decisions. Candidates further benefit from the personalistic features of political competition, since electioneering practices and media coverage of campaigns in Latin America increasingly tend to place the candidate's persona at the center of the contest (see Skidmore 1993).

Most importantly, the cultural traits and the nature of the presidential office lead voters to highlight leadership attributes and personal biographies. Candidate-centered elections are congenial to presidential systems since "the presidential candidates do not need and often do not have any prior record as political leaders" (Linz 1994: 11). In Linz's view, candidates "may not be identified with a party with an ideology or program and record. . . . The choice is often based on an opinion about *one* individual, a personality, promises, and—let's be honest—an image a candidate projects" (1994: 11; italics in original). If this interaction of institutional design and campaigning style is extremely functional in eliciting voters' candidate-centered calculations, it is even more so under conditions of financial distress. Generalizing to the whole region, O'Donnell describes presidential elections as contests where "presidents get elected promising that they—strong, courageous, above parties and interests, *machos*—will save the country. Theirs [will be] a 'government of saviors' (*salvadores de la patria*)" (O'Donnell 1992: 12; italics in original). Voters are therefore asked to choose the individual who is most fit to take charge of the country's destiny, leaving considerations such as party affiliation or class identity aside.

The peculiar advantage of candidates' attributes as decisional clues is expressed, for example, by the fact that candidates outperform political parties as factors explicitly motivating the choice of electors. Survey data in seven different contests show that candidates are often the primary criterion of decision of voters *vis-à-vis* political parties: on average, voters are twice as likely to refer to candidates than to parties as sources of decision.[32] Interestingly enough, if at first the data may suggest a correlation between the magnitude of this ratio and the persistence of electoral politics (with the sole exception of Panamá), longitudinal data from Brazil leaves this impression unsettled. From the opening elections of 1982 to the 1989 presidential elections, national samples of Brazilians were asked to explain their choice as based on parties or candidates. The pattern is rather clear: in 1982, the pro-candidate ratio stood at 1.2; in 1985, it went up to 3.8; by 1988, it was 3.2; and by 1989, it picked up to 5.7.[33] As a corollary, one could say that rather than materializing the influence of partisan cues, the development of democratic politics created a more beneficial landscape for the consolidation of candidates' attributes as key sources of decision.

Also, candidates can be expected to remain more salient not just as a result of the absence or weak presence of factors such as parties, but ironically by virtue of their very presence. If it is true that presidential elections, by their very nature, are contests centered on the quality of political individuals, a focus on personalistic features does not necessarily imply open hostility to political parties. Candidates may benefit from exploiting their public persona, as well as from relying on their linkages to partisan structures. In some ways, this duality qualifies the tendency to associate rising partisan independence with the emergence of political outsiders as candidates, illustrating how some strong candidacies are built by stressing "anti-party" sentiments (e.g., Collor in Brazil, Fujimori in Perú, Chávez in Venezuela). But one should not miss how other strong candidacies may successfully compete by free-riding on the additional recognition effect provided by parties (e.g., Menem in Argentina, Caldera in Venezuela). Parties may provide a "surplus" benefit in making candidates the core decisional clue of voters.

One way of providing empirical evidence for such relationships is using Pearson's correlation coefficient which measures the degree of co-dependence between our available measures of candidates evaluations and partisanship.[34] According to the data, sympathetic views of the incumbent candidate achieve a rather high Pearson's correlation of .67 with the personal identification with the ruling party, and a somewhat moderate correlation of .43 with an aggregate measure of incumbent party strength (see Chapter 4). Conversely, Pearson's correlation between appraisals of the major opposition contender and partisan identification with the opposition hits a coefficient of .73, while the correlation of the former with the party strength measure for the major opposition force reaches a coefficient of .62. A summary portrait of the connectedness between candidate-centered guidelines and partisan clues is achieved by correlating the net differences of each variable: the Pearson's coefficient reaches .75 with the subjective measure of net partisanship and .45 with the aggregate measure of net party strength.[35]

The basic message conveyed by these correlations is that candidates and parties are far from always competing in a zero-sum game as decisional clues. They may live together as relevant sources of electoral guidance, although considering the higher visibility of the former, this can only help candidate clues to become even more accessible and instrumental to voters.

It is clear from the discussion above that voters and electorates can resort to a plurality of decisional clues upon which to nurture their political choice and that certain decisional clues are more influential than others in shaping the voting decisions of citizens in Latin America. The key question is how these clues fare when considering their effects at the same time and what dynamics can be distinguished under different electoral scenarios. Addressing these issues requires to shift focus from voter rationality and decisional clues to methodology and theoretical models of electoral choice, which are discussed in the next chapter.

NOTES

1. Unfortunately, standard measures of political knowledge are hard to find for the whole region as cross-national public opinion studies are far more an exception than a rule. Still, preelectoral polls such as those conducted by CID-Gallup and Belden&Russonello in Central America throughout the 1980s, and the data reported in scholarly work like Cros Beras (1985) for the Dominican Republic, Alducin (1992) for México, and Meneguello (1993) sustain this assertion. Thereafter, for the sake of simplicity, all figures are presented in rounded form unless otherwise noted. Also, all cross-national averaged figures are presented as unweighted rates unless otherwise noted.

2. CIMA, "Barómetro Iberoamericano II," July 1993, 2–4.

3. Corporación Latinobarómetro, "Latinobarómetro I," *Press release* 1995, <http://www.latinobarometro.org> (July 1995).

4. Latinobarómetro, "Latinobarómetro I," 1995.

5. CIMA, "Barómetro Iberoamericano IV," November 1994, 3–4.

6. CIMA, "Barómetro Iberoamericano II," 5–6.

7. CIMA, "Barómetro Iberoamericano III," November 1993, 7.

8. Latinobarómetro, "Latinobarómetro I," 1995.

9. If no answers and no responses are pooled together with the overtly cynical views, altogether these yield an average of 43 percent.

10. Latinobarómetro, "Latinobarómetro I," 1995.

11. World Values Survey, "World Values Survey II," (http://www.worldvaluessurvey.com/statistics/index.html), 1992; LatinoBarómetro, "Latinobarómetro I," 1995.

12. The survey question asked read, "Would you say that changes in this country should be made in an accelerated or gradual manner?" and was asked of urban samples of thirteen Latin American countries (in seven of them twice) during 1993, thus amounting to a total number of twenty cases. Both predictors—one, a measure of the proportional difference in inflation rate relative to the previous year, and the other, a weighted-by-month-of-the-survey measure of per capita income growth rate—explain almost fifty percent of the variance of the net difference of proportions between those endorsing the "gradual" alternative minus those in favor of the "accelerated" option. Only the first predictor (inflation) achieved statistical significance at conventional levels greater than $p < .05$, with a negative unstandardized coefficient of $-.20$, which implied that as inflation was proportionally higher over time, less people were willing to prioritize gradualism over radicalism. By the same token, support for "accelerated changes" was bound to fall as inflation lowered and per capita income grew (although the effect of the latter was non-significant). These calculations are based on CEPAL (1995) and CIMA, "Barómetro Iberoamericano II" and "III", 1993.

13. For such an interpretation of the 1988 and 1994 Mexican elections, see Colosio (1993: 155); Adrianne Appel, "Though Unhappy, Mexicans May Vote for the Ruling Party," *The Christian Science Monitor*, 15 August 1994, 14; and Editorial, "El Cambio, NO", *Proceso*, 23 August 1994, 1. For the 1993 Venezuelan election, see David Scott, "Venezuela Prepares for Watershed Presidential Election Sunday," *The Christian Science Monitor*, 3 December 1993, 12. For the 1994 Brazilian election, see Editorial, *Jornal do Brasil*, 4 October 1994, 1–2, and Pinto (1994: 96–97); for the 1995 Peruvian election, see *DESCO Resumen Semanal*, Appendix 2, 18 April 1995, 1–2. For the 1995 Argentine election, see Editorial, *El Cronista Comercial*, 19 May 1995, 14.

14. For an extended discussion of the concept of "judgmental heuristics," see Sniderman et al. (1990). For a partial rebuttal of the universality of this notion in light of the development of political skills by Western electorates, see Dalton and Wattenberg (1993). For a critique of views assuming that reliance on decisional clues permits uninformed voters to behave like fully informed electors, see Bartels (1996).

15. Even in those few cases like Brazil, where authoritarian rule allowed party politics to evolve and motivate people to count on judgmental heuristics (e.g., MDB as the "party of the poor," ARENA as the "party of the rich," see Lamounier 1980), the stability of these developments was crumbled by successive changes in the electoral legislation and party system.

16. Latinobarómetro, "Latinobarómetro I," 1995.

17. This evidence comes from an incomplete set of countries where publics were unable, or unwilling, to place themselves on a standard seven or ten-point scale of ideological self-identification. Due to the data incompleteness, the evidence has an illustrative rather than a representative value. The percentage ranges of "non-ideologues" (defined as those who were unable to identify ideological concepts and place themselves at some point of the continuum) were 46–47 percent in Argentina (1989–1995), 45–69 percent in Brazil (1989–1994), 30 percent in Chile (1993), 41 percent in Colombia (1982), 56 percent in México (1994), 43–52 percent in Perú (1990–1995), 14–25 percent in Uruguay (1989–1994), and 19–24 percent in Venezuela (1983–1988). For sources, see Appendix G.

18. Looking at the changes in the Gini index during the 1980s for some of the larger electorates of the region, the trend was towards greater inequality: Argentina switched from .389 to .461, Bolivia from .479 to .515, Brazil from .574 to .625, and Perú from .427 to .438 (Edwards 1995: 257). Interestingly enough, exceptions to this rule are found among longstanding democracies like Colombia and Costa Rica.

19. Latinobarómetro, "Latinobarómetro I," 1995.

20. See Appendix G.

21. See, for example, Wiarda (1992: 324–27) on the belief in the natural hierarchy of social or functional groups and the overall importance of these groups; Eisenstadt and Roniger (1984: Chapter 6) and Roniger (1990) on patron–client relationships and exchange of particularistic benefits; and Morse (1992: 88–90), McDonald and Ruhl (1989: 341–344) and others on personalism embodied in the figure of the "Machiavellian leader" or *caudillo*.

22. Interestingly, comparing non-partisanship over time renders very weak support for the argument that sees effective partisan socialization as a function of the tempo-

ral opportunities for party development offered by continuous democratic governance. Considering the average proportions of non-identifiers for the first and last election held in each country for which data are available (38.5 and 37.6 percent, respectively), there seems to be a null effect, or, if anything, a slight party dealignment effect as party politics endures.

23. Unfortunately, data for priority lists are not available for all forty-one contests here examined, but only for 32 elections. Another problem is that the information gaps are stockpiled in the earlier period of analysis (1982–89), suggesting the possibility of some systematic temporal bias when drawing inferences. The cases with missing data are: Bolivia, 1985 and 1989; Colombia, 1982; Costa Rica, 1990, Dominican Republic, 1982, 1986 and 1990; and Ecuador, 1984 and 1988. I suspect that a complete priority list for all elections would not present a wholly different balance in terms of the basic dimensions reviewed hereafter; yet, within the realm of economic performance issues, it might have given a greater salience to inflation-related concerns. For sources, see Appendix G.

24. This figure reflects the ratio of the number of elections in which this problem was mentioned in the first, second or third place (23 in total) to the number of elections where it was not cited (9 in total).

25. Cells with values of zero represent mentions with low priority (fourth place or farther). The category "crisis" includes mentions of "economic crisis," "stagnation," "recession," "(lack of) growth," "shortage," "budget problems," "external debt," "devaluation," and "government mismanagement." The category "poverty" includes mentions of "poverty," "hunger" and "misery." The category "crime" includes mentions of "crime," "security," "guerrilla," "violence," "terrorism" and "war." The category "social policy" includes mentions of "housing," "education," "health" and "drugs."

26. Comparability between observations is somewhat conditional due to slight differences in question wordings; for sources and wordings, see Appendix F.

27. World Values Survey, "World Values Survey II," 1992; LatinoBarómetro, "Latinobarómetro I," 1995. The information available for Argentina, Brazil, Chile and Mexico pointed out that, on average, 35.5 percent gave exclusive priority to the democratic deepening preferences in 1990–1 and 33 percent priviledged order maintainance. Five years later, the balance for the same group of countries was 36.5 and 28 percent, respectively.

28. Empirical evidence for particular countries is found in Booth and Seligson (1994), Torres (1985), Cros-Beras (1985), Catterberg (1991), Seligson and Booth (1995).

29. Consorcio Polis, "Relatório de pesquisa," IDESP, 1988; LatinoBarómetro, "LatinoBarómetro I," 1995. The question reads: "There are people who say that some heavy-handed government is necessary; others say that there is no need for a heavy-handed government. What opinion comes closer to yours?"

30. Consorcio Polis, "Relatório de pesquisa," IDESP, 1988; LatinoBarómetro, "Latinobarómetro I," 1995.

31. These results, however, should be taken cautiously, since multiple responses were possible in some of the surveys these data come from. A comparison of incumbent party sympathy and incumbent candidate sympathy should offer a more accurate description of the existing gap between the two in terms of identifiability and, as a consequence, practical utility as decisional clues. For sources see Appendix G.

32. The values were as follows: in Argentina in 1989, 55 percent for candidates and 38 percent for parties; in Brazil in 1989, 30 and 5; in Chile in 1993, 43 and 11; in Colombia in 1982, 22 and 14; in Costa Rica in 1994, 45 and 28; in Guatemala in 1985, 44 and 17; in México in 1994, 19 and 38; in Panamá in 1994, 16 and 23; and in Venezuela in 1993, 40 and 36, respectively. For sources, see Appendix G.

33. Tendências, "Encarte de Dados de Opinião Pública," *Opinião Pública* 1, no. 1, (July–August 1993): 20

34. The coefficient ranges between +1 to −1, with values close to either extreme meaning that the variation in the first measure (say, opinions about candidates) is highly dependent of the variation observed in the second measure (say, feelings towards parties). A value close to zero means that both measures are independent of each other, therefore, they lack any significant relationship.

35. In the first two cases the number of observations adds to twenty-three; in the comparison of net differences the number is twenty-two. All coefficients in the range of the .40s are significant at the level of .05; all other estimates showing higher coefficients are significant at the level of .01.

Chapter Four

Models of Electoral Choice: Measurement and Empirical Description

USING MODELS OF ELECTORAL CHOICE TO ANALYZE ELECTIONS DATA

Electorates confront the moment of decision in a context of opportunities and conditions. Thus, acknowledging the variety of decisional clues available to them to come up with a choice is all but only one step in helping us to understand what governing rules trigger their process of electoral responses. It is also necessary to uncover the structure of the competing explanations derived from a situation of multiple available sources which is done by modelling the simultaneous influences of decisional clues on the final decision.

The use of models entail the belief that specific hypothesis underlie the way we make sense of voting results. Six models of electoral choice can be offered as organized explanations of the determinants shaping the public verdict at the polls. I refer to these as affirmative voting, party voting, economic voting, democratic performance voting, political referendum voting, and candidate voting. These models are then used as the basis of analysis at both the macro and micro levels. Accordingly, focus will shift to how each model is composed and what empirical measures are used.

METHODOLOGICAL CONSIDERATIONS

Level of Analysis

Before specific models of choice can be addressed, certain more fundamental questions with regard to methodology must be settled. For one, what level of analysis is appropriate when studying elections? Each of the decisional clues that voters use to make electoral choices not only reflects special characteristics of the electoral environment, but also permits the articulation of fairly cogent responses at the aggregate and individual levels. Which of these levels is more useful? Fortunately, the answer is simple: it is only by studying both the aggregate and individual data—by looking both at the macro and the micro picture—that one can form a clear, accurate view of elections in the region.

Examining voting choice from both perspectives, macro and micro, has advantages not afforded by either of the approaches alone. It serves as an occasion to learn about the impact of objective conditions on political behavior and, at the same time, about the reasoning process through which individuals make a final decision at the ballot box. This is an extremely useful strategy in light of the shortcomings of each approach. The great advantage of a macro-level specification is that it can ignore the idiosyncrasies of individuals and, as a result, offer a patterned description of the determinants and consequences of the choices undertaken by collective entities. On the other hand, such analysis supplies half-answers to the question of how the individual voter reacts to changing circumstances and why people vote the way they do, since the data do not provide information at the level of the individual. In turn, emphasizing only micro-level data exposes the analysis to problems of spuriousness and rationalization. Although these may not be entirely avoided in aggregate analysis either, they can at least be partially checked by the degree of correspondence one encounters between micro and macro level findings. Furthermore, in view of the recentness of survey research in Latin America, a concentration on individual-level studies could only provide very limited information for the region as a whole. Thus, aggregate and individual analyses must complement each other and help determine the extent to which decision processes at both levels bring together a consistent illustration of voting choice in Latin America.

Aggregate-level examination offers insights into the major voting trends and the extent to which objective conditions and developments influence the electoral fortunes of the incumbent, as well as the ways in which different institutional and macro-economic contexts interact with those main effects. In this study, in Chapter 5, I focus on the patterns of voting choice substantiated in forty-one different presidential elections during the period between February 1982 and May 1995. Only competitive presidential elections are considered for analysis. Each election qualifies as competitive if it allows the effective presence of more than one candidate and party in the race, no significant social or political majority are formally excluded (Dahl 1971), at least thirty percent of the votes are allocated to the opposition, and it does not represent a "founding election" (O'Donnell et al., 1986), that is, the election by which democracy itself was restored. The elections analyzed here satisfy these requirements, though partial exceptions should be acknowledged for the cases of the 1989 Salvadorean and 1990 Guatemalan elections, where facilities for left-of-the-center organizations to participate were considerably restricted. For Colombia, Costa Rica, Dominican Republic and Venezuela, the first contest considered is the one closest to January 1982 (see Appendix A).

On the other hand, an examination of the individual-level effects provides an opportunity to assess the extent to which macro-level motivations are effectively translated into the voter's calculus of choice and allows direct observation of how individuals weigh the major factors structuring their decision. In Chapter 7, I examine the individual process of electoral decision-making that occurred in three different presidential contests held in Argentina, Perú and Uruguay between November 1994 and May 1995, each taking place in a distinct context in terms of both levels of political institutionalization and economic stability.

Context

Indeed, context is a key factor that must be taken into account. Voters are likely to follow one particular decisional clue more than another as a result of the structure of opportunities and incentives provided by the institutional and macro-economic contexts of their action. But one can hardly assume that everyone will react in the same way under different political and economic environments. The specific effects of political socialization, party systems and macro-economic circumstances must be considered, as they may influence the voting decision in radically different ways in different milieu. I examine the impact of context on electoral behavior and results in Chapter 6.

Incumbent Voting

As discussed in previous chapters, electoral choice in the region essentially boils down to voting for or against the incumbent. Accordingly, the focus of our empirical study is explaining the variation of the fortunes of the incumbent party –thus, the percentage of votes gathered by the incumbent party will be our dependent variable across this research. Keeping this in mind, the general model of choice on which all specific models are based, regardless of the level of analysis chosen, can be stated as follows:

$$\text{Incumbent Vote} = f(\text{Economic Clues, Non-Economic Clues})$$

which indicates that the incumbent vote-share is a function of the effect exerted by economic and non-economic clues over voters.

SIX MODELS OF ELECTORAL CHOICE

Considering the discussion in the previous chapter about how, and to what extent, decisional clues may be effectively present, six models of electoral choice can be distinguished. These models are derived both from previous discussion by literature and my review of the performance and leverage of the decisional clues.

Arrayed according to their embodiment of long-term and short-term factors, the models can be labeled as affirmative voting, party voting, economic voting, democratic voting, political referendum voting, and candidate voting. Each of these models offers an explanation of voting behavior that can be tested empirically, either at the aggregate or individual level or both. By examining elections data through the prism of these models, while at the same time taking context and the basic assumption of incumbent voting into account, we can arrive at parsimonious explanations of electoral behavior in Latin America. The models presented below form the basis of the discussion in the following chapters, as data from the elections under study are examined and the theoretical constructs are put to the test to see which of them can—and to what degree—account for election results in Latin America. First, however, we must look closely at the models of electoral choice and the different sets of variables and measurements they entail. It is these variables that lend themselves to empirical testing and will be examined in subsequent chapters.

Affirmative Voting

Voters may define their electoral options by simply repeating prior choices, that is, deciding their vote "affirmatively" (see McDonald and Ruhl 1989: 14), or rather contrarily, purposely choosing the alternative to the one in office. Motives are numerous: the high costs of acquiring and updating political information, the incidence of cultural predispositions favoring inertial and ritualistic behavior which result from either "a desire not to alienate the powerful" (McDonald and Ruhl 1989: 14) or a deep-seated adversarial attitude towards government.[1] Prior voting is the variable that, at the aggregate level, captures more substantially the effects of longer-term factors over the magnitude of public endorsement to incumbents.

The affirmative voting model assumes that electorates as a whole possess some political memory regardless of the gap between electoral schedules. Also, it takes for granted some minimal inertia in how generations are politically socialized as a result of their class and other group positions, even in the face of dramatic and rapid changes in the social structure. Occasionally, the voter may not be directly moved by class clues or by any other collective attachment or culturally derived source of affirmative or negative electoral conduct, but these elements may indirectly help to make other considerations, such as economic matters, candidates' personal attributes or partisan linkages, more salient. In this case, after controlling for the effects of other factors, one can expect a reduction in the influence of the affirmative model.

This model, therefore, represents the success of basic organizations of society in structuring electoral choice and keeping aggregated cultural orientations in balance, thus equalizing, if not offsetting, the impact of short-term forces. For grouped data, the model is empirically described by the proportion of valid votes obtained by the incumbent party in the previous presidential contest (i.e., prior vote). Therefore, the model represents a temporal, stable baseline against which to measure the changes wrought by the other short- and long-term effects.

For individual data, this model is assessed by social class of the survey respondent. This means that it takes the specific form of a class voting model, one which taps the degree to which electoral preferences covary with individuals' socio-economic status. The implicit understanding here is that social class position constitutes a particular variant of long-term factors that entail a strong stabilization, therefore, highly repeatable, of individual political choices. This variable is built as a summated index of income, household appliances, and home and car property.

Party Voting

Since electoral decisions take place in situations where political parties seek to politicize collective identities, mobilize voting loyalties and conceptualize the basic issue controversies, the magnitude of support for political continuity depends on the strength to which partisan ties with the incumbent have developed over time. The more support gathered by the party-in-office over time, the higher the return in votes that the incumbent group should be able to obtain. A similar dynamics is granted for the parties in the opposition.

This model posits partisan attachments as long-term, stable, structurally founded political trends that back up individual political choices. Of course, there is an assumption here that the opportunity for parties to politicize electorates has been present—a situation that is somewhat uncommon for countries under review, since most of them held elections against a backdrop of longstanding authoritarian experiences and a social structure drastically affected by the economic crisis of the 1980s, which further revamped previous partisan alignments. Moreover, matters such as how entrenched in the existing political culture political parties are, how publicly crystallized and stable their policy profiles are, and how seriously they are taken by the very same politicians running for office are critical in anticipating variations in the efficacy of the party model.

The model is assessed by a single variable named party strength, which represents a measure of the aggregate level of partisanship as expressed by a weighted average of the partisan vote gathered by the incumbents at the congressional level, prior and coincidental to the presidential contest, adjusted for turnout and null and blank votes (see Table 4.1). In principle, this measure seems to tap more closely a dimension of the structural stability of alignments revealed in terms of enduring party potency in the electoral arena, rather than an indication of individual attachments to the incumbent force. Nonetheless, its content validity is confirmed by a Pearson's correlation of .55 (significant at $p < .01$) with an aggregate measure of the partisan sympathies and leanings expressed by the electorate in pre-electoral public opinion studies (this later information is available for only thirty-five contests, see Table 3.1).[2]

A variable called party leanings summarizes the argument of party voting at the individual level. Admittedly, it does so somewhat poorly, since it is built upon a different measure in each country. In the Argentinean case, the question asked in surveys directly taps the issue of party identification. In the case of Perú, however, party voting is estimated by a question about prior alignments in the 1993 plebiscite on the constitutional reform set forth by the incumbent. Since the centerpiece of the reform was about allowing the president's reelection and that position was only endorsed by the president's party, this is considered as a valid proxy measure of party leanings. In the case of Uruguay, the measurement of the degree of party voting is based on the recall of the voting preferences for the 1989 presidential election. Considering the stability of partisan alignments in the city of Montevideo for the post-authoritarian period (González 1992), this variable is taken as a fairly accurate proxy of party leanings. (For survey question wordings for this and all other individual measures, see Appendix E.)

Economic Voting

Voters' sense of satisfaction is critically determined by the economic performance of the ruling party. Since a good deal of their notion of utility is closely tied to how their individual and/or collective material situations have fared under a specific administration, and since voters tend to project past experiences to the future, economic forces can be expected to draw the line between the worthiness of choosing government continuity or shifting towards a political change. Thus, in the economic model, voters make their choices as if the election were a referendum on the incumbent's economic results.

A basic assumption underlying this model is that electorates are candid in their appraisals of the economic situation; that is, they hold perceptions which replicate as correctly as possible the actual situation. However appraised, economic trends serve as a low-cost mechanism for judging the value of supporting political continuity by means of providing voters with a partial sense of the "nature of the times" under the incumbent's tenure. Of course, one has to believe that economic information is easily and accurately available through the media, and that the media coverage of news ends up being, on average, neither fully adversarial nor fully deferential.

A more critical assumption for the correct validation of this model is that the state of the economy is connected to the realm of authorities' responsibilities. Understandably, unless officials are viewed as responsible for economic conditions, they can hardly be held accountable for them. In principle, the traditional importance of the state-centered model of economic development and well-being provisions, along with the prevalence of a populist mode of income distribution and material progress in the region (see Harrison 1985; Calvert and Calvert 1989) is quite likely to secure such connection. Besides the consequences of this upon the region's economic culture, the recurrence of hermetic and top-down practices of launching stabilization shocks and the exercise of strong presidentialism may also help to render this linkage obvious in most people's minds. Concomitantly, in view of the cognitive limitations and political traditions of most Latin American voters, one can argue in favor of a second feature: the development of particularistic ties based on the exchange of votes for public goods and access to patronage resources of the state in a context of high information costs. Therefore, one may expect even among some of the least informed and inattentive members of the electorate, the maturation of a straightforward connection between private material conditions and a view of the government as responsible for these.

To explore the economic voting hypothesis at the aggregate level, four key variables, all weighted by the month of the election, can be used.[3] Given the high skeweness of most of the economic measures, these measures are recoded as categorical variables in order to achieve distributional normality (coding values in parenthesis).[4]

The first variable is the average GDP growth, measured as a weighted average level of growth of the gross domestic product during the two years preceding the election, which aims to summarize a long-term measure of economic activity. It is measured as composed of five possible values, as follows: (1) "high growth" (whenever growth reached 4.5 percent or more), (2) "slow growth" (between 2.3 and 4.4 percent), (3) "stagnation" (between 0.1 and 2.2 percent)[5], (4) "recession" (between 0.0 and −1.9 percent), and (5) "depression" (−2.0 percent or lower). In interpreting the statistical correlation between this measure and electoral outcomes, a negative sign should be read: as GDP rate increases, so does the proportion of votes gathered by the incumbent party, and vice versa.

The second variable is the average inflation, measured as a weighted average level of inflation during the two years preceding the election, which aims to capture the effects of price hikes over the relative long-term. It is also measured as composed of five values, as follows: (1) "low inflation" (whenever inflation remained at 9.9 percent or lower)[6], (2) "medium-level inflation" (between 10 and 25 percent), (3) "Latin inflation" (between 25.1 and 40 percent), (4) "high inflation" (40.1 and 180 percent), and (5) "hyperinflation" (180.1 percent or more). At the moment of examining the impact of this variable upon electoral choice, a negative sign should be read: as inflation lowers, the vote-share of incumbents increases, and vice versa.

The third variable is the level of unemployment, measured as a weighted level of unemployment during the year preceding the election, which appraises both social policy–related and individual pocketbook effects. It is also coded in five values, as follows: (1) "low unemployment" (a rate of 5.9 percent or lower). (2) "moderate unemployment" (between 6 and 8.9 percent), (3) "high unemployment" (between 9 and 11.9 percent), (4) "very high unemployment" (between 12 and 14.9 percent), and (5) "hyper-unemployment" (15 percent or more). A negative sign should be read: as the jobless rate remains low, the vote-share of the incumbent increases, and vice versa. Cut-off points tend to follow the variable's natural breaks in its cumulative distribution during these years.

The fourth variable is the inflation rate of change, measured as the difference in weighted annual inflation rates between the year of the election and the previous one, which should inform about how dynamic and retrospective-oriented public economic reflexes are. Its coding is based in seven values and goes as follows: (1) "extreme deflation" (a difference in inflation across time of −50 percent or more), (2) "strong deflation" (a decrease between −49.9 and −2.6 percent), (3) "moderate deflation" (between −2.5 and -0.1 percent), (4) "price stability" (between 0 and 2 percent), (5) "moderate inflation increase" (between 2.1 and 10 percent), (6) "strong inflation increase" (between 10.1 and 49.9 percent), and (7) "extreme inflation increase" (50 percent or higher). A negative sign should be read: as governments succeed in reducing the inflation rate from the year prior to elections to the electoral year, they can be expected to collect votes, and vice versa. Cut-off points tend to follow the variable's natural breaks in its cumulative distribution.

At the individual level, the analysis uses the respondents' evaluations of the economic situation, both at the personal and national level, and in relation to the past as much as to the future. These measures are contained in an almost identical set of questions in the polls for the three countries considered here. By making explicit the "locus" of reference and the "time frame" to which the economic variables refer, one minimizes problems of spuriousness and temporal projection (i.e., rationalization) of responses. Each particular question can, then, be viewed as addressing different dimensions of financial states, namely, retrospective personal, retrospective national, prospective personal and prospective national. Scholars have shown that these distinctions involve different types of individual calculations, as well as interactions between cultural frames and economic orientations emphasizing dissimilar aspects of choice (see Kinder and Kiewiet 1981; Paldam 1991). This diversity of responses is also a result of different motivating environments; accordingly, important differences in the effects of each specific version of the economic argument can be expected as a result of particular properties of the context such as the level of macro-economic stability preceding the contest. In addition, these distinctions provide an illustration of how voters actually process economic clues into electoral decisions.

The validity of the economic voting hypothesis is further elaborated by taking into account people's evaluation of government's economic responsibility. As already suggested, unless fluctuations in the financial states are explicitly politicized in a way that makes voters hold the party-in-office accountable for them, the effects that impressions about the economy may reveal about the electoral decision are virtually spurious (see Kramer 1983; Peffley 1985). Thus, one should observe the kind of interaction between financial considerations and responsibility attribution that substantiates a connection of the economy to the arena of electoral preferences. This is done by asking each respondent the extent to which he or she considers the government's policies liable for their own and the nation's economic fortunes. This two-step strategy of assessing the effectiveness of a model of economic voting looks, first, to determine to what extent individuals find it necessary to hold the incumbent accountable for economic records before reacting electorally to these. Second, it offers a description of individual differences in relation to the temporal and political dimensions that articulate the vote under the premise that different levels of responsibility affect differently the intensity to which individual may resort to reward or punishment when voting.

Democratic Performance Voting

Transitions from authoritarian rule to electoral democracy in Latin America might have been the product of elites' interactions (O'Donnell et al. 1986); nevertheless, they were also paralleled by growing mass acceptance of the idea of democracy. Some authors even suggest that democratization of the political culture took precedence over the democratization of the political systems (see Flisfisch 1983; Mainwaring and Viola 1984). Accordingly, given the context of collective reconstruction of democratic routines and the regained salience of political and civil liberties, one should in principle expect that electoral outcomes would reflect a response to how successfully the ruling party has made progress towards deepening citizenship. This suggests that the freer and more pluralistic the environment in which a government holds the ongoing election, the greater the support it will receive.

Nevertheless, support may not be conditioned by the extent to which the average voter qualifies the incumbent government as democratic or authoritarian, since these values are not upheld as a clear-cut polarity at the mass level. A critical premise is therefore that voters may still vindicate deepening democratization as a value but, in the face of seriously perceived challenges to the survivability of the public order, reward more strongly a government that displays authority, even if this entails some degree of authoritarian reversals in the sphere of rights and liberties. By the same token, voters who face successful incumbents in the realm of democratization may still turn their backs on them in response to an unmet demand for stronger authority, often elicited in the face of accumulating threats to political governability.

In assessing the effects of democratic performance, three variables are considered. One is the political climate during the year of the election, measured by an additive index of the assessments on political rights and civil liberties as reported by The Freedom House annual reports (Gastil 1978–91; Karatnycky 1992–95). This index ranges between 1 (high respect for freedoms and liberties) to 10 (low respect for freedoms and liberties). In interpreting correlation results between this measure and voting outcomes , a negative coefficient implies that the more free, pluralistic and inclusive the political order is in the electoral year, the more votes are harvested by the incumbent.

The second variable is the change in the political climate between the year preceding the election and the first year of the incumbent in office, measured as the change in the additive index of the political freedoms and civil liberties as reported by The Freedom Forum annual reports (Gastil 1978–91; Karatnycky 1992–95). The higher the negative values, the greater the steps in a democratic direction; the higher the positive values, the more authoritarian the performance of the government. In interpreting results, a negative sign implies that as governments deepen democratization (compared to the level they inherited), political support increases; conversely, a positive sign means that the public reacts favorably as governments get tougher.

The third variable is the level of ideological polarization between major parties contending for office, as ascertained by Dix (1989) and Mainwaring and Scully (1995). This indicator is measured by four values: (1) "low polarization" (i.e., Costa Rica across the 1980s-1990s); (2) "moderate to low polarization" (i.e., Argentina, Colombia, and Honduras, mainly); (3) "moderate to high polarization" (i.e., Bolivia, Dominican Republic, Ecuador, Mexico, and Venezuela); and (4) "high polarization" (i.e., Brazil, Perú, El Salvador and Nicaragua) (see Table 4.1). In interpreting results, a negative sign suggests that as the level of polarization increases, electoral ratification of the incumbent shrivels.

Due to the lack of appropriate data, this model cannot be tested at the individual level at this time.

Political Referendum Voting

Voters do not only seek (and react to) material results. They also pursue the fulfillment of expressive and symbolic goals, and an important portion of these consists of people's fascination with the qualities of political leadership exhibited by the heads of government. Through their displays of commanding authority before domestic and international conflicts, problem-solving qualifications in the realm of social policy and state affairs, and political dramatization of daily events, presidents convey an impression of ability to rule. In this way, they transmit a sense of psychic security about where the country is heading and suggest what assurances people may have if they (or their "heirs") stay in office for the coming term.

This makes of the election a political referendum, that is, a contest on the political leadership revealed by the incumbent and the impressions transmitted in regards to the overall national quality of life achieved during the incumbent's tenure. Accordingly, such elections are not contests based solely on personal charisma, issue mobilization, or isolated policy. The assumption is that cultural factors (already discussed in Chapter 3) facilitate the relevance of leadership clues and, heightened by moments of economic and political instability, may create a climate conducive to rewarding political dramatization, bold institutional and international initiatives, and/or a *caudillista* style of rulership.

The impact of the political referendum model is measured by a single variable: presidential popularity (see Table 4.2). In order to avoid problems of endogeneity and simultaneity bias, the variable to be used in the aggregate level analysis is the residualized version of the approval of the president's performance after being regressed against the four macro-economic indicators previously described. In the elections studied here, economic factors explained thirty-three percent of the variance of presidential popularity. (The only significant effect was accounted by the inflation rate of change.)

Table 4.1. Aggregate Measurements of Party Strength and Party Polarization

Country (Election Month/Year)	*Party Strength (%)*[7]	*Political Polarization*[8]
Argentina (5/1989)	46.1	2
Argentina (5/1995)	47.5	2
Bolivia (7/1985)	36.2	3
Bolivia (5/1989)	33.1	3
Bolivia (6/1993)	54.6	3
Brazil (11/1989)	77.4	4
Brazil (10/1994)	31.2	4
Chile (12/1993)	56.7	3
Colombia (5/1982)	55.7	2
Colombia (5/1986)	41.2	2
Colombia (5/1990)	49.2	2
Colombia (5/1994)	54.0	2
Costa Rica (2/1982)	47.3	1
Costa Rica (2/1986)	57.9	1
Costa Rica (2/1990)	50.9	1
Costa Rica (2/1994)	50.9	1
Domin. Rep.(5/1982)	52.7	3
Domin. Rep.(5/1986)	51.7	3
DominicanRep(5/1990)	46.6	3
DominicanRep(5/1994)	34.2	4
Ecuador (6/1984)	42.0	3
Ecuador (1/1988)	19.7	3
Ecuador (5/1992)	19.4	3
El Salvador (3/1989)	36.7	4
El Salvador (3/1994)	46.4	4
Guatemala (11/1990)	51.0	2
Honduras (11/1985)	53.7	2
Honduras (11/1989)	50.0	2
Honduras (11/1993)	55.5	2
México (7/1988)	73.0	3
México (8/1994)	52.0	3
Nicaragua (2/1990)	63.5	4
Panamá (5/1994)	40.3	2
Perú (4/1985)	54.4	4
Perú (4/1990)	59.4	4
Perú (4/1995)	55.0	4
Uruguay (11/1989)	41.4	3
Uruguay (11/1994)	39.4	3
Venezuela (12/1983)	42.2	3
Venezuela (12/1988)	56.5	3
Venezuela (12/1993)	48.3	3

Domin.Rep.: Dominican Republic

Sources: Nohlen (1993); *Keesing's Record of World Events* (various years); Dix (1992); Mainwaring and Scully (1995).

For the individual data, presidential approval is first regressed against the set of basic economic evaluations, and then the "economics-free" residualized values of the variable are used as predictors. For Perú, the economic variables accounted for twenty-eight percent of the variance of presidential popularity; for Argentina, for forty-three percent of the variance; and for Uruguay, for only twelve percent.

It is important to note that presidents sought reelection in only five of the contests reviewed here (and data for presidential popularity is available for only four of these), which minimizes the problems of concept overlapping between support for the president and electoral endorsement. Also, since most measures of presidential popularity were taken in a period between three and six months from the elections, one can safely regard these data as estimating the long-term governmental leadership aspects with a minimal distortion produced by short-term events or campaign-related effects.

Candidate Voting

Since elections are contests between individual politicians who tend to dramatize their public persona as a global synthesis of the major controversies of the time, the personal attributes of candidates play an important role in determining electoral outcomes. The media's focus on personal character and the "horse-race" aspects of the election only reinforces candidates as decisional clues. Furthermore, cultural traditions of fascination with charismatic personages permit candidates' personal attributes to become a major source of decision.

All things considered, the more visible the candidate is, the higher will be his or her electoral advantage over the party's, and the more votes he or she can be expected to collect. Still, this does not indicate a zero-sum kind of tension between candidates and partisan clues, since the former's effect can only anticipate greater support in votes to the incumbent if some degree of party ties are already developed.

To assess candidate-related influences two measures can be used. One is an index of net candidate salience, which measures the net difference (between the incumbent and the principal opposition) of an additive index assessing the historical timing of the candidate's party (that is, whether the party was created as an institutional vehicle for personal electoral purposes or had an institutional history traceable years before the election), the extent to which the candidate's leadership has been contested in primaries (or whether it emerged undisputed), and the nature of the candidate's previous personal and professional records (that is, whether he or she could resort to some reservoir of prestige based on family or office-holding backgrounds). The basic candidate salience index ranges for incumbent and opposition between 0 ("no salience," as when (a) the candidate's party had a history prior to the restoration of democracy or 1982, (b) the candidate had to go through a process of primary selection or double simultaneous vote, and (c) he or she could not ride upon any extraordinary personal or professional antecedents) and 3 ("high salience," as when (a) the candidate's party was created exclusively for the current electoral race, (b) he or she did not have to test his or her leadership credentials against other would-be candidates within the same political force, and (c) the candidate could take advantage of public knowledge of him or her as former president of the country).[9] The net candidate salience index can range from +3 ("high salience" for the incumbent candidate) to −3 ("high salience" for the opposition candidate).[10] As such, this index attempts to tackle the extent to which personality-related and charismatic forces were present and, if they were, whether they had any influence at all. In interpreting results correlating this index with electoral outcomes, a positive score means that the ruling party benefited electorally from having a highly candidate-centered strategy of competition, compared to the one displayed by the opposition; conversely, a negative value shows that the opposition successfully ran the contest upon a candidate-centered campaign.

The other measure is the net candidate advantage of the incumbent, which assesses the net difference (between the incumbent and the principal opposition) in terms of the vote difference obtained at the congressional level (as measured by a weighted average like the one described for party strength) and at the presidential level. This second index assumes, then, that the edge in votes obtained by the presidential ticket compared to the same party's congressional ticket represents the existence of unambiguous candidate-related effects linked to the individual biography or political position. Thus, if positive, the higher the scores of the correlation between this measure and the vote percentage received by the ruling ticket, the greater the incumbent candidate's effect; if negative, the higher the scores, the greater the opposition candidate's effect. In Chapter 5, I assess this variable in two forms: initially, for all forty-one cases, I use the original values. When I replicate the analysis testing the political referendum model (for a smaller number of cases), in order to remove collinearity with presidential popularity and inflation rate of change,[11] I use the residualized version of the net candidate advantage measure, after it has been regressed against these two variables.[12]

As an indirect way of probing for this measure's content validity I tested a correlation with an aggregate indicator of net candidates' evaluation drawn from public opinion studies for twenty-two electoral occasions. Coefficients indicate that each of the two indexes used (net candidate saliency and net candidate advantage) entails different meanings.[13] Thus, whereas net candidate advantage seems to identify the extra-partisan appeal of a ticket (i.e., how

Table 4.2. Public Opinion Indicators of Presidential Popularity and Measures of Candidate Performance

Country (Election Month/Year)	*Presidential Popularity*	*Net Candidate Advantage*	*Net Candidate Evaluation*
Argentina (5/1989)	44	−5.9	−8
Argentina (5/1995)	42	6.6	N/A
Bolivia (7/1985)	N/A	−16.6	N/A
Bolivia (5/1989)	N/A	0.9	N/A
Bolivia (6/1993)	21	−25.8	−18
Brazil (11/1989)	8	−54.6	N/A
Brazil (10/1994)	40	13.2	N/A
Chile (12/1993)	58	17.1	42
Colombia (5/1982)	48	−11.8	N/A
Colombia (5/1986)	13	−16.4	−11
Colombia (5/1990)	51	14.3	N/A
Colombia (5/1994)	54	−12.2	N/A
Costa Rica (2/1982)	4	−17.2	−21
Costa Rica (2/1986)	51	−6.0	1
Costa Rica (2/1990)	75	−5.2	2
Costa Rica (2/1994)	33	−5.3	8
Domin.Rep.(5/1982)	N/A	2.0	N/A
Domin.Rep.(5/1986)	N/A	−2.2	N/A
Domin. Rep.(5/1990)	N/A	8.3	N/A
Domin.Rep.(5/1994)	43	2.7	6
Ecuador (6/1984)	10	−19.7	N/A
Ecuador (1/1988)	18	−4.8	N/A
Ecuador (5/1992)	15	−23.2	N/A
El Salvador (3/1989)	32	−20.8	3
El Salvador (3/1994)	50	11.2	16
Guatemala (11/1990)	21	−13.6	−14
Honduras (11/1985)	56	−2.0	N/A
Honduras (11/1989)	35	−7.5	−18
Honduras (11/1993)	53	−11.2	−2
Mexico (7/1988)	32	−0.4	N/A
Mexico (8/1994)	64	1.6	34
Nicaragua (2/1990)	39	−23.5	−15
Panama (5/1994)	22	2.7	31
Peru (4/1985)	7	−33.8	N/A
Peru (4/1990)	19	−24.0	N/A
Peru (4/1995)	66	32.6	N/A
Uruguay (11/1989)	13	−0.6	−19
Uruguay (11/1994)	29	−8.4	−4
Venezuela (12/1983)	14	−15.4	−5
Venezuela (12/1988)	30	−1.9	24
Venezuela(12/1993)	14	−16.9	−10

Domin.Rep.: Dominican Republic
N/A: not available
Sources: See Appendix G; Nohlen (1993); *Keesing's Record of World Events* (various years).

much candidates are preferred over parties), net candidate salience seems to ascertain what it takes for an individual to reach the position of candidate of a party.

At the individual level, I skip this test, because in two of the contests the presidents sought reelection (which would have made this measure highly collinear with any evaluation of candidates), but also because of lack of data availability.

Each of the models of electoral choice presented above offer a potential argument to explaining why people—at both the aggregate and individual levels—vote the way they do. In order to make a transition from the theoretical discussion of electoral determinants to the empirical analysis of the underpinnings of results at the ballots, focus was placed on how each model is likely to affect the voting outcomes and, specially, how each model can be observed and identified in the context of Latin American politics and the available data.

The questions arising, now, shift to the capabilities of each of these models to account for the electoral outcomes recorded in the region since the process of democratization unfolded. What is the prevalent order of their mutual relationships? In what way or ways do they interact with different contextual conditions? To answer these questions, we must test each of the six models in absolute and relative terms, probing their explanatory power under various politico-institutional and macro-economic environments.

NOTES

1. For a preliminary discussion of "negative voting" in Brazil and Venezuela, see Guilhon Albuquerque (1992) and Torres (1985). Curiously, rather than interpreted as the other side of the same coin, McDonald and Ruhl see "protest voting" as an entirely different concept of voting behavior (see McDonald and Ruhl 1989: 14).

2. A further proof of validity is rendered by another moderate-to-high $r = .53$ Pearson's correlation (significant at $p < .01$) between a measurement of net party strength (i.e., incumbent's minus major opposition's) and an homologous measure of net party identification. Obviously, this denotes that the respective values for major opposition party are importantly correlated as well ($r = .66$, $p < .01$).

3. Initially, I considered twelve measures for economic activity: real average wages, quarterly, yearly and biannually average inflation rates, hyper-inflation occurrences, inflation rate of change over the year prior to election, economic growth measured on same year as election, as a two-year average and as rate of change, per capita economic activity rates measured both as levels or rates of change, and the unemployment rate. However, the effects of many of them were poor or problems of collinearity between indicators systematically appeared. Besides, it did not make

sense from a conceptual point of view to include all of them. I therefore settled on the four variables discussed here. These variables remain non-collinear to each other, except for the moderate collinearity between both measures of inflation ($r = .45$, $p = .001$) and between the biannual average measures of economic activity and inflation ($r = .43$, $p = .002$). The decision to weigh them by the month of election follows Remmer's (1991) strategy, in order to build upon her initial work and to make consistent gains in the empirical findings over time and across different number of cases. Sources: *The Economist* Intelligence Unit for the quarterly assessments of inflation; and the Economic Comission for Latin America and the Caribbean (CEPAL) and the Inter-American Development Bank (IADB) annual reports for all other variables.

4. Square root and logarithmic transformations did not yield much more symmetrical distributions, while other more powerful transformations were avoided given their less intuitive interpretability.

5. The cut-off point around two percent fits the region's average population growth during the period under consideration, therefore if economic activity adds up to about two percentual points, it means that the per capita rate of growth remained zero.

6. The reader should remind that the economy in Latin America of the 1980s and 1990s was characterized by far higher levels of inflation compared to the rates of today, as well as to the standards of Europeand and North American countries. As a result, cut-off points across values for this measure tend to follow the variable's natural breaks in its cumulative distribution during this period.

7. The party strength represents a weighted average of partisan support obtained by the incumbent party (or coalition) in the previous two congressional contests. It represents the percentage of valid votes going to the ruling party for the lower house, weighted by turnout. For a few cases without data available and holding a proportional representation system (for example, Brazil from 1990 onward), I use the proportion of partisan seat-share which should denote a very close approximation to the actual percentage of votes received.

8. Scores for political polarization follow Dix's (1992) and Mainwaring and Scully's (1995) classifications.

9. Whenever the candidate was son or daughter of any previous president or he or she has held a key ministerial or internationally prestigious office during the period immediately prior to the administration voted in, the score assigned was equivalent to 0.5. A similar score was given to candidates facing only one competitor at the intra-party level, and whenever the party's historical life dated from the post-authoritarian period onwards, yet preceded the election in progress.

10. This situation is not verified in this sample since it would suppose that the party or coalition in government has been completely dismantled and a wholly new force had been created for the specific electoral occasion. See Appendix H for full results.

11. Pearson's correlation coefficients stood at .57 ($p < .01$) and $-.37$ ($p < .01$), respectively for a total number of thirty-six cases.

12. These two variables accounted for over thirty-four percent of the variance of the original variable. In standardized coefficients, presidential popularity and the

differenced inflation rate yielded values of .41 and −.38, respectively (both significant at $p < .01$).

13. Pearson's correlation between the net difference in candidates evaluation and net candidate advantage stood at an impressive $r = .74$ (significant at $p < .01$). Conversely, correlation with net candidate salience was merely $r = .08$ (not significant even at $p < .10$). In both cases, coefficients were calculated upon a total number of twenty-two cases. Pearson's correlation between both aggregate measures, for all forty-one cases stood at low $r = .26$ (significant at $p < .06$).

Chapter Five

Aggregate-Level Analysis of Electoral Outcomes in Latin America

From the early 1980 to the mid-1990s, hopes remained high in the new democracies of Latin America that elected leaders could help the economy become stronger, governments could behave more democratically, societies could get better organized across party lines, and the quality of political outcomes would more closely resemble people's preferences. However, as the road towards regularization of electoral rule and democratic consolidation often deviated from this ideal path, building political support was not an easy task. What accounts for the differences in support achieved by the incumbent forces? Which models of voting behavior are most efficient in capturing the variety of motivations and clues guiding electorates in Latin America?

In this chapter, I analyze data from forty-one competitive presidential elections to address the question of what forces determine the voters' choices for political continuity. After explaining my methodology, I look at the general characteristics of the elections under examination. I then examine the effectiveness of each major argument of voting in explaining electoral outcomes. In particular, I focus on the issue of whether voters articulate their decisions around what the economy dictates or whether they resort to other explanations of non-economic nature. In the next chapter, I present a follow-up discussion of how voting patterns behave under dissimilar contexts.

METHODOLOGY

At the aggregate level, the dependent variable is assessed by the share of the valid votes received by the incumbent party or coalition. (In all cases with run-off elections, the data refers to the first round; similarly, whenever a coalition of parties constitute the incumbent force, the summed proportion of votes obtained by each single party is considered). This method offers a direct measurement of the degree to which electorates back up an option for political continuity or change, and it is one of the most standard ways in which the study of voting functions has been operationalized. If, as argued, voters exert only incumbency-oriented voting, it will suffice to know what leads them to endorse the party in office or reject it.

Forty-one competitive presidential elections held in seventeen different Latin American countries between February 1982 and May 1995 constitute the units of analysis (see Appendix A). This period comprises the largest number of regularly free and competitive contests for the top office of government ever held in the region. It is also unique in its economic and social contours after the late-1981 default of México on its external debt payments, which spurred the most critical times that Latin America has had to face since the 1930s.

Aggregate models of choice allow detection of the overall patterns underlying electoral support for political continuity in the region, and ordinary least squares (OLS) technique enables the statistical testing of those patterns behind the incumbent vote-share. This statistical tool will permit both to ascertain the explanatory power of each model of the varying percentage of votes collected by the incumbent in the region, as well as the assessment of the simultaneous interplay of all models replicating real-life situations of electorates being submitted to multiple and concurrent sources of choice (the reader interested in in-depth discussion of this methodological approach can refer to Appendix C).

Eleven variables are initially used to explain variations in support for the incumbent across the forty-one elections held between 1982 and 1995 in Latin America. This selection of independent variables follows the arguments developed when inferring the different electoral models. Admittedly, the choice is in itself a controversial matter, since a good deal of the disagreement on the subject comes from the idiosyncratic manner by which scholars have specified their models in each analysis. As Miller (1989), Paldam (1991) and others have acknowledged, much of the diversity in results about voting functions springs from using different indicators, using different lags, weighting data diversely, appraising complex political phenomena through simplistic dummy variables, or overtly ignoring some critical variable.[1]

In formal terms, the influence of the eleven variables can be summarized with the following general model structure:

$$\begin{aligned} VS = \alpha &+ \beta_1(\text{Prior Vote}) + \beta_2(\text{Party Strength}) + \beta_3(\text{GDP growth}) \\ &- \beta_4(\text{Inflation level}) - \beta_5(\text{Inflation Change-Rate}) \\ &- \beta_6(\text{Unemployment}) - \beta_7(\text{Political Climate}) \\ &- \beta_8(\text{Political Climate Change-Rate}) - \beta_9(\text{Political Polarization}) \\ &+ \beta_{10}(\text{Net Candidate Salience}) + \beta_{11}(\text{Net Candidate Advantage}) + \epsilon \end{aligned}$$

where VS represents the incumbent's vote-share in terms of the percentage of valid votes cast in favor of the ruling party or coalition. The coefficient α represents the value of the intercept, and the concept labeled ϵ symbolizes the unmeasured influences not included in the equation. Coefficient β_1 represents the impact of the affirmative voting argument, β_2 reflects the effect of the party voting model, β_3 through β_6 indicate the impact of the economic model in their different expressions, β_7 through β_9 illustrate the relevance of the democratic performance model, and β_{10} and β_{11} indicate the impact of the two indexes feeding the candidate voting model.

A further exploration, however, reveals that a trimmed version of the major hypothetical explanatory models seems not only to fit better the numerical evidence and the empirical patterns of relationships thereby unfolded, but also contributes to a more parsimonious understanding of the phenomenon under study. Thus, after reviewing the impact that this initial set of variables had upon the forty-one electoral results, I use more compact version of the previous models with only five major explanatory variables (namely, prior vote, inflation change, political climate change, party strength, and net candidate advantage), each summarizing one particular argument to be tested. Finally, a sixth variable, presidential popularity, is entered for a subset of cases, to sketch the effect of a political referendum explanation of voting.

In formal terms, the aggregate model takes the following shape:

$$\begin{aligned} VS = \alpha &+ \beta_1(\text{Prior Vote}) + \beta_2(\text{Party Strength}) + \beta_3(\text{Inflation Change-Rate}) \\ &- \beta_4(\text{Political Climate Change-Rate}) + \beta_5(\text{Presidential Popularity}) \\ &+ \beta_6(\text{Net Candidate Advantage}) + \epsilon \end{aligned}$$

where each coefficient symbolizes a different model. It is important to note that once presidential popularity is included, the measure of net candidate advantage is entered as a "residualized" variable (that is, with the partial effects of presidential popularity and change in the inflation rate removed). These two modifications are referred to in the text as the extended trimmed version of the models.

For all variables in the tables presented in this and next chapters, three pieces of information are offered: the parameter estimate, b, which is the unstandardized OLS regression coefficient; the statistics, SEb, which stands for the standard error of the parameter estimate; and β, which is the standardized OLS regression coefficient. Summary statistics concerning how well the theoretical models fit the data are discussed in the text. In addition, let be said that no major collinearity problem exists at the level of either the trimmed version of the models for the whole sample or its extended restatement for the subsample already specified. As Table 5.1 shows, except for the moderate correlation between party strength and prior vote ($r = .50$, $p < .01$ for $n = 41$; $r = .48$, $p < .01$ for $n = 36$),[2] all other coefficients remain below .40. This

Table 5.1. Matrix of Product–Moment Correlations between Aggregate Independent Variables

	Prior Vote	*Party Strength*	*ΔInflation Rate*	*ΔPolitical Climate*	*Candidate Advantage*
Prior Vote		.50[a]	.15	−.11	−.14
Party Strength	.48[a]		−.21[c]	.06	−.01
ΔInflation Rate	.23[c]	−.16		−.19	−.37[b]
ΔPolitical Climate	−.12	.06	−.20		.20[c]
Candidate Advantage	−.20	−.22[c]	.00	.08	
Presidential Popularity	.29[b]	.31[b]	.00	.18	.00

[a]Coefficients are significant at $p < .01$
[b]Coefficients are significant at $p < .05$
[c]Coefficients are significant at $p < .10$
Coefficients located above the main diagonal refer to the estimates for the original trimmed version of the models (N = 41); coefficients located below the main diagonal refer to the extended trimmed version (N = 36).

assures that whatever the effect a model holds, this impact is authentic and not a product of the projected impact of other contending arguments.

DESCRIBING THE ELECTIONS PROFILES

Latin American voters have been, on average, mild supporters of political continuity in an electoral sense. As a whole, voters granted thirty-six percent of the valid votes to the incumbent forces at the presidential level, a figure that on special occasions could grant to office-holders the largest minority, or at least an opportunity for a run-off election. The incumbent vote-share reveals a standard deviation of 15.3 percent, which means that there was plenty of room for dramatic demonstrations of both support and repudiation of political continuity. As it stands, that dispersion value means that in almost seven of every ten elections (i.e., 68 percent of cases comprehended within one standard deviation) results could have fallen between 11 and 51 percent[3] —that is, between a humiliating expression of voters' anger and a gratifying assurance of reelection.

Table 5.2 summarizes how other forces behave, on average, across all these presidential races. For example, a look at the electoral background in terms of prior votes shows the extent to which a phenomenon of "swing votes" prevailed. Furthermore, when observed in conjunction with the level of party strength, it hints at the fact that incumbents reach office blessed by an inflated amount of electoral support.[4] It seems logical that after getting elected with a margin of votes that greatly exceeded their partisan strength, authorities had nowhere to go but down, unless short-term factors heavily discount the natural trend towards re-equilibrium. This view of events is further reinforced by the magnitude of the dispersion of the prior vote variable.

The average value of party strength suggests that almost one in every three voters (28.05 percent) leans towards the incumbent force in a regular manner. This reveals that some degree of partisan continuity has articulated the distribution of preferences. Also, as its dispersion is lower than that of incumbent vote-share, party strength may be interpreted as an important stabilizing force over mass electorates.

Short-term forces undermine such stability. Take democratic performance, for example. Bearing in mind that a negative sign signifies that democratic progress took place when comparing the year preceding the election and the first year of the incumbent in office, the average value for the rate of change in the region's political climate (i.e., −0.46) indicates that—as a whole—electorates have seen advances in democratization, and authorities have been for the most part responsive to the post-authoritarian plea for political amelioration. Yet, as I will discuss later, this is not to say that emphasis on democratization constituted a strong vote-getting strategy. Whereas the overall trend worked in a direction towards improvement of conditions for pluralism and citizenship, considerable heterogeneity (as measured by the standard deviation) also showed up. Thus, considering only sixty-eight percent of the cases (i.e., one standard deviation) would yield situations with some governments sliding into mild authoritarian regressions (i.e., a value of 1.70) and others going forward down the road to full democracy (i.e., a value of −2.62).

Another major short-term force driving results, the president's appeal, also shows an intuitive pattern. In its original values, the percentage of popularity of the president gets extremely close to the proportion of votes collected by the incumbent. However, as its variance is larger, the emphasis on presidential leadership can only introduce an additional measure of incertitude to the inherent volatility in political support.[7]

Economic performance has not been a stabilizing force either. In broader terms, the grouping of elections held under both unfavorable and auspicious economic conditions shows a somewhat distorted picture of what average voters were undergoing at election time. This picture becomes evident when contrasting the behavior of the economy, especially inflation-related measures, in times of growth against times of economic slump. When all contests are aggregated, the indicator of economic activity positions itself half-way between "slow growth" and "stagnation," leaning more heavily towards the latter. The long-term measure of inflation falls closer to the category labeled as "Latin inflation," that is, between an annual index of 25 and 40 percent.

Table 5.2. Central Tendency Measures of Dependent and Independent Variables for the Analysis of Aggregate-Level Determinants of Presidential Electoral Outcomes in Latin America, 1982–1995

			Institutionalization				*Party system*				*Economic Context*			
	All cases		*High*		*Low*		*Two-Party*		*Multiparty*		*Crisis*		*Prosperity*	
Variables	Mean	Stddev	Mean	Stddev	Mean	Stddev	Mean	Stddev	Mean	Stddev	Mean	Stddev	Mean	Stddev
Incumbent Vote-Share	35.95	15.29	41.19	10.74	31.43	17.36	40.42	10.79	30.78	18.20	28.78	13.35	42.14	14.35
Prior Vote	46.34	13.21	49.89	7.67	43.28	16.15	52.55	7.47	39.15	14.86	47.63	12.94	45.23	13.64
Party Strength	28.05	10.09	31.89	8.64	24.75	10.27	31.18	7.88	24.42	11.32	26.58	9.44	29.32	10.68
Average Annual GDP Rate	2.26	3.65	3.31	2.73	1.34	4.14	3.49	2.71	1.19	4.06	NA	NA	NA	NA
Average Annual Inflation	2.85	1.35	2.58	1.22	3.09	1.44	2.86	1.36	2.84	1.38	3.53	1.31	2.27	1.12
Unemployment Rate	2.41	1.20	2.21	.92	2.59	1.40	2.54	1.30	2.26	1.10	2.42	1.12	2.41	1.30
Inflation Change-Rate	3.66	1.82	3.63	1.64	3.68	2.01	3.73	1.80	2.84	1.38	4.47	2.04	2.95	1.29
Political Climate Change-Rate	−.46	2.16	−.21	2.10	−.68	2.23	−.23	1.38	−.74	2.82	−.89	2.13	−.09	2.16
Presidential Popularity[5]	−.00	15.01	1.72	15.32	−1.92	14.89	4.57	14.96	−5.10	13.74	−.01	15.18	.00	14.94
Presidential Popularity[6]	34.00	19.05	37.70	19.44	29.82	18.27	36.84	19.57	30.82	18.51	24.40	17.83	40.86	17.15
Net Candidate Advantage[5]	−7.16	15.34	−5.57	9.75	−8.54	19.04	−8.38	11.34	−5.76	19.21	−13.55	14.82	−1.65	13.83
Net Candidate Advantage[6]	−.00	13.24	1.63	9.79	−1.83	16.40	−3.62	11.17	4.04	14.50	−5.70	14.07	4.07	14.94
N =	41		19		22		22		19		19		22	

Mean represents the arithmetical mean of the variable.
Stddev represents the standard deviation of the variable.

Efficacy in fighting prices hikes over time (as measured by the difference in annual inflation rates) cancels itself out as a byproduct of the aggregation, placing its mean value half-way between a "moderate deflation" and "price stability." Finally, unemployment levels before elections remain between moderate and high.

Lastly, the arithmetic mean of candidate-related forces for all competitions shows that the basic strategy of the major opposition parties to unsettle incumbents has consisted in relying on a strong candidate-oriented campaign. This is how I interpret the average negative values for this variable which means that presidential tickets of the party-in-office have been systematically outpaced by a greater candidate appeal of the challenger.

TESTING ECONOMIC AND NON-ECONOMIC VOTING

Let us now turn to the reasons why Latin American electorates have chosen to endorse the ruling party with the intensity they did. In assessing properly the relative importance of each voting model, it is appropriate to focus on three summary sources of the goodness of fit: 1) the amount and statistical significance of the increase in coefficient of determination (the adjusted R^2, which informs us about the proportion of the variation of the votes going to the incumbent explained by each model); 2) the extent to which each model contributes to diminishing the spread of errors relative to the predictive power of the mean (standard error of the estimate or SEE); and 3) the extent to which each argument helps to shrink the average absolute error in predicting the percentage of votes obtained by the party-in-government.

As a way of organizing the tests of the comparative explanatory power of each voting hypothesis, we can check the systematic effect displayed by each individual set of variables describing a different argument. This is accomplished by looking at the estimated regression coefficients for each indicator used in the operationalization of each model, discounting for the fluctuations of prior voting. Such assessment provides information about the non-random effect of each argument tested in explaining the electoral fortunes of the incumbent. Table 5.3 summarizes the information at this level.

A preliminary assessment of this model's effects, as described by the adjusted coefficient of determination, indicates that only five percent of the variance in the incumbent vote-share is accounted by prior vote. In other words, the unexplained variance between prior vote and the incumbent vote-share is substantially large and can be left to be explained by the other factors of interest. This is good news for the practical relevance of a study like this. Incidentally, it suggests that the alarm over recurrent incumbency turnover in

Table 5.3. Assessing the Effects of Competing Models of Electoral Choice in Latin America, 1982–1995 (Full and Trimmed Versions, N = 41)

Variable	*Affirmative Voting b (SEb)*	*Party Voting b (SEb)*	*Democratic Voting b (SEb)*	*Economic Voting b (SEb)*	*Candidate Voting b (SEb)*	*Full Version b (SEb)*	*Trimmed Version b (SEb)*	β
Prior Vote	.32[b] (.18)	.08 (.19)	.25[c] (.17)	.45[a] (.15)	.48[a] (.10)	.31[a] (.11)	.35[a] (.09)	.30
Party Strength		.64[b] (.25)				.40[b] (.14)	.38[a] (.12)	.25
Political Climate			2.30 (1.52)			1.16 (.89)		
ΔPolitical Climate			2.30[b] (1.05)			1.35[b] (.48)	1.40[b] (.46)	.20
Polarization			−5.35[c] (2.87)			−2.34 (1.59)		
Inflation Rate				−10 (1.84)		.51 (.99)		
GDP Rate				1.35[b] (.62)		.13 (.36)		
Unemployment				1.53 (1.64)		.18 (.95)		
ΔInflation Rate				−3.74[a] (1.19)		−1.56[b] (.73)	−1.84[a] (.61)	−.22
Candidate Salience					2.88[c] (1.66)	2.98[b] (1.33)		
Candidate Advantage					.74[a] (.09)	.58[b] (.08)	.65[a] (.07)	.65

Intercept	20.87[b]	14.25[c]	28.44[b]	22.30[c]	19.82[a]	19.74[b]	21.11[a]
	(8.56)	(8.44)	(11.37)	(11.41)	(4.96)	(7.81)	(4.24)
Adjusted R^2	.05	.17	.22	.41	.68	.84	.84
	(.05)	(.19)	(.20)	(.28)	(.52)		
Standard Error	14.86	13.93	13.45	11.69	8.58	6.08	6.13
	(14.68)	(13.78)	(13.63)	(13.00)	(10.58)		
Prediction Error	11.64	10.44	9.94	8.38	6.69	4.02	4.39
	(11.64)	(10.63)	(10.34)	(9.99)	(8.47)		

[a]Coefficients are significant at $p < .01$
[b]Coefficients are significant at $p < .05$
[c]Coefficients are significant at $p < .10$
Goodness of fit measures in parenthesis stand for the respective models without adjusting for the prior vote baseline.

the region may have reflected a pattern of consistent deviation between the large margins by which governments originally reached office and the large "swing" votes by which they were removed from power in the next round, rather than an intrinsic weakness of democracy.

Looking at the comparative performance of the other models points out the explanatory edge held by the argument for candidate voting. This hypothesis accounts for almost seventy percent of the fluctuation in political support going to the incumbents, while cutting almost by half its error dispersion (i.e., from an original standard deviation of 15.29 to one of 8.58). In terms of prediction, this argument alone foretells an average absolute error of less than seven percentage points (i.e., 6.69) in relation to the actual results. A quick look at the dynamics of candidate effects over voting shows that electoral outcomes do not tribute to the historical or prestige salience of competitors (as captured by the net candidate salience indicator), which displays a poor statistically significant influence. Indeed, the impact of the candidate-related hypothesis comes from the net candidate advantage variable alone, which works in favour of gathering votes to the ruling party inasmuch as the party's candidate has the upper hand.

Second in importance is the economic voting hypothesis. Its salience may partially result from the higher number of explanatory variables used, but it nonetheless is capable of reducing the uncertainty on the overall spread of the incumbent vote-share by 3.6 percentage points. Of the four measures encompassing this model, only two display statistically significant effects: the evolution of inflation and the level of growth for the national economy. Looking at the signs of coefficients proves that the incumbent ticket may expect to collect votes only when the prices have lowered and the economy shows expansion.

The option for continuity expressed in the number of votes for the party-in-government is also significantly shaped by factors of political nature like party strength and the political climate surrounding the election. Individually, the effect of aggregate party alignment suggests that for every three percentage points the ruling party received in subpresidential elections, it can expect to add almost two percentage points of support in presidential contests ($3 * .64 = 1.92$). However, the overall explanatory power of this argument is rather weak compared to that of others (only likely to explain 17 percent of the votes gathered by the ruling party), which falls in line with the lack of opportunities for full partisan socialization among most electorates of the region.

On the other hand, ambiguous effects are found in relation to the impact of democratic performance clues. Its explanatory power is mild (22 percent of the variance in incumbent vote) and is mainly attributable to changes in the political climate of each country. Moreover, this variable's coefficient sign suggests that the tougher (rather than democratic) the government has become, the more votes its presidential ticket is likely to harvest. Surprising as this might sound, there is a consistent pattern of incumbents who, after deepening democracy, lose people's support at the voting booths; after all, one expects voters to have become sensitized electorates about the value of democracy. (I shall return to this point later.) Ideological polarization is the only other variable of this model with some additional influence on voting. One would expect a pre-electoral scene of high polarization to serve against the incumbent's best interest, since this may be interpreted as signal of incapability to ensure full-scale governability. This hypothesis is confirmed by the negative sign of the coefficient.

As a preliminary approach to the patterns underlying popular choice, the data presented in Table 5.3 reveal that decisional clues hold distinctive effects for each model. Yet no single argument can summarize the complex multiplicity of forces shaping the vote. This simple revelation must serve as a warning against reducing voting results to unidimensional factors. Moreover, it can help to make visible the limitations of single-minded views of elections for contexts comprising more than one country, one election and one temporal point. For example, although conventional wisdom holds both the 1989 and 1995 electoral results in Argentina as reflections of retrospective economic voting alone (the former in the form of "punishing" the incumbent, the latter in the form of "rewarding" it),[8] a look at the difference between the incumbent vote-share that a pure economic model would predict and the actual proportion of votes obtained should underscore the curtailed leverage of such argument. Whereas the 1995 contest could be very closely predicted by paying attention only to the macro-economic performance (a difference of less than one percent with the actual results), the predicted fortunes of the ruling party in 1989 were over fifteen percentage points off the mark. In other words, while a voting model solely based on macro-economic performance predicted 17.4 percent of votes, the Radicals were able to pool 32.5 percent.

Such examples speak to the need to contemplate other explanations when circumscribing the analysis at the aggregate level. Notably, the 1989 outcomes in Argentina are closer to the percentage forecast provided by the party strength model or the candidate effects model (a difference to actual results of less than four and six percentage points, respectively), which clearly points to the importance that party and candidate-related factors had in determining the outcomes of that particular election. As this case illustrates, reliance on unidimensional factors can lead to grossly erroneous results. And if such approach cannot offer accurate predictions in one country, it is not hard to imagine how the errors could be compounded when dealing with many countries and elections.

ASSESSING THE RELATIVE IMPORTANCE OF COMPETING EXPLANATIONS

A more compelling way to test for the relative incidence of each explanation of electoral returns is to have all hypotheses be controlled for each other. By analyzing them in this way, we can gain a broader sense of the actual weight of each argument as well as of the ways in which these arguments affect each other's impact on the vote.

Table 5.3 shows the changes experienced by the estimates of one particular argument when the variables representing a rival argument are incorporated as controls. The column titled Full Version condenses the relative importance of each variable within each model after being controlled for all other factors' presence altogether. Among other findings, this analysis shows that, even when other economic and non-economic influences are present, the effects of prior alignments expressed by past election choices and partisan connections retain considerable influence in explaining the percentage of votes going to the incumbent ticket. The estimates show that votes obtained in the previous presidential election are positively and significatively correlated with the current vote-share of the incumbent, as is also the case for the measure of aggregate partisan strength.

Results also show that the better the economic outlook in terms of high growth, low inflation, and greater reduction in the cost of living, the more votes the party-in-office may expect to collect. However, the data retain some unexpected patterns of influence. For example, no one of the economic effects reach statistical significance when other factors are also included. What is more, whereas one may have expected a negative relationship with increases in unemployment dragging electoral support away from government, the situation is just the opposite. This latter characteristic, of course, lowers any theoretical concern about the role of unemployment in this discussion; however, this should not excuse one from making sense of its possible meanings. An immediate interpretation for such a case calls to mind the Italian example in which a similar pattern was verified (Belluci 1985), and which simply reflected the hidden potential of clientelistic voting underneath economic voting explanations. Similarly, when electorates have undergone situations of repeated and/or enduring high inflation manifested in real-life scenes of economic ungovernability, and realized that economic stability and social peace can be restored by means of harsh stabilization policies, tolerance for the joblessness side of the equation may increase and endure. Such a pattern may represent a collective preference for a particular equilibrium point in the Phillips curve: a tendency to ignore unemployment if accompanied by price stability (see Stokes 2001).[9]

Rather unexpectedly, governments less committed to an amelioration of the political climate seemed rewarded with votes rather than punished. This finding contradicts the rationale positing that electorates see utility satisfaction in democracy-deepening efforts. Some scholars, however, might not be surprised, since such effects hint at the trade-offs encountered by electorates facing contexts of economy-driven tensions and social upheaval (Acuña 1994; Gamarra 1994). Others may interpret them as tapping hidden cultural trends rewarding some authoritarian behaviors of leaders (see Conaghan 1995; Carrión 1998). In this view, elections are plebiscites of the incumbent's capacity to assure public order and to keep social uncertainty at a minimum, rather than to advance political and citizenship-related goals of collective self-actualization (see Torre 1993; Payne 1995). In sum, Latin American electorates judge civilian authorities upon their aptitude to resolve the old dilemma of how much democracy and how much government are needed, and proceed to vote accordingly.

The negative (and non-significant) coefficient of ideological polarization seems consistent with the inherent conservatism of the above view: as political confrontation skyrockets in pre-electoral times, the incumbent is likely to be blamed and thereby punished, reinforcing the notion that there is an electoral premium on maintaining public order as a good in itself; yet, such effect seems better captured by the longterm evaluation of how the overall political climate of the country has evolved during the ruling party's tenure.

Finally, candidate-related influences also nurture the ultimate outcome of presidential elections, but only the net candidate advantage measure does so with statistical significance.

In addition to pointing to these specific insights, the data also illustrate the prevailing heterogeneity within each particular argument. We learn, for instance, that when adjusted for the inflation rate of change and the level of economic activity, plus the long-term alignments captured by the prior vote measure, the jobless rate and the average biannual inflation rate do not help to reveal any significant effect on the electoral fortunes of incumbents. This confirms that, during the early stages of democratic development throughout the 1980s and 1990s, the economic sensitivity of electorates was meaningfully captured by over-time comparisons of economic performance related to the cost of living.

In a like manner, the relative importance of the candidates' salience variable suggests that there is room to think of personality-driven politics as domestic developments somewhat hostile to the institutional background surrounding the elections. Not surprisingly, then, the net candidate advantage stands out as highly significant and strong.[10] Having said that, the institutional aspects of Latin American elections are safeguarded by the role that over-time partisan alignments held upon voting results.

How do the general arguments rival one another? To what extent is each model relativized or reinforced by the broadening of the explanations of electoral results? Comparing columns 1 and 3 of Table 5.3, for example, shows that the economic voting hypothesis not only contributes significantly to a better understanding of why electoral results vary but also helps to strengthen the type of affirmative voting effect (by enhancing the statistical significance of the prior vote's coefficient). In so doing, it also provides more substantive significance to the overall relationship: as one would expect, if affirmative voting results from both structurally determined alignments and cultural trends of political inertia and conformism, then the macro-economic conditions can only reinforce such a pattern by introducing government performance as a cost-saving source of decision for electors looking for additional clues of how to vote. Electoral conformism may, then, be turned into some sort of economic conformism. A different way to state this is to say that unless economic conditions are so obviously worse that they succeed in deviating electorates from their regular choices, one can expect outcomes to be significantly driven by inertia.[11]

Once other political forces are incorporated as joint explanations, as in the Full Version model, the effects of all previous economic influences attenuate, as their impact is shared with (when not made viable through) these other variables. After indicators of democratic performance, partisanship and candidate voting are incorporated, economic influences are considerably moderated. Indeed, holding all other arguments constant, the impact of economic voting is limited to the administration's success in fighting inflation. On average, incumbents can expect a decrease in over three percent of the valid votes whenever inflation performance deteriorates from levels of "price stability" to "strong inflation increase" (that is, to the point of jumping two categories and bringing price indexes up by a range between 10.1 and 49.9 percentage points).

Consistent with historical patterns and contextual conditions during the 1980s and 1990s, Latin American electorates show high sensitivity to the inflation-related efficacy of governments; less obviously, they seem relatively immune to how much economic activity precedes the election or how collective a problem unemployment becomes. Still, an important caveat suggested by a country-level inspection of the way pieces of the economic argument perform seems to indicate that there may be different thresholds of economic tolerance across national electorates. Thus, even if economic indicators get below certain levels their electoral influences may remain innocuous (for example, in Argentina and Uruguay, this occurs with lower levels of growth across time). Conversely, once economic factors reach certain levels their electoral effect may become explosively important (for example, a boost in inflation during the year preceding the contest). Thus, while two situations of economic activity, one characterized as "recession" and the other as "depression," may not necessarily lead to different electoral outcomes (as suggested by the lack of statistical significance of the GDP growth coefficient), a similar comparison of inflation performance over time between a situation of "price stability" (a price hike between zero and two percent) and "extreme inflation increase" (a rise of fifty percent or more) is bound to provoke an erosion of almost five percent of the valid votes ($3 * -1.56 = -4.68$), all other conditions held constant.

Unlike economic variables, all other factors in the Full Version are modestly changed in size and significance. Prior vote (which seems to be encompassed by party strength to the point of becoming non-significant in the Party Voting model) remains at the very same level it started, anticipating one percentage point of valid votes for every three percentage points harvested by the incumbent in the previous contest. As such, it represents an important stabilizing force amidst the marked changes in policy profiles and political coalitions by the parties-in-office, as well as given the fluctuations in how satisfied the public is with incumbents' performance.

In spite of the pervasive sense of partisan malaise in Latin American (already documented), party effects on voting persist and succesfully compete with the alternative explanations of electoral choice. In the Full Version model, the regression coefficient indicates that, on average, aggregate party loyalty contributes substantively to the electoral performance of the incumbent, thus further reassuring the impact of political, long-term forces upon elections results.

From Table 5.3, the candidates' appeal emerges as the decisional clue voters rely most heavily upon. In the Candidate Voting model, both indicators remain significant. More so, compared to the performance of the Economic Voting model, the introduction of candidate effects into the Full Version model doubles the explanatory power of vote outcomes: a highly significant adjusted R^2 increase from .41 to .84, while it improves the overall fit of the model by reducing the standard error to plus or minus six percent.[12] As expected, the greater the incumbent candidate's margin of votes over his or her party's compared to the major opposition candidate's, the greater the electoral support for the government's presidential ticket. The coefficient for net candidate advantage clearly speaks of the importance of personality-related factors. This importance is further confirmed by the role that candidate salience plays in explaining electoral results: for every situation in which the incumbent candidate enjoyed some charismatic latitude over the major competitor, one could predict an increase of about three percentage points in votes.[13]

In brief, the complex matrix of forces instrumentalizing support for political continuity reveals candidate-related factors to be the ones of major relevance.

This picture seems consistent with the limited informational resources and socialization opportunities that impair the development of long-term and issue performance clues in the region. It is also consistent with traditional insights from political culture theory stating that Latin American collectivities are fascinated with charismatic and highly personalistic leadership in the realization of their political decisions.

A PARSIMONIOUS LOOK AT COMPETING EXPLANATIONS

The picture presented above successfully synthesizes the hidden nuances behind any interpretation of electoral outcomes in the region, except that it fails to provide a truly parsimonious view of the phenomenon. On the one hand, the cases-by-predictors ratio is too low to become a functional and statistically appropriate summary of the relative impact of each model; on the other hand, several variables simply fail to play any role in furthering our knowledge about what moves the fortunes of the government at the ballot box. Both considerations are addressed in the last column of Table 5.3, where a Trimmed Version model is presented. In view of previous information obtained, only the relevant variables are kept. The basic rule followed was to drop all variables that did not achieve statistical significance (at $p < .10$) in the full multivariate model presented in Table 5.3-Full Version model. The only exception was made with the "net candidate salience" variable, which was dropped due to a) its comparatively less straightforward interpretation relative to "net candidate advantage"; b) its previous statistical behavior when entered into a Candidate Voting model alone (revealing a non-significant impact); and c) the need to keep each model explained in the simplest form possible. The resulting five models are reproduced in a way that brings about a simpler and clearer view of the forces shaping the election.

This Trimmed Version keeps the single variable-based arguments of affirmative and party voting as they have already been presented, and qualifies the measurement of the economic, democratic performance, and candidate voting hypotheses by representing them with the most statistically and substantively significant variables: the change in the inflation rate, the change in the index of the political climate, and the net candidate advantage for the incumbent, respectively. This revision affords a neater overview and more efficient understanding of the main effects at work without a loss of either much information or explanatory power.[14] Also, it reveals that no dramatic changes occurred in the strength of each estimate after eliminating all redundant information.

In terms of competing arguments, the information conveyed by the beta weights of the Trimmed Version model clearly points out the explanatory edge of the candidate voting hypothesis, which more than doubles the impact exerted by any other argument. The conclusion that follows is that electoral outcomes in Latin America throughout the 1980s and up to mid-1990s outlined first and foremost a model of choice structured around the personality assets of the candidates.

The institutional drawbacks of a candidate-centered decision-making are somewhat balanced by the significant and positive effects of longterm factors such as prior vote and party strength. Both influences acted upon electorates as stabilizing forces that contributed to maintaining the pace of institutional development despite the strong economic oscillations and continuous social tensions of the 1982-1995 period. As important as that, the resiliency in voting patterns across elections captured by prior vote represents something more than mere partisan rationalization. Rather, it may be understood as a cultural trait of the electorates of the region that raises the odds of aggregate inertial responses when voters decide whether to favor political continuity or change.

The model of economic voting plays an important role in explaining ballot outcomes in Latin America. However, contrary to much speculation, it is neither the sole cause of voting nor the most relevant factor. Controlled for the effects of all other arguments, its estimate endorses the notion that poor performance on a matter very sensitive to electorates, such as inflation fighting, can only drag support away from the incumbent.[15] A number of examples illustrate this rationale: Argentina in 1989 and 1995, Brazil in 1989 and 1994, Bolivia in 1985 and 1993. These results show that electorates hold their governments accountable for their economic efficacy, and that the loss of votes for mismanagement in inflation policy may be lethal for the incumbent's aspirations to reelection. Still, other determinants of choice also do come decisively into play, attenuating the economy's electoral consequences.

The way governments have handled the political environment—that is, the extent to which they have promoted or restricted democratic development—also provides a relevant decision rule at the aggregate level, although one operating in a rather anti-political fashion: briefly stated, as incumbents become tougher over time, they are more likely to obtain more votes.[16] References to Colombia in 1990, Venezuela in 1993, Peru in 1994, or Dominican Republic in 1994 are certain. Interpreting this pattern from a cultural perspective seems inevitable; yet, the conditions among which many elections were held (civil wars, presence of guerrilla and narcoterrorism, popular uprisings and food riots, swelling poverty and high crime rates, poorly checked military forces and tutelage over the civilians, etc.) may point out a complex situation in which authoritarian moves by civilian authorities may indicate to the electorates a strong will for political governability and regime survival rather than the opposite. One can therefore speculate that under these specific conditions, insofar as there is some tendency to reward uncivic initiatives with votes, the deployment of a series of de-democratizing actions in pre-electoral times may prove to be a successful (although contingent) model of political capitalization.

TESTING INTERACTION EFFECTS BETWEEN COMPETING EXPLANATIONS

Since the aim of this study is not just to come up with a parsimonious understanding of the subject but to achieve a realistic general model of electoral choice, interaction between competing explanations must be investigated, to see if voting effects by one model are sharpened or downplayed when considering the interplay of this factor across specific categories of a second competing model. I test four interaction terms.

The first one is computed for the inflation rate of change and the political climate rate of change. The expectation is that different rates of success (or failure) in controlling inflation over time might encourage lower (or higher) uses of politically repressive devices (for example, inflationary upsurges may be followed by food riots and looting, which in turn may naturally drive governments to impose restrictions upon civil liberties). The use of these devices may then project distinctive effects over the electoral fortunes of incumbents.

The second interaction term, between party strength and the differenced rate of inflation, relies on the assumption that a meaningful presence of partisan alignments in society might pave the way to the enhancement of government's performance in key economic matters such as inflation reduction, anticipating political benefits at the voting booths. Conversely, different degrees of economic deterioration might be suspected of intensifying partisan dealignment trends which, in time, might also affect the distribution of electoral support.

The third interaction term assumes that the distribution of the incumbent candidate advantage might vary for the different levels of governmental success in controlling inflation over time, the reasoning being that success in the economic field might become a party's commodity and thus make unnecessary the nomination of a strong personality candidate (unless, of course, the president were seeking reelection). Conversely, under adversarial economic conditions, the party-in-office might bet upon a charismatic leader to stage a strong candidate-centered campaign as an attempt to offset its poor record. This reasoning may collide with the standard "strategic politician" hypothesis (see Jacobson and Kernell 1981), which postulates that strong candidates enter only in electoral races after concluding that economic conditions, among other factors, would eventually become an asset rather than a liability. Although this argument may have been at work in Latin America, it has cohabited with another, more folkloric version of "strategic politicians." This home-grown version sees office-seeking leaders as charismatic riders of people's expectations for the arrival of a "savior of the country," an expectation that becomes particularly acute as economic hardship increases and ethical criticisms of the political class escalate.

Finally, the last interaction between partisan support and candidate advantage is built upon the supposition that the weaker the party's aggregate endorsement over time, the higher the incentives to appeal to strong personality candidates to mobilize extra votes.

None of these terms prove to be significantly related to the dependent variable when controlled for the main effects. The huge bivariate correlations at the .90 or higher level between the last two interaction terms and the share of votes going to incumbents are pulverized after adjusting for the effects of the original variables. What it is even more substantial, no interactions produce major alterations in the way each original variable influences electoral outcomes—except for the drastic reduction to non-significance of the political climate measure after introducing the first two multiplicative terms.[17] The minimal alterations brought by the inclusion of the interaction terms speak, again, of the robustness of the findings discussed above.

TESTING THE POLITICAL REFERENDUM MODEL

The inclusion in the equation of the variable assessing the extra-economic leadership provided by the incumbent helps to paint a broader picture of the forces determining electoral outcomes. This new description results from both the direct effect of presidential approval on the incumbent vote-share and the changes it forces in the way candidate effects should be appraised.[18] As data availability remains limited to only thirty-six of the forty-one elections so far reviewed, a separate discussion is provided, as a sample-based extension of the Trimmed Version model already discussed (see Table 5.4).

In this new examination, the variability of the incumbent vote-share gets slightly higher than for the original universe of forty-one elections ($std.dev._{36} = 15.76$ versus $std.dev._{41} = 15.29$), which makes logical to find some light increase in the standard error estimate of this revised model ($SE_{36} = 6.34$ versus $SE_{41} = 6.13$). Nonetheless, the model's goodness of fit measure remains at exactly the same point, adjusted $R^2 = .84$, which suggests that the main contribution of this extended Trimmed Version is to better illustrate the complexities underlying fluctuations in political support.

Overall, improving the general model specification by incorporating the political referendum hypothesis (measured by presidential popularity) offers a qualitatively more refined sense of the cross-pressures confronted by electorates (see Table 5.4)

On the one hand, the patterns articulating voting results remain very similar to those for the forty-one elections in relation to each major predictor's estimates (after discounting for prior vote effects).[19] This result tells us that for all the modifications involved, the broader argument remains fairly robust. On the other hand, as the gap in the strength of the coefficients reveals, this re-specified version suggests that the heuristic approach to voting behavior in Latin America can be better served by first separating long- and short-term forces, and then distinguishing between economic and non-economic effects. Thus the first cut separates those influences that involve a time-intensive prerequisite to develop (i.e., the socialization opportunity for partisanship to emerge, the crystallization of cultural trends and political traditions involved in the prior vote measure, or the comparison for democratic achievements between administrations) from those of a short-term nature (economic achievements, political leadership and candidates' attributes). In fact, a comparison of standardized coefficients shows a cut between long-term forces (ranging between .18 and .26) and short-term forces (ranging between .39 and .50). The second cut distinguishes between reliance on economic performance and dependence on symbolic utilities embodied in manifestations of political leadership or the attractiveness of candidates' biographical and political personas.

The extended Trimmed Version of the models also helps the economic explanation to gain more ground, although this argument still falls behind the candidate-related effects. Interpreting the values of this version, one can say that, with everything else held constant, for every ten points of incumbent's net candidate advantage over his or her opponent's, there is an expected average return of six percent more votes for the ruling party ticket (10*.61 = 6.1). In a like manner, when comparing one election held under a situation of "strong inflation increase" in the annual price rate to another of "price stability," there is an average expectation that the incumbent vote loss for the first scenario will be almost eight percentage points higher than for the second scenario (2*−3.94 = −7.88). Similarly, for every five percent rise in the non-economic popularity of the president, the party-in-office can expect, on average, to harvest an additional two percentage points in votes (5*.41 = 2.05).

The relative strength of these estimates means that electoral results are not shaped by decisions of either instrumental or symbolic nature alone. Electorates react in relation to data they receive (i.e., an urgency to stabilize the economy, a need for a strong-willed authority, impressionistic information

Table 5.4. Assessing the Effects of Competing Models of Electoral Choice in Latin America, 1982–1995 (Extended Trimmed Version, N = 36)

Variable	*Affirmative Voting b (SEb)*	*Party Voting b (SEb)*	*Democratic Voting b (SEb)*	*Economic Voting b (SEb)*	*Political Referendum Voting b (SEb)*	*Candidate Voting b (SEb)*	*Extended Trimmed Version b (SEb)*	β
Prior	.28	.06	.34[c]	.43[b]	.10	.40[b]	.29[a]	.26
Vote	(.19)	(.20)	(.18)	(.16)	(.17)	(.17)	(.10)	
Party Strength		.62[b]					.34[a]	.23
		(.27)					(.12)	
ΔPolitical Climate			2.73[b]				1.25[b]	.18
			(1.06)				(.49)	
ΔInflation Rate				−4.81[a]			−3.94[a]	–
				(1.25)			(.64)	.45
President Popularity					.56[a]		.41[a]	.39
					(.16)		(.08)	
CandidateAdvantage						.59[a]	.61[a]	.50
						(.18)	(.08)	
Intercept	23.11[b]	16.10[c]	21.71[b]	33.66[a]	31.59[a]	17.45[b]	27.53[a]	
	(9.32)	(9.29)	(8.66)	(8.34)	(8.36)	(8.43)	(4.77)	
Adjusted R^2	.03	.14	.17	.31	.28	.24	.84	
Stand. Error	15.49	14.59	14.35	13.08	13.32	13.71	6.34	

[a]Coefficients are significant at $p < .01$
[b]Coefficients are significant at $p < .05$
[c]Coefficients are significant at $p < .10$

about candidates, a declining politicization of group and class identities) and in relation to the sources of decision they lack (i.e., poor socialization experiences of partisanship, inconsistent preferences for democratic performance). This implies that a plurality of reasons articulates the final voting decision with different intensity. Thus, electorates do not ignore material clues when they consider using the election as a referendum on the political leadership of the government. Nor do they disregard perceptions of the nation's sense of direction (as captured by the political leadership indicator) merely because they show susceptibility to economic circumstances. Likewise, one should not expect that voters' attention to candidate's appeals would make outcomes less dependent on financial states.

Such multidimensional sensitivity reflects the plurality of sources of political capitalization available for incumbents. This diversity can be illustrated by simulating electoral scenarios. In theory, setting all variables to their mean values would yield an incumbent vote-share of 31.3 percent. This value underestimates by less than five percentage points the grand mean reached for the whole sample (that is, corresponds to an average absolute prediction error of 4.68). There may be multiple reasons for this, such as unmeasured factors not included in the general model (e.g., issue proximity), the trimmed nature of each specific model (which left aside some variables of interest for the sake of parsimony), and the measurement errors of some of the predictors included. All these effects are, therefore, contained in the error term. Let's simulate a situation of strong inflation increase. Here, one can anticipate an average proportion of incumbent votes of 21.9 percent, with all other variables held constant.[20] Naturally, such a downturn in relation to the average pattern—9.4 percent—seems to justify the popularity of economic explanations.

On the other hand, this dramatic "free fall" in support for the ruling party is not doomed to happen if incumbents motivate electorates to ponder other decisional clues. For example, an energetic display of initiative and commanding authority by the president in the realm of domestic and foreign policy (especially if it echoes matters that the public judges to be of high priority) would make people trust that, despite the dire state of the economy, the public order is assured and the party-in-office has the capacity to make decisions. Then, whenever events allow the president's approval to reach, for example, 58 percent (that is, 14 percentage points above its average level), one can expect a cancellation of the negative effects provoked by the economic crisis (a predicted incumbent vote-share of 31.5 percent).[21]

If it is true that such levels of popularity are hard to accomplish when financial distress abounds, it is also true that presidents and their parties count on numerous opportunities and resources to strengthen their political leadership (e.g., nationalism, fight against crime or terrorism, party mobilization, etc.) . In a similar way, incumbents may attempt to offset negative economic trends by relying heavily on a candidate-centered campaign, likely to produce a reasonable advantage over their major contenders. Thus, for example, whenever the net advantage for the incumbent candidate exceeds by 7 percentage points the opposition's, those negative effects coming from a poor economic situation can be overcome (that is, vote-share of 31 percent is again attained).

Typically, incumbents resort to more than one asset to enhance their chances of reelection. Even if financial conditions seriously worsen before elections, incumbents can still hope to compensate by relying on a partisan fidelity higher than average (say, 33 percent rather than just 28.5), staging a series of politically bold, approval-boosting decisions (say, raising popularity to 40 percent, which corresponds to about 7 residual unit scores), and nominating a candidate able to match up his or her opponent's advantage (say, to reduce the difference to zero). In such circumstances, incumbents can still expect to obtain about 31.1 percent of the valid votes, on average.[22]

In summary, both economic and non-economic variables are key in shaping support for the incumbent party at the ballot box. To contend that economics is all that matters is to set up the wrong assumptions about how average electorates produce decisions and to ignore the actual voting experience of Latin America. Given the fact that elections convey, ultimately, a decision about support or rejection of political continuity, the presence of important non-economic factors does not come as a surprise.

Economy is a critical variable for understanding fluctuations in incumbent support at the polls. But the evidence so far analyzed also shows that once the impact of the economy is controlled for other determinants that are non-economic in nature and scope, it fails to lead the explanatory race. Moreover, not all forms of measuring economic effects are equally important: the rate of change of inflation over time stands out as the most salient. These conclusions are in fact pretty consistent with the scattered substantiation produced by other Latin Americanists who place inflation as the most efficient measure of economic voting and underscore the limited influence of this approach after adjusting for the impact of political forces (see Remmer 1991; Rius 1992; Carrión 1998). Conversely, the electoral fortunes of ruling parties are highly responsive to the political leadership displayed by the head of the government. This indicates that a general sense of the quality of life achieved by the nation, beyond economics, as captured by the president's popularity, is an important yardstick against which voters decide whether or not to grant a new chance to the current authorities.

Candidate effects emerge as the strongest explanatory argument. The importance of these effects underscores the weight of cultural traditions that make personalistic traits the most effective vehicles of politicization. It is also consistent with a picture of poor partisan socialization resulting from the resiliency of authoritarian politics in the region. In this regard, as long-term forces are structurally handicapped in influencing voters (although they are still capable of having limited influences on voting), the prevalent reasons for choice reside in short-term factors.

These findings defy a good deal of conventional wisdom about economic voting in Latin America. However, several limitations in the assessment of the economic voting argument have to be acknowledged. First, there may perception gaps with regards to objective conditions and that cannot be appraised using aggregate-level analysis. Second, the effect of macro-economic performance tackles only retrospective forces, while one may speculate that electorates may be more prone to react to promises and the prospective performance. Third, individualistic pocketbook-oriented reasoning may be at play, which is missed by the intrinsically sociotropic nature of the macroeconomic indicators.[23] Fourth, electorates may actually have an economic memory extending longer than the two-year period assumed here, judging performance across administrations rather than only intra-administration successes or failures. Finally, there may be obstacles to holding governments fully responsible for the economic performance, resulting from factors as varied as acknowledged dependency on external powers or international market instability, the institutional structure of the country, lack of trust in elections, and low confidence in the economic responsiveness of parties.

All these eventualities may handicap a more substantive salience for the economic voting argument. Yet they must not conceal the fact that macroeconomic conditions surveyed by conventional standards fare but second when compared to other non-economic effects. In order to narrow down the discussion of effects in a manner that is both theoretically sound and empirically feasible, the next chapter examines how each of the models of electoral choice behaves under different institutional and macro-economic conditions.

NOTES

1. Of course, there are many others sources of error in aggregate analysis. Among those related to the specification aspect, one can also point out to the proportionally higher measurement error involved in non-economic variables (generally assessed through dummy variables that model specific political events) compared to those estimating economic conditions and performance, something that in principle should benefit a higher effect of the latter by comparison with the former. Paradoxically, one may suspect that, given some of the flaws and biases present in the way macroeconomic data is collected in less developed countries, the gap in measurement error

between economic and non-economic variables should be smaller, thus permitting the latter to reveal a more substantial impact.

2. I would contend, though, that this level of correlation does not involve a severe problem. Actually, these coefficients are, according to conventional standards, well below any serious risk of collinearity. Furthermore, when controlled for all other arguments, each one behaves very independently of the other.

3. That is, fifteen percentual points below the average value of 36 percent, equalling eleven percent, or above the average value, thus equalling fifty-one percent of votes.

4. This is suggested by the greater distance between prior vote and party strength (over 18 percentage points) compared to the differences between prior vote and incumbent support (less than 8 points) and party strength and incumbent support (close to 8 points).

5. Values correspond to those of the residualized version of the variable for a total number of thirty-six cases. Cases add up to nineteen for the group of highly institutionalized and bipartisan systems (which in the latter group leaves three cases as missing), and seventeen for the group of poorly institutionalized and multiparty systems (which in the former leaves five missing cases and in the latter two). Among the groups of economic crisis and prosperity, this variable amounts fifteen and twenty-one cases, respectively.

6. Values correspond to those of the original variable for a total number of thirty-six cases.

7. As expected from the assumption of homoscedasticy, the residualized version of presidential popularity (after regressed against economic variables) presents a zero mean value. Still, as indicated by the size of its standard deviation, the new variable retains quite a bit of its original variability, which confirms the resiliency of the instability introduced by leadership factors.

8. See Catterberg and Braun 1989; Editorial, "El Mandato de las Urnas," *Clarín*, 16 May 1995, 12.

9. An alternative interpretation could have resorted to the argument of distinctive "party policy expertise" (see Hibbs 1987), that is, that the incumbent party still receive votes, even if confronting negative economic results in unemployment, as a result of their perceived expertise on some other economic area (for example, control of inflation). However, a background of citizens cognitive limitations in appraising party policy expertise, poorly developed partisan profiles, and the dominance of incumbent-oriented voting suggests to discard this explanation.

10. Interestingly, the "net candidate salience," which holds a more obviously personalistic and antiparty content, projects itself rather weakly onto the "net candidate advantage" variable (i.e., product-moment correlation of .26, significant at $p = .05$).

11. For example, if one leaves out those economic variables with non-significant effects and assumes zero growth ("recession") and no major improvement in anti-inflationary policy (zero change) preceding the election, the party-in-office may still be likely to harvest, on average, over 22 percent of the votes (see the intercept) plus slightly less than half the proportion of votes that brought it to incumbency (see prior vote).

12. In terms of average prediction error, the Full Version model reduces by more than half the proportion of incumbent votes missed by the model of Economic Voting (from 8.38% to 4.02%).

13. This evidence somewhat attenuates the extended belief that independent newcomers, political entrepreneurs and showbizz personalities emphasizing their lack of political past as a virtue had the electoral upper hand across the region since the mid-1980s.

14. Actually, this version provides a picture very similar to the original one: it explains the variability in outcomes at an identical rate (84 percent), while contributing to a similar improvement in the fit as measured by the minimization of the spread of errors (down to an average error of +/−6.13 percent). Furthermore, its average prediction accuracy remains very high, over 95 percent (e.g., 100-4.39 = 95.61) in absolute terms.

15. Such downscaled effect is not a methodological artifact coming from the different levels of measurement used for the economic and non-economic variables (i.e., categorical among the former but interval among the latter). If, in principle, these measurement features of the first constructs might have resulted in a reduced variance (and, therefore, a lower statistical effect) relative to the latter, this proved to be inconsequential in practice. After reordering all variables presented in the trimmed version (see Appendix D) into five categories to match the scale of the economic variables measured as biannual averages, and including both annual inflation and annual GDP levels, the same picture remains: neither the average yearly inflation rate nor the average yearly GDP rate are significant at conventional levels, while all other variables remain statistically and substantively important. Furthermore, comparing standardized coefficients, the edge of candidate effects remains intact, the relevant though secondary role of the inflation change-rate continues, the relative trailing of the democratic issues in regards to the other arguments is confirmed, and minor variations of order are verified for the party strength and prior vote effects. This examination confirms the reliability of the findings already discussed.

16. It is important, however, to bear in mind that the mode for this variable falls in the "no change" value, concentrating 29.3 percent of the cases. Those elections held on the eve of any sort of democratic improvement over the previous period comprise 39 percent of the sample, whereas those surrounded by a worsening of the political conditions make up the remaining 31.7 percent. In a like manner, linear readings of this variable's impact may sometimes be misleading, as illustrated by the Honduran election of 1985. On that occasion, the incumbent party successfully harvested enough votes to stay in power in spite of President Suazo Cordova's authoritarian drives; but the election of liberal José Azcona to the presidency rather than Suazo's protegé, Mejía Arellano, in the context of an electoral system of double simultaneous vote, actually looked more like a choice for change than for continuity (see Rosenberg 1989).

17. Pearson's correlations of political climate rate of change with the interaction terms between inflation and political climate, and inflation and party strength stand at .93 and .89, respectively, revealing collinearity problems which depressed the impact of the main effect on the vote. Quite interestingly, the latter value suggests a pattern

by which whenever party support remains low, inflation-reduction efforts are bound to fail, a situation that when repeated over time may complicate governability and the administration's survival in office, thus prompting the incumbent to resort to increasing coercion. This may become even more true if, as revealed by the non-significant impact of the interaction term and the significant effect of the political climate variable, such a move may pass unnoticed to voters and the "showing toughness" tactic may end up being handsomely rewarded with votes.

18. As discussed in Chapter 4, conceptual and statistical reasons suggest "decontaminating" the "net candidate advantage" variable from the influences of presidential political popularity and inflation performance over time, rendering a new variable with new values.

19. This similarity is remarkable considering that, due to data unavailability, the sample of 36 elections analyzed here misses cases mostly from the pre-1990 period, thus posing a potential problem of period- related biases for the findings. Fortunately, all in all, this seems not to be the case.

20. This value comes from adding the values for the following equation:

$$21.9\% = 27.53 + .29(47) + .34(28.5) + 1.25(-.42) \text{ -}3.94(6) + .41(.00) + .61(-7.95)$$

where the left-hand side value represents the resulting incumbent vote-share (21.9%) and the right-hand side of the equation corresponds, in order, to the addition of the intercept value and the estimates for prior vote (set to its mean), party strength (set to its mean), the change in the rate of the political climate (set to its mean), the change in the annual rate of inflation (set to the "strong inflation increase" category), presidential popularity (set to its mean), and net candidate advantage (set to its mean).

21. Fifty eight percent of approval corresponds to roughly twenty units in residual scores. The resulting average electoral outcome (31.3%) is a product of setting all variables to their mean values except for inflation and presidential popularity, rendering the following structure:

$$31.3\% = 27.53 + .29(47) + .34(28.5) + 1.25(-.42) - 3.94(6) + .41(20) + .61(-7.95)$$

22. This results from adding the corresponding estimates with the following values:

$$31.1\% = 27.53 + .29(47) + .34(33) + 1.25(-.42) - 3.94(6) + .41(7) + .61(0)$$

23. Unfortunately, measures which might come closer to the individual economic experience, such as purchasing power parity or real wages, were either not available for the whole range of years here studied or were measured at wholly different levels in each country (e.g., in some countries covering urban areas, in others only the manufacturing sector, in others only the service sector of one of several major urban centers), all of which would have made comparisons unmeaningful.

Chapter Six

Taking Contextual Differences into Account

Different institutional and macro-economic environments furnish different structures of opportunity for the effective development of the decisional clues triggering the vote. It is therefore safe to assume that electorates voting under dissimilar contextual conditions will find available, will be motivated to follow, and will make use of divergent informational shortcuts and sources of decision. Put succinctly, people voting under different conditions make their choices differently. This view is shared by a number of scholars, such as Powell and Whitten (1993), who insist that contextual distinctions must be taken into account when attempting to make sense of the inconsistency of effects in cross-national studies of voting, particularly of those focusing on economic arguments.

In this chapter, I explore how the models of electoral results perform under varied situations of political institutionalization, party systems and macro-economic activity. After reviewing theoretical and methodological considerations, I examine the way in which each argument interacts with the major features of the institutional context surrounding forty-one presidential contests. I then replicate the analysis for the subsample of cases for which information about the political leadership of the incumbent can be added. A second review of contextual effects focuses on how situations of recession and growth furnish different opportunities for the electorate. This analysis aims at discovering whether or not the conventional wisdom about the presence of "protest" voting (as illustrated by asymmetrical responses to circumstances) is verifiable.

CONTEXTUAL EFFECTS: THEORETICAL UNDERPINNINGS AND METHODOLOGY

People´s political life does not unfold in a vaccum. The stimuli that develop their voting preferences, the availability or saliency of decisional clues to use, the constraints to use elections to reveal a deep-seated value (or to substitute the lack of core beliefs for narrower and shallower orientations) refer to outcomes related to their environment of decision. Three spheres represent the key environmental influences present in Latin America throughout the years here examined: the level of economic stability or instability upon which electorates lived, the structure of the party systems that articulated the electoral disputes, and the degree to which political life in each country followed clear-cut institutional lines, that is, predictable and formal rules of political organization and control. These three contextual effects summarized the critically different scenarios observed across the region, submitting different national electorates to somewhat dissimilar opportunities and conditions.[1]

The Effect of Political Institutionalization

Highly institutionalized contexts facilitate a clear division of roles and responsibilities among incumbent parties, opposition forces and the remaining branches of power. This explicit division makes it easier, at least in theory, for voters to glimpse the extent to which attribution of responsibility should fall into governments' hands or not and, consequently, hold the incumbent accountable for all major developments (Mainwaring and Scully 1995). In this way, a connection between economic performance and electoral decision can easily develop.

Economic voting is also likely to occur under institutionalized systems because of the greater chances that parties may develop stable policy profiles that voters can identify. Also, as in the case of advanced democracies, political independence may push voters to structure their choice around government outcomes. Party voting can be expected to exert an unambiguous and substantive effect, since this type of context provides opportunities for partisan socialization. Candidate voting, on the other hand, is likely to play a relatively marginal role, since room for personalistic politics is limited and a practice of collegial, consensual and highly professionalized paths of selecting party candidates usually dominates. In principle, these circumstances should keep the role of presidential prestige in time of election fairly limited; on the other hand, given the intrinsically greater expediency in keeping the president liable for achievements in the extra-economic domain, some systematic leadership effect may show.

In relation to democratic performance, highly institutionalized regimes do not leave much space for further advancement of civil liberties and political rights. On the other hand, these regimes do certainly shut down any attempt at reversing such liberties and rights. Therefore, in contexts characterized by high institutionalization, these matters can be expected to look more like constants than variables.

Situations characterized by inchoate party systems offer a different array of effects. Since rules and formal procedures are less binding between leaders, the public and party organizations, and political linkages are forged through personal contacts and material benefits, candidate voting gains primacy. Frequently, its pivotal role is a consequence of the existence of parties as exclusive instruments for the advancement of the political will of individual leaders. Party voting, on the other hand, is marginal to the process of decision, not merely as a result of the poor conditions for the development of partisan identities among the people, but also because of the structural difficulties in converting social cleavages into partisan alignments.

Economic voting may work rather ambiguously in such situations. Given the fact that responsibility attribution is difficult to achieve, economic performance may remain without political overtones. On the other hand, since the general characteristics of poorly institutionalized systems do not leave many other clues to voters besides short-term forces, one should grant the existence of some degree of reaction to accomplishments in the realm of finances. Still, the prevalence of clientelistic arrangements may hinder the presence of straightforward effects of the economy, since numerous individuals may rely more heavily upon particularistic channels of assuring material benefits in exchange of votes, ignoring the trends at the national level.

Finally, people's receptivity to charismatic authority and the relative easiness of deciding the vote according to the commanding ability of the president is likely to confer a central position to the model of political referendum. Also, one can expect considerable sensitivity to successes on the road of democratization as a result of the rhetorical salience of democratic issues among the media, partisan factions, and the anti-authoritarian social movements that pushed forward the transition.

To explore these interactions empirically, I split the sample of pre-electoral contexts into two groups according to levels of partisan institutionalization. Those with a score of 1 comprise situations characterized by "high institutionalization", while all others are considered to be "weakly institutionalized."[2] The list of all countries appears in Table 6.1. For the individual level discussion, to be developed in Chapter 7, each country under study is taken

Table 6.1. Descriptive Values of Political Institutionalization and Party System Format

Country (Election Political Month/Year)	*Political Institutionalization*[3]	*Number of Effective Parties*[4]
Argentina (5/1989)	1	2.57
Argentina (5/1995)	.5	4.54
Bolivia (7/1985)	0	4.15
Bolivia (5/1989)	0	4.36
Bolivia (6/1993)	0	3.92
Brazil (11/1989)	0	2.78
Brazil (10/1994)	0	8.68
Chile (12/1993)	1	5.06
Colombia (5/1982)	1	2.06
Colombia (5/1986)	1	1.98
Colombia (5/1990)	1	2.45
Colombia (5/1994)	1	2.97
Costa Rica (2/1982)	1	2.38
Costa Rica (2/1986)	1	2.27
Costa Rica (2/1990)	1	2.21
Costa Rica (2/1994)	1	2.21
Domin.Rep.(5/1982)	.5	1.99
Domin.Rep. (5/1986)	.5	2.25
Domin.Rep. (5/1990)	.5	2.53
Domin.Rep. (5/1994)	.5	3.05
Ecuador (6/1984)	0	3.97
Ecuador (1/1988)	0	7.63
Ecuador (5/1992)	0	6.99
El Salvador (3/1989)	.5	2.40
El Salvador (3/1994)	.5	3.03
Guatemala (11/1990)	0	2.98
Honduras (11/1985)	1	2.17
Honduras (11/1989)	1	2.12
Honduras (11/1993)	1	2.00
México (7/1988)	.5	1.82
México (8/1994)	.5	2.22
Nicaragua (2/1990)	0	2.28
Panamá (5/1994)	0	3.79
Perú (4/1985)	0	2.46
Perú (4/1990)	0	2.32
Perú (4/1995)	0	2.99
Uruguay (11/1989)	1	2.93
Uruguay (11/1994)	1	3.35
Venezuela (12/1983)	1	2.65
Venezuela (12/1988)	1	2.42
Venezuela (12/1993)	1	2.83

Domin.Rep.: Dominican Republic
Sources: Nohlen (1993); *Keesing's Record of World Events* (various years); Dix (1992); Mainwaring and Scully (1995).

to represent a different situation, with Uruguay of 1994 at one pole, Perú of 1995 at the other, and Argentina of 1995 placed half-way of each pole (see Appendix B).

The Effect of Party Systems

Since systems that are predominantly organized in two-party formats allow for a better identification of the incumbent's responsibility for performance in general, macro-economic and democratic outcomes can be expected to be influential in these contexts. To the extent that the president's approval is founded on the management of extra-economic matters, it is also likely to play an important role in shaping voters' choice. These conditions tend to limit the variance of the partisan influences, so low party voting can be expected. Actually, much of the effect of party voting is likely to be captured by prior vote record, rendering the affirmative voting argument very effective. In addition, candidate voting should present attenuated effects.

On the other hand, multipartism makes it harder for electorates to assign responsibility for performance, since the sources to blame or credit are multiple. Accordingly, economic voting, along with democratic and leadership performance voting, is likely to be deflated. Furthermore, given the higher costs involved for voters in terms of following each party's standings on the issues of the day, defaulting on affirmative voting clues can be expected to be important. By the same token, partisan forces may be diminished, leaving the door open to candidate-related influences, although at a moderate level.

I identify party systems following the Laakso-Tagaapera index of the number of effective parties in the Lower House previous to each presidential contest and dividing the index into two groups. One group comprises those elections held within a predominantly two-party system, holding an index equal to 2.75 or lower (ranging from 1.82 before the 1988 Mexican elections to 2.65 before the Venezuelan elections of 1983). The second group includes those elections held within a predominantly multiparty system, holding an index equal to 2.76 or larger (ranging from 2.78 before the 1989 Brazilian elections to 8.68 before the 1994 contests in that same country).

The Effect of Macro-Economic Circumstances

Good and bad economic times are not only expected to enhance or deflate different arguments of voting behavior but also to predispose individuals differently in the way they appraise economic information as a decisional clue. Times of recession and/or economic discontinuity are likely to increase individuals' sensitivity to respond electorally based on how they might have done financially. Therefore, pocketbook and retrospective reactions should prevail in light of the minimal attention and predictability of policy programs under situations of downward instability, as well as the trauma that hyperinflation upsurges created in few of the countries with the larger electorates of the region. In theory, the policy unpredictability blurs the chances of prospective economic voting. Concomitantly, hyperinflation experiences impair considerations of sociotropic nature, given the priority attained by considerations of personal survival. On top of this, economic distress under inchoate party systems may induce voters to rally against the incumbent to a greater extent than would be normally the case, since no partisan anchoring sentiments are developed. The political translation of economic grievances does not become merely an option for punishment, but may reflect a skewed orientation against the ruling party.

Situations of economic ungovernability leave room for the active intervention of the incumbent through economic plans and stabilization shocks. Often, when interacting with poorly institutionalized systems, presidents develop these programs autonomously, bypassing party and congressional authorities. Since economic policy becomes personalized, the attribution connection is greatly simplified. Furthermore, this situation reinforces the centrality of the president's political leadership and the candidates' attributes.

When prosperity reigns, the urgency to choose a government on the basis of economic criteria depends on the recent record of the country. Incumbents naturally seek to politicize the economy. Since voters' personal conditions are not immediately threatened, their voting decision is more likely to be based on the financial state of the country. For the same reason, forward-looking orientations may take place. But citizens are risk-averse, which inclines them to ponder the past as well and reward the incumbent party for its achievements in this area.

Economic circumstances do not guarantee a symmetrical certification of the ruling party for its positive and negative attainments in the economic field. Even if prosperity is moderate among conditions of economic stability, one may speculate that voters may react to material conditions in light of the adroitness to which they can link financial states to government politics. Previous features of the state-centered model of development in the 1980s, as well as the active engagement of the Executive power to privatize the economy and decentralize social services thereafter, ensures that public perception of economic fortunes will rest on the incumbent party's actions, both at the personal and societal levels.

I assess the overall macro-economic situation according to the behavior of the average annual rate of the gross domestic product. The sample is split in two: elections held in times of "crisis" (a weighted GDP rate between +2.9 and −9.5 percent, that is, situations ranging from stagnation to depression in per capita terms) and in times of "prosperity" (a weighted GDP rate between +3.1 and +8.4 percent, that is, situations ranging from small progress to economic expansion in per capita terms).[5] By proceeding in this way, I am also able to explore the existence of asymmetric responses to the incumbent economic performance. At the individual level analysis of Chapter 7, countries are aligned according to the level of economic discontinuity (see Appendix B).

CONTEXTUAL CLEAVAGES AND MODELS OF ELECTORAL CHOICE

The notion that electorates who make decisions under dissimilar institutional and macro-economic settings do not operate in the same way is confirmed by the data. A look at Table 5.2 in previous chapter reveals that each milieu yields a particular scenario of electoral choice in terms of the intensity of support for political continuity or change. To begin with, highly institutionalized contexts offer a greater solace for incumbents compared to inchoate party systems, as two-party systems do relative to multiparty structures. The difference reaches ten percentage points. Divergence further extends to the degree of fluidity in pro-incumbent support: weakly institutionalized and multiparty systems show close to double the dispersion displayed by politically developed and bipartisan regimes.[6]

Different institutional configurations also yield different magnitudes of political habits (such as prior vote) and partisan traditions. As a rule, long-term sources of political support are stronger among institutionally advanced and bipartisan orders. A pattern of affirmative voting seems particularly stronger among two-party systems. Naturally, then, as prior vote and party support seem consistently associated with institutional characteristics, as does incumbent vote-share, it is reasonable to speculate that some pattern of systematic covariation may be present for these three sets of variables. Also, as expected, volatility across elections is greater among less politically developed and more pluralistic systems—almost twice as large as the one observed among opposite circumstances.

In the area of democratic performance, highly institutionalized systems, by definition, fully warrant political rights and freedoms to their citizens, thereby offering almost no room for improvements. Both the lower amount of positive change and the lower dispersion of this variable illustrates this situation. Conversely, most inchoate party structures are coincidental with newly democratized regimes, that is, political orders still in the process of consolidating citizenship entitlements and liberties. These different structures of opportunity are highly consequential for the subsequent variability in government performance in deepening democracy across situations. Interestingly enough, the same pattern is reproduced across different party systems.

Table 5.2 also makes obvious that institutional contexts are not neutral in terms of the economic conditions they house or promote. Highly institutionalized and bipartisan regimes are more effective in securing growth. Elections held in inchoate party systems, in turn, are more prone to be encircled by greater inflation rates and levels of unemployment. Multiparty systems, on the other hand, are more effective in keeping prices low by the time of elections. The question of whether this entails an inherently greater efficacy of multiparty systems to deal with inflation or the presence of greater political constraints over authorities in two-party systems to generate efficient deflationary political cycles, however, still remains to be answered.

Profiles of incumbent political leadership and candidates' appeal also present systematic differences across institutional conditions. The ruling authorities benefit more under high institutionalization, but the pattern in terms of the party systems is ambiguous. Whereas two-party formats give to political leadership a greater saliency, they assure the incumbent nominee a lower advantage over his or her rival relative to that he or she might have in a multiparty system.

The different effects imposed by institutional conditions on the way determinants of electoral decision perform in the region are replicated by macroeconomic circumstances. Distinguishing contests by the level of economic crisis or prosperity that surrounds them illustrates another gap in how models of choice behave. The abyss across economic contexts is remarkably seized by the 13 percentage points that separate the political endorsement of the incumbent whenever good times precede the election, compared to a situation of economic downturn.

The data reveal several differences. For one, presidents ruling under prosperity can expect a sort of "honeymoon" effect, which extends popularity for economic reasons to performance in extra-economic arenas, as suggested by the average presidential approval of 41 percent. That bonus rarely exists for presidents ruling in times of economic slump, forced to "administer the crisis" (average approval of 24 percent). After removing the effect of economic factors on the president's popularity, the residual scores show a consistent pattern of positive values in times of growth and negative values in time of decay. In addition, each environment evokes a different reaction to candidates' attributes. Bad times pave the way to a greater advantage for the challenger, whereas times of progress reduce such edge to almost zero.

Interestingly enough, situations of crisis and prosperity do not leave room for the articulation of specific trade-offs in terms of policy outcomes. Economic slowdowns in pre-electoral moments are usually accompanied by greater, not lower, rates of inflation in the short and long run, compared to situations of economic advancement. Furthermore, levels of unemployment remain pretty much the same across situations. Indirectly, this picture hints at the limited opportunities that Latin American leaders have had to stage efficacious political business cycles prior to presidential elections. These policy constraints co-exist with a lack of clear-cut differences between macroeconomic backgrounds and the magnitude of prior votes and party strength. Since the latter are measures with a temporal lag that precedes the assessment of economic activity, whatever the intensity of political traditions and alignments may be, they are unlikely to grant a differential leverage to incumbents in terms of their abilities to manage the economy to their favor.

Finally, it appears that times of crisis—not prosperity—are more prone to coincide with greater democratic achievements. One reason for this is the overlap of regimes that face relative prosperity and that are highly institutionalized, a quality which by definition does not allow much progress on democratic matters. Another plausible reason is the electoral strategy followed by incumbents. Oftentimes, economic downfall is accompanied by social turmoil and ungovernability, but in electoral circumstances heavy-handed initiatives are withheld until the ballots are counted. Not rarely is it left to the winner of the elections to straighten things out, often by resorting to authoritarian means.

TAKING ACCOUNT OF DIFFERENT INSTITUTIONAL CONTEXTS

Table 6.2 summarizes the interplay between environmental conditions and the initial and extended trimmed versions of the models. For the initial trimmed versions, the interaction between models and specific institutional features largely enhances the explanatory power of voting outcomes. (This is presented at each column of the Table with the indication "initial".)

As a rule, electoral arguments respond differently to institutional cleavages. Both bipartisan and highly institutionalized regimes are able to offer a more precise understanding of electoral choice than situations of multipartism and poor political development with regards to how well the arguments summarized by the trimmed versions fit plausible explanations of electoral support. Comparing summary statistics across the board, highly developed and two-party systems reduce the amount of uncertainty to an average of plus or minus 4.9 and 4.8 against an average proportion of uncertainty of plus or minus 5.2 and 6.8 for poorly developed and multiparty systems, respectively. (In terms of mean prediction error, bipartisan and highly institutionalized sys-

Table 6.2. Institutional Contexts and Models of Electoral Choice in Latin America, 1982–1995*

	Level of Political Institutionalization								*Type of Party System*							
	Low				*High*				*Two-Party*				*Multiparty*			
Models of Choice	*initial b(SEb)*	β	*extended b(SEb)*	β	*initial b(SEb)*	β	*extended b(SEb)*	β	*initial b(SEb)*	β	*extended b(SEb)*	β	*initial b(SEb)*	β	*extended b(SEb)*	β
Affirmative Voting	.27[b] (.11)	.25 (.13)	.16 (.17)	.25 (.20)	.94[a] (.17)	.67 (.20)	.93[a] (.14)	.66 (.13)	.25	.17	.21	.14	.29[b]	.24	.23	.19
Party Voting	.46[b] (.19)	.27	.55[c] (.25)	.33	.22 (.18)	.18	.23 (.20)	.18	.44[b] (.17)	.32	.37[c] (.19)	.25	.34[b] (.16)	.21	.22 (.17)	.14
Democratic Voting	1.54[c] (.72)	.20	.71 (.92)	.10	−.64 (.69)	−.12	−.60 (.78)	−.12	1.26 (.87)	.16	.69 (1.06)	.09	1.27[3] (.64)	.20	.63 (.67)	.10
Economic Voting	−2.06[b] (.86)	−.24	−4.09[a] (.81)	−.44	−2.61[a] (.75)	−.40	−3.30[a] (1.01)	−.50	−1.29[3] (.67)	−.22	−3.67[a] (.90)	−.58	−2.20[c] (1.07)	−.23	−4.78[a] (1.03)	−.46
Political Referendum			.44[b] (.14)	.34			.10 (.10)	.15			.22[b] (.09)	.29			.65[a] (.17)	.45
Candidate Voting	.69[a] (.09)	.75	.72[a] (.13)	.62	.22 (.14)	.20	.21 (.16)	.19	.51[a] (.10)	.53	.65[a] (.14)	.63	.71[a] (.10)	.75	.49[a] (.15)	.38
Intercept	23.04[a] (4.55)		27.86[a] (6.25)		22.60[a] (9.23)		−1.08 (10.08)		22.94[b] (8.44)		32.71[b] (10.92)		23.87[a] (6.11)		35.56[a] (6.96)	
Adjusted R^2	.92		.92		.80		.79		.81		.82		.85		.87	
Standard Error	5.01		5.44		4.78		4.97		4.72		4.93		7.08		6.63	
N =	22		17		19		19		22		19		19		17	

*Trimmed version of models presented in two formats: *initial* and *extended* (without and with referendum sub-model, respectively).
[a]Coefficients are significant at $p < .01$
[b]Coefficients are significant at $p < .05$
[c]Coefficients are significant at $p < .10$

tems exceed in accuracy multiparty and inchoate party systems: in percentage points, 3.18 and 3.36 versus 3.39 and 4.27, respectively.)

Institutionalization

The various arguments presented in the trimmed versions perform differently under each particular context. Highly institutionalized regimes, for example, prove to be an island of specific effects. First, candidates' appeals have a negligible influence. Second, the political referendum argument reverses the modal effect, which defies the "toughness rewarded" hypothesis (although it does not achieve statistical significance). Finally, there is a high incidence of economic performance on people's choice. All this suggests that societies whose political systems are highly developed permit both a higher degree of economic accountability and a lower tolerance for any authoritarian deviation undergone by their governments.

In addition, under highly institutionalized regimes, patterns of voting achieve greater stability, which reflects the larger impact of the affirmative model. Actually, a look at the beta weights confirms that prior vote is the leading force behind the outcomes, whereas the unstandardized coefficient points out a close to one-to-one ratio in the votes collected by the incumbent party over time. Furthermore, given the more intensive loading of partisan contents in the measurement of affirmative voting, the former is likely to show a high collinearity with the latter, thus depressing the effects of party strength.

Incumbents in less institutionalized systems are subject to a different combination of models of voting. Since by definition parties are poorly structured, the slightest difference in partisan stability within this group has a greater impact than among highly institutionalized systems. Consequently, party alignments can produce significant differences in the odds for political continuity. Still, this may entail some puzzlement: after all, why should partisan support play any role over time in a situation characterized by inchoate political organizations? A tentative answer is that, in contexts of poor institutionalization, party strength should be thought of less in terms of structural partisanship and more as a proxy of patron–client ties that are formally channeled through an enduring pattern of exchange of electoral support for private access to patronage and individual or group benefits. For examples of this pattern in Latin America, see Rosenberg (1989), and Conaghan (1994).

Still, among inchoate party regimes, no matter how much greater the comparable sensitivity to partisan forces might be, the core influence in voting is borne by candidates' attributes. Candidate-related clues account for the twelve points difference in the explanatory power of the general model when contrasted to the fit attained under politically developed orders (an adjusted R^2 of .92 for the former versus one of .80 for the latter).

Among elections held in poorly institutionalized systems, incumbents are held accountable for performance, but neither to the extent nor in the direction that their counterparts in highly institutionalized regimes are. If economic performance is a relevant decisional clue for voters, it is so even more strongly in politically developed contexts, as a comparison of beta weights reveals (−.24 in the group of low institutionalization versus −.40 in the group of high institutionalization). On the other hand, democratic performance achieves some statistically significant effect over vote, but in a way that assures electoral compensation for tough leadership. Lower levels of institutionalization help governments to diffuse blame for policy inefficacy while raising the stakes for the display of unambiguous signs of authoritative rulership. This explains in part why the effect of economic management may appear weaker and why incumbents may expect to lose votes, rather than to win them, if the only sign of progress they exhibit is limited to the democratic arena.

These conclusions above illustrate the substantial implications contained in institutionalization differences for the debate on the degree of effective accountability in new democracies. Generally speaking, performance may be a more indeterminate source of decision among politically underdeveloped systems. This situation makes incumbent's political survival contingent upon the presence of other sources, such as the character of the contending candidates or the displays of political leadership by the president. As expected, fewer opportunities for partisan socialization and a less clear attribution of responsibility for performance leave voters to rely upon highly personalistic references. Given the circumstances, these clues become the sole sources that can effectively provide order amidst the uncertainty of who is capable of assuring some basic degree of satisfaction. Quite likely, a vicious cycle may derive from this situation, since "where personalistic disputes reign supreme and party labels are insignificant, those who win elections feel less restrained in how they govern" (Mainwaring and Scully 1995: 25). Accountability thus achieves a different operational meaning when it depends on candidates' charisma and weighs not what the government has done for democracy but what it has done for law and order.

Party Systems

Let us now turn to the interplay between models of choice and the predominant types of party system. A common supposition holds that two-party systems facilitate the identification and attribution of responsibility for good and bad performance (Downs 1957), whereas multipartism helps diffuse this kind of linkage (Lewis-Beck 1988). However, Table 6.2 shows that there is hardly any evidence of differential economic voting effects across party systems. In either case, for the initial trimmed version of the models, the efficacy in fighting price fluctuations over time reveals a statistically dubious impact upon the distribution of political support. Some differences of degree are, nonetheless, worth noting. If we compare two elections held under a multiparty system, one preceded by a "moderate deflation" and another one by a "strong inflation increase," and keep everything else constant, we can expect an average loss of 9 percentage points in the second situation ($4^* -2.20 = -8.8$). The same comparison for bipartisan systems would yield a smaller loss of about 5 points ($4^* -1.29 = -5.16$). The resulting 3.6 percent difference does not always seem innocuous, if we recall that on many occasions this gap forced run-off elections (for example, in El Salvador in 1994) or signified the incumbent's defeat (for example, in Uruguay in 1994). Consequently, such disparity of effects reveals that economic sensitivity among electorates is not totally indifferent to the predominant type of party system.

The influence held by candidates' attributes transcends the specifications of party formats, in the sense that, when contrasted with other arguments, they still lead the explanatory race. On the other hand, the effect of contenders' appeal is greater in multiparty structures, first, because its estimate is larger, and second, because its size is much bigger compared to the next influential source of decision than it is among bipartisan regimes. Differences exist in the expected direction: two-party systems are slightly less driven by personalistic forces in comparison with multiparty settings. These differences are better understood when taking into account the estimates for the affirmative and party models. Wherever two-party systems dominate, aggregate party support naturally becomes the second largest effect shaping the incumbent's fortunes, foretelling nearly one additional percent in votes for every two points of continuous support over time ($2^* .44 = .88$). Less salient is the comparative role of this argument within multiparty contexts.

Another contrast is present in relation to governments' performance on issues of citizenship advancement: among two-party systems a non-significant estimate is the rule, whereas multiparty orders show an inclination to accept manifestations of authoritarianism. As speculated earlier, accumulated social tensions and governability-menacing conflicts resulting from anti-inflationary policies may push rulers to increase their reliance on heavy-handed tactics to assure social peace and public order. This kind of pattern may ultimately find a lukewarm reception for the poor quality of democratic accomplishments among voters. An exemplary case is the Bolivian election of 1989, where stabilization policies made of economic governability a precious good but also ignited social unrest and widespread crime. This led, in turn, to placing law-and-order considerations as top priorities of large majorities, thus helping to legitimize the subsequent coercive response of the government. To be sure, the high return of votes to Paz Estenssoro's party may speak loudly of the success in bringing inflation down, but also of the favorable image of "tough leadership" conveyed by the official team (see Conaghan 1992; Gamarra 1994).

Finally, the intensity of candidate voting reveals a clear-cut covariation with the nature of the party system. Clearly, multiparty systems are more likely to be subject to candidate effects than two-party regimes. Among the former, the ratio of the impact of candidate attributes to the next effect of importance (i.e., prior vote) measured in beta weights stands at 3.1 to 1. In bipartisan contexts, such a ratio stands at only 1.6 to 1 (with party strength as the next effect of importance). This pattern clearly reflects the particular overtones of multiparty systems in presidential regimes characterized by weak organizational capabilities and a heavy dependence upon a style of politics based on *caudillismo*.

No serious changes are recorded after improving the specification of the models. These results are illustrated by the respective columns labeled "extended" in Table 6.2. The inclusion of the political referendum model and the revised version of the candidate voting does not produce major fluctuations in the estimated coefficients, except for the enhancement of the impact of economic voting in all situations and the partial weakening in the relative effect of candidate voting within multiparty systems.

Economic performance gets stronger as more "economic-free" information, such as presidential popularity and candidates' attractiveness, is incorporated into the general model. Within poorly institutionalized systems, economics becomes second to candidate-related considerations as a source of electoral decision, doubling its original impact (from −2.06 to −4.09). Within highly institutionalized systems, there is also an improvement of the effect of economic outputs over voting, but it takes place in a more attenuated fashion (from −2.61 to −3.30). These nuances are ignored by the differences across party systems. In both two-party and multiparty contexts, the effect of government efficacy in fighting inflation more than duplicates in relative terms compared to its impact in the initial trimmed version. Furthermore, among multiparty systems the effect of economic voting unsettles the leading role of candidate voting (-.46 versus .38), whereas under two-party regimes it closely follows the influence of the personalistic appeals of the runners (−.58 versus .63).

The inclusion of political leadership considerations also affects the way in which democratic performance clues shape the vote. Among inchoate party systems, the drop of the estimate for political climate rate of change to statistical non-significance suggests that the effects originally attributed to the conduct of the government in the field of political rights and civil freedoms are somehow captured by the presidential popularity variable. Elections held under these circumstances predict an additional three percentage points in valid votes for the incumbents for every extra seven percentage points in the approval of the president (7* .44 = 3.08), holding everything else at mean values. Conversely, political leadership considerations are ineffectual among highly institutionalized contexts. Moreover, the resemblance of effects across all models of voting with the initial trimmed version is remarkable. Here, both longstanding group alignments captured by prior vote and economic performance views remain the critical decisional clues affecting people's choice.

In a like manner, political leadership weighs more heavily on electoral outcomes whenever many political parties, rather than few, structure the political scene. An increase in ten percentage points in the popularity of the president assures and additional 6.5 percent in valid votes in multiparty contexts, against only 2.2 percent in two-party structures. In the case of multiparty politics, the extra-economic aptitude of the incumbent force matches its economic qualifications, as shown by the standardized coefficients (−.46 for the change in the inflation rate relative to .45 in the approval of the president). This combined effect deflates the relevance of candidate clues. It also drives toward statistical non-significance the effects of other elements requiring a long-term temporal dimension to become effective (that is, prior vote, party strength and attainments in the political climate of the nation).

This combination of effects has not passed unnoticed; some Latin Americanists studying the less institutionalized systems in the region have keenly emphasized the linkages between strong political leadership and developments in the economic sphere. As Gamarra (1994: 7) suggests, "the [economic] "threshold of crisis" [in Latin America] was successfully transcended by leaders who exerted an uncommon capacity to govern. Their feats were accomplished not by altering the rules or changing institutions . . . , but by using their command over the institutional features of a given system, concentrating power at the executive level, and deploying enough strength to implement policy."

In two-party systems, in contrast, leadership considerations are far from challenging the economic and candidate arguments. Rather, these considerations stand as a second-rate factor, with a statistical effect proximate to that of party voting. This means that bipartisan orders are, first of all, domains of economic accountability and personal character; yet, if those two attributes become relevant they accomplish so not at the expense of making the effect of partisan factors insignificant.

In sum, as the data in Table 6.2 conclusively demonstrate, electoral choice is not indifferent to the type of institutional order that predominates in society. Under each specific regime, some models achieve greater salience than others. Furthermore, when improving the specification of the measurement model by including political leadership effects and decontaminating candidates' attributes from economic influences, different arguments prevail for the different statuses of political development and partisan organization. The question to be addressed now is whether different macro-economic circumstances reproduce such an heterogeneous pattern of influences.

ELECTORAL OUTCOMES UNDER CRISIS AND PROSPERITY: TESTING FOR VOTING ASYMMETRIES

A tacit assumption of aggregate models is that electorates behave similarly under situations of economic distress and prosperity, even though common sense would indicate otherwise. In reality, the empirical evidence for countries of the region yields ambiguous results (see Seligson and Gómez B. 1989; Pacek and Radcliff 1995).

A look at the interplay between macro-economic environments and both the initial and extended trimmed versions of the models points out the existence of serious asymmetries in the way people articulate their electoral choices and, in particular, the way they make use of economic clues. As Table 6.3 reveals, there is a systematic contrast between the highly significant effect of economic performance in contexts of crisis and the lack of statistical significance under conditions of growth. This dissimilarity indicates that Latin American publics hold a different sensitivity to economic matters depending on the circumstances. Whenever bad times precede the election, voters take serious note of the ability of the rulers to manage inflation and, if government fails, they tend to punish it mercilessly. A comparison of estimates reveals that the average loss in votes for increases in the inflation rate over time amounts to almost 5 percentage points in situations of crisis versus 2.5 percentage points in situations of economic expansion. This also means that if changes take place in a deflationary direction, incumbents will be rewarded with comparatively fewer votes when financial conditions improve. On the other hand, as good times arrive before an election, voters stop reacting with an eye on the economy, shifting their focus to other matters.

These findings support the notion that electorates behave ungratefully, responding unevenly to the government's economic performance. In other words, voters appear biased in the direction of ignoring the incumbent's anti-inflationary progress in good times, but they do not miss the chance of throwing the rascals out at the first sign of economic ineptitude during periods of recession. This behavior falls in line with McDonald and Ruhl's (1989: 14) contentions that "protest voting," that is, the tendency to sanction governments harder than to reward them, is a generalized practice in Latin America. It also matches Pacek and Radcliff's (1995: 753) findings on the existence of asymmetric reactions to the economy in Third World electorates.

As a rule, conditions of economic stagnation or recession in per capita terms make voters indifferent to democratic performance and partisan clues. Whatever the ascendancy these factors may have under normal circumstances, they are not likely to explain much of the electoral response whenever economic decline becomes the rule. Times of economic slump are, therefore, likely to motivate voters' apathy before accomplishments in the realm of democratic progress. Holding non-significant estimates under different model specifications means that electoral outcomes simply remain independent of

Table 6.3. Competing Explanatory Models of Electoral Outcomes under Different Macro-Economic Contexts in Latin America, 1982–1995*

	*Macro-Economic Contexts***							
	Crisis		*Prosperity*		*Crisis*		*Prosperity*	
	Initial				*Extended*			
Models of Choice	*b (SEb)*	β	*b (SEb)*	β	*b (SEb)*	β	*b (SEb)*	β
Affirmative Voting	.55[a] (.17)	.53	.31[c] (.17)	.30	.45[c] (.22)	.43	.28 (.18)	.26
Party Voting	.19 (.22)	.13	.40[b] (.19)	.30	.22 (.26)	.15	.37[c] (.20)	.27
Democratic Voting	.29 (.73)	.05	1.65[c] (.91)	.25	.46 (.89)	.08	1.37[c] (.98)	.21
Economic Voting	−2.51[a] (.66)	−.38	−.34 (1.46)	−.03	−4.79[a] (.89)	−.70	−2.52 (1.45)	−.22
Political referendum					.39[a] (.11)	.41	.39[a] (.13)	.39
Candidate Voting	.67[a] (.09)	.74	.64[a] (.12)	.62	.66 (.14)	.65	.57[a] (.15)	.44
Intercept	18.19[a] (5.67)		18.41[b] (6.90)		25.73[a] (7.51)		23.94[a] (7.83)	
Adjusted R^2	.85		.76		.83		.75	
Standard Error	5.11		7.07		5.90		7.33	
N =	19		22		15		21	

*Trimmed version of models presented in two formats: *initial* and *extended* (without and with referendum sub-model, respectively).

**Mean Incumbent Vote-Share under Crisis (28.8 %) and under Prosperity (42.1%); average Absolute Prediction Error: under Crisis (1.70%) and under Prosperity (5.24%)

[a]Coefficients are significant at $p < .01$

[b]Coefficients are significant at $p < .05$

[c]Coefficients are significant at $p < .10$

any fluctuation of this factor. On the other hand, under times of growth, democratic performance voting achieves significance in a direction that conforms to the popular wisdom that as long as the economy runs well, electorates may tolerate authoritarian drives.

Besides reacting strongly to the economic aptitudes of office holders, voters look for guidance in the personality of the candidates or in the longstanding political traditions captured by prior voting alignments. The data confirm theoretical suppositions about the political strategy of leaders in presidential elections. The evidence of candidate voting effects that are stronger under troubling financial conditions than when good times prevail contradicts the standard argument of "strategic politicians" as developed by Jacobson and Kernell (1981). Instead, it sustains the notion that a situation of economic downturn is capable of arousing people's expectations for a "savior of the country," thus leaving the door open to the rise of strong candidates.

It is interesting to note that the inclusion of presidential popularity considerations does not reveal a divergent impact across situations. This effect indicates that no matter what the financial circumstances, political leadership is always a valuable resource to which voters resort. Concurrently, after one takes the model of political referendum into account, substantive modifications occur in regards to other decisional clues. For example, in times of crisis, economic performance ends up surpassing candidate voting. In addition, affirmative model type of reactions become less important which witness to the force of political circumstances to erode past alignments whenever hardships persist. By the same token, when prosperity is the rule, the acknowledgment of political leadership weakens the effect of long-term forces such as prior vote and partisan alignments. It also raises the relative impact of economic matters, but not to the point of making these factors statistically significant. Last but not least, as one takes into account political leadership considerations during good times, one can expect a substantial reduction in the relative influence of candidate voting. Even though incumbents' fortunes still respond primarily to character attributes of the contenders (a beta weight of .44), those fortunes are very likely to depend on the popularity of the president as well (a beta weight of .39).

In summary, the data confirm that voters are affected by contextual conditions in developing their electoral choices. Differences in the environment imply different opportunities and information availability to the public. For example, economic performance becomes more salient under situations where attributing economic responsibility to government is easier or whenever financial grievances make of the economy a critical point of reference. On the other hand, as the institutional framework allows the incumbents to diffuse responsibility, or as prosperity alleviates pressures for material security and stability, economic arguments weaken substantially.

The same diversity of interactions between contexts and models of choice occurs when political leadership considerations are observed. When partisan pluralism and weak political development prevail, voters are quite likely to approach contests as a referendum on the quality of the political situation the country achieved under the current administration. Under such situations, leadership clues simplify the complexity of politics to voters in a very efficient manner. Similarly, as financial conditions improve, presidential popularity may also become a more relevant decisional clue, as a result of the secondary role economic considerations play. A comparable dynamic extends to those forces involving long-term effects, such as party strength and prior alignments. These factors covary more intensely with political support as environmental conditions permit, first, some degree of variability in the values of these measures and, second, an opportunity for a process of political socialization by social groups and parties to become effective and autonomous from economic emergencies.

Analysis of the institutional and macro-economic contexts within which presidential contests take place allows us to fine-tune our understanding of the different voting arguments and the ways in which they relate to electoral choice in the region. But to form a complete picture of voting behavior, we need to explore how specific arguments of voting mobilize not only national electorates but also individual voters under heterogeneous contexts.

NOTES

1. Occasionally, changes at any of these three contextual spheres in one country during this period of 1982-1995 resulted in one same electorate subject to markedly different environmental influences from one election to another one.

2. The sources are Dix (1992) and Mainwaring and Scully (1995: Chapter 1). Levels of institutionalization result from a composite index accounting for the stability of interparty competition, the social rootedness of partisan forces, the salience of party organizations in structuring the electoral process, and the continuity in party policy identity.

3. Scores for political institutionalization follow Mainwaring and Scully's (1995) classification. For the first construct, a value of 1.00 means high institutionalization or political development, a value of .5 represents an intermediate level, and a value of 0 signifies a poorly institutionalized or inchoate party system.

4. The number of effective parties is computed according to the Laakso-Taagepera index for an adjusted-by-valid votes averaged measure of electoral support at the congressional level over time (e.g., lower house). It is derived by squaring each party's (or coalition) share of seats, adding all of these squares, and dividing 1.00 by this number: $N_s = 1/\Sigma \rho_i^2$, where N_s is the effective number of parties expressed in seats

and ρ_i is the fractional share of seats of the *i*-th party. An index of 2.57, like in the case of Argentina in 1989, for example, means that the number of effective parties exceeds two but remains below three.

5. Of course, this implies pooling cases with different degrees of crisis and prosperity. However, since the cut-off point (3 percent) remains highly proximate to the average population growth rate (2.2 percent) and leaves out an equivalent number of cases in each group, it makes sense to set the division in this way. The average GDP growth rate for the first group stands at −.70 (n = 19) and for the second group the mean stands at 4.81 (n = 22).

6. Reasons explaining this may vary for each feature, however. Among weakly institutionalized systems, the intrinsic character of non-consolidated democracy makes it reasonable to find more electoral volatility. On the other hand, the reason leading to vote instability among multiparty regimes may be found in the inherent need to build different electoral and ruling coalitions for every new electoral occasion.

Chapter Seven

Individual-Level Analysis of Voting Behavior in Three Latin American Countries

Electoral outcomes are aggregate products of what collective entities decide. From an aggregate-level perspective, a focus on electoral choice illustrates the patterns structuring the way electoral masses respond. But aggregate analysis can hardly be satisfying to one who wants to explore the mystery of political behavior, since it only conveys oblique information about how individual voters undergo a process of reasoning and decision-making before making a political choice explicit.

This chapter complements the previous discussion of aggregate voting patterns with an analysis of three instances of electoral behavior at the individual level, based on electoral survey data collected in Argentina, Perú and Uruguay. Individual-level data supply the evidence about the specific processes voters work through before deciding whom to support. More obviously, this approach provides clues about how people actually perceive objective reality and how their perceptions become politically consequential.

An analysis centered on individual level data offers important benefits in dealing with models of choice, particularly when considering the impact of economics, given the multiplicity of calculations that might orient the individual's decision. How sensitive are individuals to economic matters relative to non-economic affairs in deciding whom to support? Do citizens more closely resemble the figure of the pocketbook voter, relying solely on personal experiences, or do they ponder the national situation more heavily? Are economic expectations the basis of the elector's decision, as Downs conjectured, or do individuals conform more to a type of voter described by Key, choosing based upon "past events, past performance, and past actions" (1966: 61)? Individual-level analysis allows us to answer such questions.

METHODOLOGY

At the individual level, the dependent variable is measured by the voting intention (or reported vote) verbalized by survey respondents. In order to evaluate the individual-level determinants of the vote choice, particularly the connection between economic perceptions and support for the incumbent, relative to other influential forces, the analysis is based upon electoral survey data collected in Argentina, Perú and Uruguay. Although three different national elections can hardly take account of the variety of nuances underlying the process of vote choice during the span of time for all contests and countries covered in the aggregate analysis, these cases can at least illustrate some of the main behaviors exhibited by Latin Americans in making up their minds at the polls.

These three countries are thus relevant because of their dissimilarities in both economic backgrounds and profiles of political institutionalization in the post-authoritarian period following the ten years after each country returned to democracy (see Smith et al. 1994; Mainwaring and Scully 1995). Furthermore, such picture of variations crystallize at a moment of simultaneous presidential elections across the three nations, which replicates a controlled experience while makes it safe to assume that the major controversies striking the region's electoral experiences are reasonably contained (see Appendix B).

In all cases, samples were drawn from the voting-age population (that is, 18 years old or older) of the major urban centers—Capital and Greater Buenos Aires, Lima and Greater Lima, and the city of Montevideo—following a random selection of sampling areas, blocks and households, with quota adjustments for sex and age at the respondent level. (It is worth noting that Federal Capital and Greater Buenos Aires areas comprise about thirty-eight percent of the national electorate of Argentina. Similarly, Lima and Greater Lima comprise slightly over thirty-five percent. The city of Montevideo hosts almost fifty percent of the Uruguayan national electorate.) The number of cases (weighted number of cases in parenthesis) for Argentina was 245 (265); for Perú, 519 (537); and for Uruguay, 191 (187). In Perú and Uruguay, fieldwork was conducted prior to election day, twenty days before the April 1995 contests in Lima and five weeks before the November 1994 elections in Montevideo. In Argentina, fieldwork was conducted within two weeks after the presidential elections of May 1995 were held.[1] In each country, a local polling institute implemented the study, including a specific battery of questions upon personal request of the author.[2]

Individual sources of information originating in different countries but obtained with similar research instruments and designs for a relatively homogeneous time-period allow for invaluable comparisons at the individual level, since the same analytical technique can be used to assess the relative impact of each major voting model. In such analysis, it is also possible to test multiple arguments of explaining voting by means of multivariate statistical models, thus assuring that whatever cross-national variations are found are not a result of methodological artifacts but of substantive differences.

Since the criterion for how individuals process their electoral decisions rests on the assumption that they approach the ballots as a binary choice between supporting or opposing the incumbent, the dependent variable takes the form of a dichotomous variable. The premise of linearity, therefore, must be discarded and logistic regression techniques should be employed. Considering these assumptions and the multivariate approach here pursued, Pearson's product–moment correlation and binomial logistic regression techniques are used here.

In discussing the multivariate data, two pieces of information are used: the partial correlation coefficient (named "Correl" in the tables in this chapter), which summarizes the pure effect of each variable upon the vote holding constant the impact of all other variables; and the estimated chances of supporting the incumbent party (versus dumping it) for every one category change in the explanatory variable (named "Chance" in the tables). The statistical significance of all coefficients is indicated in superscripts in all the tables. Furthermore, two other measures are presented to assess the fit of the data to the model: the percentage of votes gathered by the incumbent party and by all forces in competition that were correctly predicted by the model; and the chi-square–based goodness-of-fit measure, with its respective probability value, which informs the extent to which the model significatively departures from a perfect fit.

In formal terms, the individual-level model takes the following theoretical enunciation:

$$\pi(\text{VS} = 1) = \frac{e^{(Z)}}{1 + e^{(Z)}}$$

$$\begin{aligned}
\text{where Z} = \propto &+ \beta_1(\text{Personal Retrospective}) + \beta_2(\text{Personal Prospective}) + \\
&+ \beta_3(\text{National Retrospective}) + \beta_4(\text{National Prospective}) + \\
&+ \beta_5(\text{Personal Retrospective * Responsibility Attribution}) + \\
&+ \beta_6(\text{Personal Prospective * Responsibility Attribution}) + \\
&+ \beta_7(\text{National Retrospective * Responsibility Attribution}) + \\
&+ \beta_8(\text{National Prospective * Responsibility Attribution}) + \\
&+ \beta_9(\text{Presidential Approval}) + \beta_{10}(\text{Partisanship}) + \beta_{11} \\
&(\text{Social Class}) + \epsilon
\end{aligned}$$

and where $\pi(\text{VS} = 1)$ refers to the probability of voting in favor of the incumbent party rather than against it, and $e^{(Z)}$ represents the exponential function of the linear combination of independent variables disaggregated in the previous equation. When exponentiated, each coefficient β represents the factor by which the odds of supporting the incumbent party rather than the opposition should be multiplied and thus estimated.

A discussion of the underpinnings of responsibility attribution can offer a window for exploring the actual mental process connecting economic perceptions and electoral choices at the individual level. Below, I discuss responsibility attribution in the hope of illuminating the issue of how much asymmetry is present in reacting to economic conditions.

In this context, I will first address the issue of fairness in the politicization of economic matters by appraising the degree of blame or credit ascribed to office-holders, given the particular way of judging the economy. In theory, negative coefficients among those evaluating conditions as "worse" imply that as financial states are perceived with more pessimism, the government will be exempted from responsibility. Negative coefficients among those having a positive impression ("better") mean that financial betterment will not be credited to the government either. On the other hand, positive coefficients for those seeing things as "worse" mean that as states go downhill, blame rises, whereas for those appraising circumstances as "better," they mean that these people are more inclined to credit the government for the improvement.

Furthermore, whenever the coefficient for those holding pessimistic views is greater than the one among the optimists, it implies that governments are more harshly blamed under dire straits circumstances than credited under prosperity. Conversely, if coefficients are larger among those perceiving things as getting "better," it means that governments will enjoy proportionally more praise for good performance than reproach for mismanagement. If coefficients remain about the same magnitude, voters are willing to condemn the authorities in the face of economic distress as intensively as to trust them for improvements.

A second issue assessed is the extent to which conditions perceived as "good" or "bad" elicit cogent responses such as approving or sanctioning the incumbent regardless of government liabilities. Theoretically, negative coefficients among those evaluating conditions as "worse" indicate that as financial states are perceived with more pessimism, incumbents will be increasingly contested. Conversely, among those appraising circumstances optimistically, positive coefficients anticipate more votes for the government.

Let it be said, as well, that whenever coefficients among pessimists exceed in magnitude those recorded among optimists, incumbents will suffer more for poor results or prospects than they can expect to enjoy for economic betterments. On the contrary, if coefficients are larger among those perceiving things as improving, the party-in-office can count on more votes from the group of electors content with the economic situation than what it may expect to lose from those dissatisfied with it.

The last issue discussed is the extent to which economic satisfaction (or dissatisfaction) gets translated into electoral rewards (or sanctions) for different levels of government responsibility. Negative coefficients among those judging the situation as "worse" can be expected to indicate that pessimism forewarns incumbent losses. On the other hand, positive coefficients among those holding an optimistic view of the economy entail a greater predisposition to make explicit the electoral gratitude to the government.

Finally, coefficients among pessimists that exceed in magnitude those recorded among optimists point to a negative asymmetry, that is, a greater loss of votes among those perceiving reality negatively than gains among those with a positive view of the economy. On the other hand, if coefficients are larger among those perceiving things as improving, it means that positive asymmetry prevails, that is, the ruling party will be rewarded for good results to a greater proportion than it will be punished for bad results. Lastly, as in all previous cases, a case of similar magnitude coefficients should be interpreted as one of symmetry between conditions, liability and electoral choices. If coefficients remain non-significant, other arguments than economic voting must be pursued.

ASSESSING INDIVIDUAL ECONOMIC VOTING

A cursory survey of the scholarly debate on the determinants of voting in Argentina, Perú and Uruguay reveals how central economic voting arguments have become. In reviewing the contests held in Perú throughout the 1980s, Dietz concludes that "voting their pocketbooks has been clearly at work" (1987: 157–158). For Catterberg and Braun, the 1989 election results in Argentina are also best illustrated by the economic voting argument: "the electorate evaluated the Radicals performance on a strictly economic basis . . . two months before the elections, the people demanded a change in the economic policy of the government, while at the same time they regarded their vote as a way of achieving such a change." (1989: 366–367).

Rial, on the other hand, discussing Uruguayan elections during the 1980s, argues that the clientelist version of economic voting, that is, the exchange of electoral support for private benefits, "has suffered a serious reversal" (1986: 261–262). Echoing Rial's conclusions for the 1989 presidential contest, Canzani contends that [if] the evolution of the economy seemed to be a key element in the political scene [of other countries], this element seemed absent in Uruguay, where five years ago a party in government that had improved some aspects of the economic situation was defeated at the ballots. This event could be interpreted as a defense of the relative autonomy of politics in relation to economics (1995: 8).

These evaluations uncover the multidimensional character of the economic voting argument. Do voters who structure their choices upon their views of the economy weigh their personal situations more heavily than the nation's, as Dietz implies, or is it more the opposite case, as one may infer from Rial's argument? Moreover, are voters resting their decision only upon retrospective views, as the first part of Catterberg and Braun's statement suggests, or should one also consider voters' expectations, as these authors later propose?

Heterogeneity is intrinsic to notions of economic voting and encompasses part of the reasoning that motivates voters to rely on economic clues. At certain times, voters may react to their pocketbook situations, while at others, they may respond to the economic situation of the country. Occasionally, voters may look backward in deciding whom to vote for; other times, they may be inclined to ponder who will do better in the future and forget about the past, which is impossible to remedy. Acknowledging this diversity of frames of reference is also a first step toward recognizing the flexibility of the economic voting argument.

Still, one needs to validate the electoral consequences of such heterogeneity of views through verifying the extent to which economic impressions are actually politicized. To what extent is the party-in-government judged responsible for the progresses or relapses in the different economic spheres? Answering this question becomes essential, since only a clear attribution of responsibility can make economic orientations a logical parameter upon which to base the decision to endorse or not to endorse the incumbents at the voting booths. The bottom line is that in any circumstance, voters are assumed to follow a decision rule which consists of attributing—or not—economic responsibility to the government before imbuing their choice with their impressions of financial reality.

Beyond these considerations, electoral preferences in Argentina, Perú and Uruguay have also been understood in light of extra-economic forces. In Uruguay, the relevance of partisanship and the president's personal prestige are decisive (González 1992). Among Peruvians, leadership considerations have a strong response, as revealed by citizen approval of Fujimori's counter-insurgency policy, presidential acts to discipline the political establishment, and the "rally around the flag" effect provoked by the short-timed war against Ecuador in 1994-95 (Carrión 1998). Finally, in Argentina, candidate and leadership effects are of key importance. Mainwaring, reviewing the 1989 Argentine presidential elections, underlines their saliency in concluding that "Radicals were so discredited [for their economic failures] that it was only because of the ability of their candidate, [Eduardo] Angeloz, to run a good campaign that he was able to pull in thirty-seven percent versus Menem's forty-seven percent of the votes" (1995: 157).

INDIVIDUAL-LEVEL VERSIONS OF ECONOMIC VOTING

Individual voters of specific nations replicate the trends seen for the region at two levels: they follow similar decision rules with similar intensity, thus confirming aggregate findings, while they also made their choices reflect the idiosyncratic stimuli unfold by national conditions in different ways, revealing how important their context is in shaping their calculus of voting.

A summary of the variety of economic voting arguments in effect in the three countries under examination, during the mid 1990s is presented in Table 7.1. A picture of comparative heterogeneity in the way economic considerations are related to individuals' vote choice emerges. In the case of Perú, for example, all partial correlation coefficients are highly significant with a similar impact of sociotropic and pocketbook orientations over the vote, no matter the time-frame of reference. No single calculation captures their vote in its entirety. Rather, Peruvians[3] proceed to link their economic optimism with a pro-incumbent choice. This behavior suggests that each impression developed about the economy is authentic, that is, that perceptions of national conditions are not simple rationalizations of personal fortunes; nor are expectations about the economy mere projections of what has already happened. On average, for each voter who sees financial conditions more optimistically (say, switching from the "about the same" category to the "better" one), the odds of issuing a pro-incumbent vote, rather than anti-incumbent one, double.

The picture of the Argentinean voters differs in that they heavily weight their expectations for the future state of the economy in deciding whom to support. Here, a pro-incumbent vote represents a bet in favor of the political alternative more able to ensure, according to the perceptions of the electorate, a more prosperous economic order. Thus, among those expecting an improvement in the national economy, the chances that they will reelect the president are four and a half times higher than their likelihood of backing the opposition.

The Uruguayan case shows a radically different landscape. Only those concerned with the oscillations of their own pocketbooks connect their views of the economy to their electoral preferences. Other economic impressions are unable to mobilize political support. The overall weakness of the economic voting approach here is eloquently summarized by the proportion of pro-incumbent votes correctly predicted by the model: only five out of every 100 votes harvested by the Blanco party.

Table 7.1. Individual-Level Versions of the Economic Voting Model in Perú, Argentina and Uruguay

Model Versions	*Perú*		*Argentina*		*Uruguay*	
Simple Version	*Correl*	*Chance*	*Correl*	*Chance*	*Correl*	*Chance*
Retrospective Personal	.14[a]	1.92	.03	1.63	.10[b]	1.82
Retrospective National	.17[a]	2.18	.11[b]	1.96	.00	1.36
Prospective Personal	.08[b]	1.67	.13[a]	2.76	.00	1.15
Prospective National	.15[a]	2.47	.23[a]	4.51	.00	.72
% Incumbent Votes Correctly Predicted		92.6		85.4		5.0
% Total Votes Correctly Predicted		79.7		84.9		77.8
Goodness of Fit	495.93	p = .58	275.48	p = .09	175.03	p = .03
Complex Version	*Correl*	*Chance*	*Correl*	*Chance*	*Correl*	*Chance*
Retrospective Personal	.08[b]	1.57	.03	1.67	.00	1.29
Retrospective National	.15[a]	2.01	.09[b]	2.18	.00	1.44
Prospective Personal	.08[b]	1.69	.06	2.01	.00	1.19
Prospective National	.15[a]	2.65	.19[a]	3.45	.00	.82
Responsibility* Retrospective Personal	.04	1.27	.00	1.14	.10[b]	1.73
Responsibility * Retrospective National	.00	1.05	.00	.94	.00	1.04
Responsibility * Prospective Personal	.00	.97	.03	1.32	.00	.96
Responsibility * Prospective National	.00	.93	.00	1.25	.00	.76
% Incumbent Votes Correctly Predicted		89.6		84.6		15.0
% Total Votes Correctly Predicted		78.3		86.4		78.9
Goodness of Fit	485.22	p = .66	259.31	p = .21	175.23	p = .23

[a]Coefficients are significant at $p < .01$.
[b]Coefficients are significant at $p < .05$.

The model of economic voting shows a much better fit among Argentineans and Peruvians, predicting correctly 85.5 percent and 92.6 percent of the votes going to the party-in-office, respectively. Such a divergence confirms that there is an inverse correlation between levels of political institutionalization and economic stability, and the intensity of economic voting.

A standard reaction to these findings is to blame not voters but the analyst for not taking account of the degree to which governments are held liable for such economic oscillations. Re-specifying the model by including the extent to which voters held incumbents accountable for the economic conditions is the logical step. By and large, no major changes occur once this is accomplished. Neither in Argentina nor in Perú does making attribution linkages explicit reach statistical significance, which suggests that, here, circumstances act in such a way as to smooth the automatic blaming of the government for economic conditions.[4]

Surprisingly, making the economic voting model more complex, and better specified, weakens rather than strengthens responsibility attribution. Uruguayans are a slight exception. Among them, it becomes salient that pocketbook voting is, in actuality, dependent upon holding the government responsible for the oscillations of private finances. Once this linkage is fashioned, the direct impact of personal economic conditions on vote choice vanishes. Here, the progress involved in specifing better the terms of the model becomes evident in the rise of pro-incumbent votes correctly predicted as going from five to fifteen percent.

This complex relation between the ways in which individuals assess the different facets of the economy, the degree of responsibility they attribute to the ruling party for economic successes and failures, and, consequently, their disposition to support or remove incumbency at the ballot box as an act of political accountability and reasoning point to the importance of mental processes governing an individual's decision-making before choosing an electoral option.

LINKING ECONOMIC GRIEVANCES TO POLITICAL DECISIONS

When attempting to discern the decision rules followed by individuals in relation to the economy, three key questions should be answered. First, to what extent do voters hold governments equally responsible for their own positive and negative impressions about the economy? Second, do voters tend to turn against incumbents when the economy is bad more readily than they become supportive in good times? Third, to what extent does the acknowledgment of government's responsibility for the economy make a "punishment" vote during bad times more likely than a "reward" vote in good ones?

Table 7.2 (a) provides clues to the first question, that is, whether or not voters tend to blame their governments for grievances in the same proportion that credit them for prosperity. Overall, diversity reigns among the national publics. Peruvians, for example, tend to look at government benevolently, or at least exonerate it for economic downturns, as the lack of statistical significance of their

Table 7.2(a). Individual-Level Linkages between Economic Perceptions and Government Responsibility

	Retrospective Evaluations				*Prospective Evaluations*			
	Personal		*National*		*Personal*		*National*	
	Better	*Worse*	*Better*	*Worse*	*Better*	*Worse*	*Better*	*Worse*
Countries								
Perú	.26[a]	−.20[a]	.28[a]	−.22[a]	.37[a]	−.03	.51[a]	.00
Argentina	−.06	.31[a]	.10[c]	.18[a]	.19[a]	.23[a]	.22[a]	.14[a]
Uruguay	−.17[a]	.08	.07	.25[a]	.03	.20[a]	.21[a]	.26[a]

[a]Coefficients are significant at $p < .01$.
[b]Coefficients are significant at $p < .05$.
[c]Coefficients are significant at $p < .10$.

coefficients suggests. At the same time, signals of economic progress, whether backward or forward-looking, personal or collective in scope, are automatically credited to the incumbent's performance. In contrast, Uruguayans follow a more pessimistic pattern of behavior: while they tend to personalize the motives behind financial success at the private level, they are prone to condemn the government for the failures perceived at the national level. Thus, the ruling party can expect to get only a partial vindication from those holding positive expectations for the collective situation in the near future.

Argentineans occupy a middle-road position: they blame incumbents for poor results, but give them the credit for situations perceived as positive. Only when it comes to fluctuations at the level of individual finances do asymmetries appear, with slumps charged to the party-in-office but upswings ascribed to personal efforts or fortuitous events.

These data offer a general overview of the diversity of cognitive processes related to economic circumstances, but how electorally consequential are these processes? One way to approach this query is by examining the bivariate correlations between economic perceptions and voting intentions, as it is shown in Table 7.2 (b). The main issue to address here is whether or not voters tend to punish their governments for grievances in the same proportion that reward them for prosperity.

In some ways, this analysis refreshes the information conveyed in Table 7.1, but with a clearer stipulation of the direction of the effects. Once again, the Uruguayan sample departs from expectations, since most coefficients achieve no significance. This result may imply that asymmetries found in matters of responsibility attribution do not automatically transpose into electoral ingratitude, the reason being that the economy simply does not play a major role.

Among Argentineans and Peruvians, the economy–vote correlation follows a more intuitive and consistent pattern: both past and expected progress are

Table 7.2(b). Individual-Level Linkages between Economic Perceptions and Support for the Incumbent

	Retrospective Evaluations				*Prospective Evaluations*			
	Personal		*National*		*Personal*		*National*	
	Better	*Worse*	*Better*	*Worse*	*Better*	*Worse*	*Better*	*Worse*
Countries								
Perú	.32[a]	−.39[a]	.44[a]	−.37[a]	.34[a]	−.31[a]	.42[a]	−.26[a]
Argentina	.20[a]	−.43[a]	.39[a]	−.45[a]	.58[a]	−.42[a]	.62[a]	−.52[a]
Uruguay	.25[a]	−.09	.15[b]	−.10[c]	−.06	.02[a]	.04	.00

[a]Coefficients are significant at $p < .01$.
[b]Coefficients are significant at $p < .05$.
[c]Coefficients are significant at $p < .10$.

accompanied by a vote of confidence in the government, whereas setbacks are punished with a pro-opposition vote. Notably, among Argentineans, the intensity with which government is sanctioned at the polls for economic relapses surpasses whatever electoral bonus it may get for financial improvements, but this applies only to the retrospective dimension. Once future-oriented considerations are observed, the incumbents overcome previous imbalances by acquiring more votes for optimistic expectations than what they lose for signals of economic pessimism.

Is there a significant difference in the degree to which ruling parties are granted or denied votes when they are held liable for the state of the economy? Table 7.2 (c) addresses that question by integrating the previous pieces of information. By splitting the samples into two groups according to the intensity to which government is held economically responsible, previously found relationships can be further tested for robustness.

Among those attributing virtually no responsibility to the authorities, the rationale is straightforward: if oscillations in the economy are not seen as a byproduct of governmental policies, it makes no sense to employ this criterion to reward or punish the party-in-office. This is what the picture of coefficients below conventional levels of statistical significance suggests. Conversely, among those holding incumbents liable for economic records, the voting connection is undeniable. Among Uruguayans, the strength of the association between betterment in the private finances and inclinations to reelect the ruling force triples, while also disclosing a relationship between sociotropic optimism and pro-incumbent vote. Among Peruvians, this specification considerably attenuates a "punishment" vote, as illustrated by the reduction in the negative coefficient between "worsening" evaluations and voting intention. Finally, a rather balanced judgment can be found among Argentineans, although one can say that the importance of prospective visions outweighs retrospective views. As these data reveal, voters put a premium on

Table 7.2(c). Individual-Level Linkages between Economic Perceptions and Support for the Incumbent across Levels of Government Responsibility

	Low Economic Responsibility of Government							
	Retrospective Evaluations				*Prospective Evaluations*			
	Personal		*National*		*Personal*		*National*	
	Better	*Worse*	*Better*	*Worse*	*Better*	*Worse*	*Better*	*Worse*
Countries								
Perú	−.05	−.27[a]	.02	−.23	.04	−.20[a]	.06	−.12[a]
Argentina	.08	.09[c]	.10[c]	−.02	.03	−.08[c]	−.08	−.10[c]
Uruguay	−.01	−.04	.01	−.08	.04	−.01	.12[b]	.03
	High Economic Responsibility of Government							
	Retrospective Evaluations				*Prospective Evaluations*			
	Personal		*National*		*Personal*		*National*	
	Better	*Worse*	*Better*	*Worse*	*Better*	*Worse*	*Better*	*Worse*
Countries								
Perú	.35[a]	−.25[a]	.42[a]	−.26[a]	.32[a]	−.23[a]	.40[a]	−.22[a]
Argentina	.18[a]	−.47[a]	.38[a]	−.44[a]	.58[a]	−.41[a]	.65[a]	−.50[a]
Uruguay	.32[a]	−.07	.16[b]	−.06	−.00	−.06	−.01	−.01

[a]Coefficients are significant at $p < .01$.
[b]Coefficients are significant at $p < .05$.
[c]Coefficients are significant at $p < .10$.

economic predictability. In this sense, future-oriented optimism is a more powerful predictor of a pro-incumbent vote than pessimism about past conditions is of a pro-opposition choice.

Generally speaking, voters tend to think first whether the government is responsible or not for the different facets of the economy before deciding for whom to vote. If they believe that the official intervention in the economy has been negligible, they resort to other considerations, extra-economic in nature, that also shape the vote. If, on the other hand, voters perceive that the government has played a pivotal role in the state of the economy, they remain open to accommodating their choice to the punishment–reward rationale.

The only partial exception to this rule is found among the Lima residents whose marked pro-incumbency bias somewhat contradicts the previous statements. Here, correlations between economic evaluations and electoral preferences systematically exhibit a pro-incumbency asymmetry, furnishing the party-in-office many more votes for positive impressions than otherwise for negative opinions. Among these electors, the prevailing reasoning is one of inertial benevolence: if conditions have improved, reelecting the president follows naturally; if conditions have worsened, there is still hope that by re-electing the government voters will find economic satisfaction.[5]

SPECIFYING NON-ECONOMIC EFFECTS

If substantial sectors of the public in Argentina, Perú and Uruguay ponder their electoral calculations with economic considerations in mind and handle their voting decision through some of the rules of reasoning described above, economic voting is still not necessarily the only explanatory model to account for how individuals make up their minds at the ballot box. Some electoral effects accounted for by economic factors might in fact spring from other variables indirectly acting upon those evaluations. In order to control for eventual spuriousness and achieve a more complete view of the forces shaping individual voting behavior, it is necessary to introduce other explanatory variables. In Table 7.3, economic voting arguments are measured against the impact of other, non-economic theories.

Table 7.3. Individual-Level Models of Electoral Choice in Perú, Argentina and Uruguay

	Perú		*Argentina*		*Uruguay*	
Revised Full Model	*Correl*	*Chance*	*Correl*	*Chance*	*Correl*	*Chance*
Retrospective Personal	.08[b]	1.74	.13[a]	2.59	.00	1.17
Retrospective National	.15[a]	2.53	.00	1.42	.00	1.15
Prospective Personal	.09[ab]	1.89	.07[c]	2.34	.00	1.13
Prospective National	.15[a]	2.89	.24[a]	6.26	.00	.77
Responsibility * Retrospective Personal	.00	1.31	.00	1.01	.06	1.79
Responsibility * Retrospective National	.00	1.16	.00	1.06	.00	1.45
Responsibility * Prospective Personal	.00	1.14	.00	1.22	.00	1.06
Responsibility * Prospective National	.00	.89	.00	1.08	.00	.74
Partisan Leanings	.16[a]	2.74	.19[a]	4.93	.17[a]	3.68
Lower Class	.05[c]	.45	−.07[c]	.16	.00	.39
Middle-Lower Class	.00	.71	−.16[a]	.07	.00	.34
Middle Class	.00	.77	−.15[a]	.06	.00	.28
Presidential Popularity	.54[a]	6.41	.32[a]	4.29	.38[a]	4.46
% Incumbent Votes Correctly Predicted	94.1		90.6		57.5	
% Total Votes Correctly Predicted	89.2		89.2		85.9	
Goodness of Fit	467.17	p = .81	203.74	p = .94	191.33	p = .03

[a]Coefficients are significant at $p < .01$
[b]Coefficients are significant at $p < .05$
[c]Coefficients are significant at $p < .10$

After comparing the proportion of cases correctly predicted in each country, it becomes evident that specification improvements translate into better predictions. The Uruguayan case offers by far the best illustration of this phenomenon: from predicting correctly 15 percent of cases supporting the incumbent under an economic voting model, the forecast jumps to an accuracy of 57.5 percent of cases when other extra-economic information is incorporated into the picture of voting behavior. Such improvement is also verified, although in much more moderate terms, among Argentineans and Peruvians. Once non-economic effects are included, an examination of the goodness of fit measure places the cases of Argentina and Perú close to a model of perfect prediction. In the case of Uruguay, however, the counter-intuitive increase in the value and statistical significance of the chi-square measure suggest that the more complete model should undergo further revision. In fact, a more careful inspection of the data reveals that once the social class and government responsibility variables are removed from the model (since they introduce "noise"), the overall gains in fit are preserved.

After controlling for the individual's socio-economic origins, his or her partisan inclinations, and his or her overall estimation of the non-economic leadership exhibited by the president, the effects of economic considerations on electoral preferences present some variations. In Uruguay, for instance, this strategy makes the already weak economic effects vanish. In Argentina, adding these controls helps to better qualify the economic influences on voting: retrospective pocketbook orientations surface, whereas the impact of expectations for personal finances evaporates. In striking contrast, the Peruvian case illustrates a situation in which the electoral leverage of economic perceptions manifests itself as authentically robust; with other effects also taken into consideration, the degree to which the economy shapes voting intentions remains essentially unchanged.

The data from all three countries show how important partisan inclinations and extra-economic leadership are in the minds of voters. Moreover, variations in the intensity of these effects match expectations related to the different levels of political institutionalization. In Perú, for each voter who leans towards Cambio 95 (instead of leaning towards the opposition or remaining politically independent), there is an average expectation that he or she will be almost three times more likely to vote for the incumbent ticket than to vote for the opposition. In Uruguay and Argentina, the corresponding chances of sympathizing with Blancos and Peronists and voting accordingly (rather than for other parties) are about four to one and five to one, respectively.

Similarly, the effect of presidential popularity on voting is much higher under contexts of low institutionalization, like the Peruvian one, which are naturally more exposed to personalistic politics. Here, among individuals holding a favorable view of the president's non-economic leadership, their likelihood to judge the incumbent candidate in positive terms raises by a factor of almost 6.5. Notably, in addition to the remarkable effect of economic optimism on voting, Fujimori's triumph at the polls seemed even more strongly inspired by a political referendum model. In comparison, the other two countries show a more moderate disposition to support the party-in-office based upon a presidential approval criterion. Yet this does not belittle its influence. Both Argentineans and Uruguayans rely on their views of non-economic performance to a much greater extent than on economic considerations when deciding for whom to vote.

Curiously, for all the changes that occurred in the social structure of Argentina in the last two decades, this country is the only one to offer some tinges of class-based voting in relation to the incumbent party: compared to upper class individuals, those belonging to middle and lower-middle classes are more reluctant to endorse Peronism.[6] Moreover, the lack of statistical significance at conventional levels in the way lower class voters behave compared to the way their upper class counterparts behave confirms the policlassistic nature of president Menem's social coalition, based on the two extremes of the social pyramid.

Social class also affects voting behavior in other ways among Argentineans. If economic explanations reveal two different profiles at play, one oriented towards how the voter's own pocketbook has fared in the past and the other one towards how the nation's economic health may look in the future, the inspection of the demographic background of each type of economic voter reveals that these two profiles are also socially different.

The first profile, characterized as the model of "peasant" voting in the literature (MacKuen et al. 1992), actually encloses the predominant way through which lower class sectors make use of economic information when deciding how to vote. This representation, in turn, is consistent with collected evidence on the higher sensitivity of the members of this group to relative changes in their incomes, which shows that every minor improvement is capable of making a major marginal difference in their living conditions, compared to other social sectors (see Hirschman 1987). Thus, economic optimism among lower classes relative to personal finances in the recent past emerges as an important force assuring the loyalty of this group to the Peronist candidates.[7]

The second profile, characterized as the model of "banker" voting (MacKuen et al. 1992), matches the rationale used by upper class voters to support the party-in-office. Holding partisan feelings constant among other variables, the electoral choice of this sector gets nurtured upon their members' association of national economic prosperity in the future with the reelection of president Menem. This class contrast might be interpreted as indicating selfish voting behavior for the lower classes and altruistic voting behavior for the upper classes, but three reasons refute this interpretation. First, forward-looking sociotropic considerations are also present among lower class voters.[8] Second, many of the optimistic expectations of the upper class at the collective level spring from positive assessments at the personal level. In other words, those expectations increase in anticipation of considerable private benefits.[9] Finally, as aggregate evidence reveals, for every additional percentage point of increase in the GDP, there is a differential marginal rise in the wealth of upper-income sectors that is several times higher than the one received by other social groups (see IEERAL-Mediterrranea 1995; Cardoso and Helwege 1992). Accordingly, it can only seem logical for members of the upper class to endorse governments in relation to their expectations for the national situation, since positive returns at this level will rapidly translate into an additional bonus for their personal welfare.

A COMPREHENSIVE PICTURE OF VOTING BEHAVIOR IN ARGENTINA, PERÚ AND URUGUAY

The data examined above reveal that, as a rule, citizens of Argentina, Perú and Uruguay react in a rational manner, pretty much as their fellow voters in advanced democracies, rewarding the incumbent with votes for what is perceived as good performance and punishing it when economic circumstances are grim. As illustrated by the contrast between Uruguayans and Peruvians, however, variations in intensity and direction exist across electorates. Among Peruvians, as among Argentineans, responsibility attribution is almost a tacit rule, barely functioning as a screening mechanism through which economic evaluations affect voting decisions. Quite likely, this results, among other reasons, from the recent experience of active presidential intervention in stabilizing the economy and redefining the model of development. On the other hand, Uruguayans are willing to tinge their vote with economic impressions only if it is clear that the government deserves the credit (or the blame). The consensual mode of economic policy-making here reduces the incentives to make government automatically accountable for financial fortunes at all levels, leaving room for the acknowledgment of exogenous (or particularistic) forces shaping the economic situation.

Diversity also exists in regards to how economic information is used. Some voters, for example Argentineans, behave on average somewhat ungratefully, blaming and punishing the government more strongly for dire straits than praising and rewarding it for prosperity. Conversely, Peruvians are markedly generous and willing to credit the incumbents for whatever positive perception they may have and vote accordingly, while absolving them for financial misdemeanors and minimizing protest votes. Finally, some voters, such as the Uruguayans, reproduce the standard pattern of advanced democracies, where symmetric attitudes prevail (Kiewiet 1983: 49; Lewis-Beck 1988: 78–79). These findings imply that the notion of protest voting based on the economy cannot be generalized. All depends on the additional political incentives that are able to mobilize people's decisions and color their subjective impressions of the economy, as well as on the degree of economic turmoil and discontinuity recently experienced.

Interestingly enough, in the election of 1995, Argentineans did not accept the major argument pushed forward by the incumbent authorities during the electoral campaign based on the notion of an "installment loan" vote ("*voto cuota*"). The basic message contained in this proposition was that only a pro-incumbent vote would assure those with credit-card installment loans for the purchase of home appliances the financial tranquility in the future that would permit them to honor their debts. In principle, this argument should have yielded a strong partial correlation coefficient between personal expectations and choice, something that has not been found when considering the whole sample. But this does not imply that Menem's campaigners failed in their proselytizing offensive. After disaggregating the effects of economic perceptions on the vote by social class, controlling for all other factors, the "*voto cuota*" emerges boldly among the lower classes. Considering those who assign high responsibility to authorities for their future personal economic situation, the group of lower class voters awaiting better times show themselves 4.6 times more likely to support the incumbent than to vote otherwise (partial correlation coefficient of .25, significant at $p < .05$). In a like manner, if we remove the evaluation of the president from the equation, the "*voto cuota*" also shows up among those with a middle-lower class background. Among them, prospects for personal well-being were strongly associated with a pro-incumbent vote; in fact, chances of supporting the Peronist government were eight times higher than of taking the opposite path. For all the tangible consequences these short-termed influences on voting may involve, one should not dismiss the importance that partisan traditions have in electoral decisions among Argentineans. In spite of the steady increase in political independence, electoral volatility and partisan dealignment (see Echegaray 1993), partisan identities still commanded an important effect (partial correlation coefficient of .19, significant at $p < .01$).

The case of Uruguay exemplifies most clearly the constraints surrounding the model of economic voting in Latin America. Here the chances of endorsing political continuity resulting from economic satisfaction are as likely as those of siding with change. In the 1994 elections, the economy was far from dividing the political waters in the view of voters. To make sense of Uruguayans' choices, one should look elsewhere—for example, at the impressions developed of the overall managerial qualities of the incumbent party or the endurance of partisan allegiances. Moreover, as a byproduct of the social homogeneity of Montevideo, no class effects are found.

As prior discussions revealed, contextual factors are essential to understanding economic and non-economic effects. Wherever inchoate party systems are accompanied by a record of economic instability, the intensity of economic voting is larger (e.g., in Perú). Indeed, such a context can hardly provide the opportunity for mass socialization that partisanship requires to affect the vote, while it subverts the social basis of most electoral alignments. Under such circumstances, perceptions of economic reality and political leadership considerations prevail.

The popularity of the president is, in all three countries discussed here, a highly significant force. In Perú, it reveals itself as the strongest single predictor of vote, reflecting the leadership provided by domestic and foreign policy accomplishments personally conducted by president Fujimori, such as the decline in guerrilla activism, the sanctions against members of the old political class, and the "rally around the flag" effect due to the war against Ecuador. In Argentina, the image of the president in relation to a variety of factors, such as administrative corruption, flamboyant style of governance, handling of military subordination and human rights issues, and active foreign policy, among others, heavily structure electoral preferences for continuity or change.[10] In this sense, each presidential contest represents a plebiscite on the political leadership of the ruling authorities.

In sum, based on the data from the elections of 1994–1995, Argentineans, Peruvians and Uruguayans articulate their choices—with different degrees of intensity—around economic perceptions. Intuitively, the intensity in economic voting covaries with levels of institutionalization and macro-economic stability. To a greater extent, and in a more homogeneous fashion, voters face the elections as opportunities to stage political referendums of the incumbent's performance. Also, the data show that partisanship is partially present. Less obvious is the influence of class voting, only visible among Argentineans. Still, a closer inspection of class interactions with economic considerations yields some positive results. All this means that, as revealed by the aggregate data and by the scholarly literature from advanced democracies, the argument for economic voting is salient for Latin Americans, but it does not exhaust the intrinsic diversity of effects underlying voting choice.

NOTES

1. Differences between the proportion of votes going to the incumbent party in the pre and post-electoral studies are rather small and fall within the reported margins of error, making of the first a reliable measure. In the Buenos Aires sample, for which a ± 5.2 percent margin of error was reported, 44.2 percent of the interviewed reported to have voted for the incumbent Peronist party, whereas the actual proportion reached 48.6 percent, thus dismissing any possibility of serious post-facto rationalization of electoral preferences. In the Lima sample, with a reported margin of error of ± 4.5 percent, 63.3 percent of the respondents (66.6 percent after proportional reallocation of undecideds) intended to support Fujimori's bid for reelection; his actual vote-share was 63.7 percent. In the Montevideo sample, with a reported ± 6 percent margin of error, the sum of votes manifested in favor of the different subtickets of the Blanco party added 21.2 percent (23.4 percent after proportional reallocation of undecideds), a figure almost matching the 21.1 percent of actual votes received. All margins of error were calculated for samples designed within a 95 % confidence interval.

2. In Argentina, it was the survey research unit of the University of Buenos Aires, CEDOP (Centro de Estudios de Opinión Pública). In Perú, it was APOYO S.A., a commercial firm with a long tradition of public opinion and marketing studies. In Uruguay, it was Marketing Investigadores S.A., a firm devoted mainly to marketing research, although with a strong interest in public opinion subjects as evidenced by their active participation in the *Barómetro Iberoamericano* project since 1992. All three firms adhere to AAPOR/WAPOR standards and code of ethics.

3. References to respondents as Argentineans, Peruvians or Uruguayans are obviously limited in scope to those residing in the areas that were sampled and should not be automatically extended to the national population as a whole.

4. The only relevant exception takes place among Argentineans with regard to the impact of their prospective personal finances expectations on vote, which loses statistical significance at conventional levels, after controlling for responsibility attribution. The initial effects may, therefore, result from spurious relationships. The relevance of this exception springs from the pivotal role played by incumbent partisans' campaigning appeals to go to the voting booths bearing in mind that only the president's reelection could warrant positive pocketbook prospects (so-called "*voto cuota*"). This point is discussed later.

5. Obviously, this thinking brings into effect non-economic factors, such as the perception of a poorly endowed opposition in matters of economic policy, the conviction that leadership qualities displayed in other arenas (e.g., the fight against terrorism) would also result in economic betterments if given a chance, or an intrinsic cultural conformism like the one reviewed at the aggregate level under the hypothesis of affirmative voting.

6. The exponential function of the log odds (chance=.06 and .07) reveals that the probability of voters belonging to middle and middle-lower classes of supporting the Peronist ticket, compared to the upper classes, is less than a tenth of their inclinations to vote against it.

7. The partial correlation coefficient of retrospective pocketbook effects on vote for this class reaches .30, which yields an estimated odds that voters with these characteristics will be 41 times more likely to vote for the incumbent than against it.

8. Controlled for all other factors, this variable presents the only other significant effect at $p < .10$, with a partial correlation coefficient of .20 (significant at $p < .07$). This yields an odds ratio of 14.3, that is, it makes those being optimistic for the nation's economic future over fourteen times more likely to vote for continuity than for change.

9. Indeed, among this group, forward-looking pocketbook considerations stand out as the only significant predictor of prospective orientations for the nation, holding constant all other economic and non-economic variables (the only exception being the measure of government's responsibility for the future financial situation of the country which also reaches statistical significance). The standardized beta coefficient reaches .37 ($p < .01$). When entered alone, the former variable explains 47 percent of the fluctuations in the later.

10. Open-ended questions of a probabilistic exit poll revealed that, among the top reasons for supporting president Menem's reelection, 20.2 percent claimed "the political performance of Menem" and "Menem's style." On the other side, 48.2 percent admitted to have voted "to support the continuity of the economic program and stability" and 13.1 percent for reasons of "partisan traditions." "Encuesta CEOP in *Clarín*, 21 May 1995: 2.

Chapter Eight

Understanding the Basis of Electoral Support in Latin America

Times of crisis or sudden changes in economic life invoke different calculations among individuals and constituencies of nascent democracies. Electoral results in Latin America reflect a process of decision-making that is complex and multidimensional, and that even under conditions of financial distress may escape from simple economic-content reactions. Macro-level and survey data for the period of 1982-1995 reveal that political considerations, as much as economic opinions, move the expectations and choices of the average Latin American voter, and variations in her living structures of opportunities, as summarized by different institutional and macro-economic contexts, turn that plurality of influences even more salient.

As such, the basis that feed the political capital of governments spring not from demanding pre-requisites of civic knowledge or difficult reasoning but from incumbents' aptitudes to favorably colour voting cues used by the majority at the moment of arriving at an electoral decision, by effectively touching both the hearts and the stomachs of Latin American voters. Certain clear patterns in how decisional clues affect the voting decision can be discerned.

REASSESSING ECONOMIC VOTING IN LATIN AMERICA

Despite the economic difficulties experienced during the 1980s and 1990s, Latin American voters did not permit economic factors to outshine the diversity of competing appeals mobilized by candidate attractiveness or partisan attachments, nor did they remain alien to longstanding cultural trends that traditionally assign priority to leadership and personality considerations. Voters were sensitive to the heterogeneity of stimuli received and, indeed, placed economic factors in an important position before developing choices, but that did not make these the sole determinants of voting.

Economic factors did play a crucial effect in determining the electoral fortunes of incumbent governments. Indeed, regardless of the level of analysis selected, individual or aggregate, performance in the economic arena had a considerable impact on voting choices. In broader terms, voters reacted rationally, rewarding effectiveness and punishing failure. Similarly, Latin Americans were not oriented by myopic reactions to recent economic performance but by relative long-term considerations. Nonetheless, some interesting gaps remained compared to the voting rationality of citizens of most advanced democracies.

Among individuals, retrospective and prospective views of the economy summarize the effects of financial forces. Less clear is the degree to which voters reacted to personal finances, except when segmented by social class, when the lower strata seemed more prone to follow their pocketbooks. Among electorates, on the other hand, the government's efficacy in dealing with the issue of inflation condenses the effect of economics. As incumbents demonstrated ability to keep prices under control, voters rewarded them with votes; if they failed to do so, voters' reproach was unavoidable. These findings are mostly consonant with other scholars' description of Western electorates, but exceptions to the general reward–punishment rule are present. At the micro level, voters economically dissatisfied with the government were not always willing to choose change over continuity. At the macro level, electorates seemed indifferent to unemployment fluctuations, despite its relative increase over time. Obviously, other considerations were mediating these anomalies, such as the perceived economic incompetence of the opposition or the informal job opportunities through which governments diffuse concern over unemployment.

I found economic factors to account for a third of the fluctuation in the support for political continuity, as expressed in votes going to the incumbents over time. This figure confirms that many voters confront elections as plebiscites on the economic capabilities of the government. However, when considering other pieces of information that voters make use of during elections, it becomes apparent that extra-economic factors are present, varied and important.

THE POLITICAL DETERMINANTS OF ELECTORAL SUPPORT

Extraordinary economic circumstances such as those experienced by Latin Americans between 1982 and 1995 were as essential for the salience of economic clues in electoral decisions as they were for the outpacing of the latter by non-economic factors. The volatile financial conditions that prevailed, in combination with people's poor level of information and longstanding cultural predispositions, highlighted voters' reliance on those decisional clues emerging as short-term forces. Thus, for example, as times of prosperity arrived, the influence of economics over electoral choice decreased and the effects of political leadership, partisanship, democratic performance and candidate appeals became more salient.

While theoretically one might expect partisan clues to be irrelevant in the Latin American context, in view of the limited opportunities for partisan socialization inherent to post-authoritarian settings and the diluted policy identity of political parties resulting from the economic crisis, the findings show that these clues did play a role. As good times superseded bad times, and a few extra years of democratic rule accumulated along the way, electorates became more prone to rely on partisan clues.

The data also revealed an interesting trade-off between what occurred in the economic and political arenas. As the economy collapsed, resulting in social turmoil and political unrest, voters did not tend to reward heavy-handed governments, nor did they support incumbents' efforts to improve the quality of democratic conditions as compensation for dire economic circumstances. In the face of recession, voters simply became indifferent to the democratic accomplishments of the incumbent. Circumstances changed, however, as the economic environment improved: in the face of prosperity in per capita terms, tolerance for authoritarian deviations rose, thus revealing a pattern of behavior that linked the notion of losses to economic performance alone (keeping the notion of democratic governance away from a domain of potential losses) and that posited economic attitudes as risk-averse for gains more strongly than for losses.

In a similar vein, no matter whether good or bad economic times prevailed, the reliance on political leadership clues to make decisions remained, on the aggregate, equally strong. This means that voters' sensitivity to government performance in extra-economic domains remained significant and intense regardless of economic circumstances. Voters did not need special incentives like a recession or depression to turn elections into political referendums on the incumbent's leadership. Indeed, given that presidential actions and omissions were the visible parameter of government effectiveness and the focus of the public's general expectations in issues that go beyond the economic realm (such as peace, domestic tranquillity, honest government, etc.), political leadership considerations constituted a core element of decision across the years.

Incidentally, this evidence also challenges the conventional wisdom about the role of popular presidents in Latin American elections. Considering the predominance of term limits and the principle of no reelection in the region, scholars have argued that Latin American political systems are extraordinarily compelled to produce capable and popular chieftains periodically and to forfeit the political capital accumulated by a successful leader, since it cannot be used beyond the leader's term of office (Linz 1994: 17). But the evidence demonstrates that the argument of political leadership remained very compelling, even though incumbents sought reelection only in five out of the forty-one contests here analyzed. This means that an effective transfer of presidential leadership to the ruling party took place, and that such political capital became accumulated as part of the party's political stock. Moreover, it is apparent that such transfer occurred with equal likelihood in both highly and poorly developed systems.

Scholars have also rejected the possibility that strong presidents and strong candidates can coexist in harmony without tearing apart their political organizations and, along the way, seriously affecting the party's appeal among voters (for example, see Linz 1994). However, electoral outcomes in Latin America show that political leadership and candidate voting may coexist and grow stronger together. The evidence is conclusive in discarding the hypothesis that between a president's popularity and candidates' appeals there is room for only a type of zero-sum relationship. It seems apparent, then, that electoral politics in the region develops more strongly as a game of political teams, in which retiring presidents and office-seeking candidates of the same party end up cooperating beyond circumstantial differences, than a game of isolated political entrepreneurs.

THE BASES OF POLITICAL SUPPORT

Symbolic aspects are at the heart of electoral politics and are as important as the instrumental aspects represented by economic performance. Whatever the contingent differences among contests might be, it is the sense of ruling abilities and psychic security conveyed by the president's popularity and the candidates' appeal that become archetypal determinants of the public's electoral considerations. Similarly, the substantive importance of candidates' attributes in molding electoral outcomes reveals the resilience of entrenched cultural tendencies favorable to the development of personalist politics.

A fundamental lesson of this analysis is that, in spite of all its intuitive logic, the argument of economic voting cannot be uncritically transplanted to new democracies. A careful assessment of the validity of the assumptions underlying such model of voting is, therefore, necessary. In operational terms, one needs to control for the influences of other contending explanations to assess economic voting effectively. At the same time, it is necessary to look at the effects of shifts in financial states from a socialization perspective to understand what causes voters to be economically sensitive. In this line of argument, fluctuations in wellbeing conditions may generate reactions among some publics, but, unless these oscillations surpass some critical threshold, they may encounter public tolerance, other issue priorities in the public mind, or competing influences by non-economic forces, all of which may result in a lessening of economic voting.

This admission of powerful extra-economic influences has direct implications for the broader debate over the economic bases of political support, especially considering that the newness of democratic governments in the region heightens the link between incumbents and political regimes. Since a central tenet of classical political research on democratic instability highlights economic efficiency as a causal factor, many observers have inferred that the systematic electoral turnover of ruling parties throughout the 1980s produced by economic mismanagement may, sooner than later, result in a wave of democratic breakdowns (Inter-American Dialogue 1989). The alert was clear: "Economic crisis represents one of the most common threats to democratic stability" (Diamond et al. 1989: 17). Moreover, prior efforts to underscore political factors in shaping the odds of regime survivability (Linz 1978) were ignored in view of the breadth of the economic emergency. The data reviewed have demonstrate that claims of economic robustness and political impotence in shaping the fortunes of governments and political systems were exaggerated. Neither political forces such as the president's leadership, partisanship, or candidates' attributes were so irrelevant nor was the economy so uniquely important. The obvious implication for studies of political stability is that support for democracy originated in something else than mere economic efficacy.[1]

Why was this the case? Although answering this question is beyond the scope of this study, one may gain insight by looking closely at the way different forces that guide voters and structure the electoral arena may ultimately work at a meta-electoral level. The relevance of the political leadership of presidents and the charismatic quality of candidates in shaping the calculus of support, amidst a scenario of economic uncertainty, demonstrates how important consequential interventions or carefully staged acts become in letting people know that someone is taking care of the nation and something is being done.

Examples abound to illustrate the diversity of expressions by which political leadership becomes salient. Pact-making efforts like the ones forged between government and opposition in Bolivia throughout the 1980s and in El Salvador since 1992 are one instance. Another is the search for governability consensus dramatized by office-seeking leaders in Brazil in 1989 and 1994 and Venezuela in 1988 and 1993. Yet, another case in point is provided by the spectacle of regular endeavors for *concertación social* (social pacts) engineered by Argentinean and Mexican presidents between government, labor and capital in the 1980s and early 1990s, or their frequent recourse to a politics of *decretazos* (executive decrees) in the face of congressional paralysis.

In sum, concerning the basis of popular support, economic fragility was effectively counterbalanced by a muscular exercise of presidential leadership and an electoral offer of strong candidates. Conversely, if governments were perceived as weak, presidents remained unpopular, or if candidates were unable to captivate majorities, incumbents were doomed to perish, the implications for the political system being that, in the face of continuous economic distress and poor political leadership, democratic rule might perish as well.

THE CONTROVERSY OVER POLITICAL ACCOUNTABILITY

The plurality of decision clues shaping electoral results also implies that voters did not hold their leaders accountable merely over economic matters. In fact, the data demonstrate that, under some circumstances, voters may care less than expected about the incumbent party's economic responsiveness and weigh more heavily its capacity to provide effective leadership in social and political matters, while remaining indifferent to the government's conduct in the domain of democratic achievements.

Such response has important implications for the ongoing pessimism over the feasibility of consolidating representative democracies in Latin America, which sees elected leaders failing to become responsible and accountable to the public concerning economic policies (see O'Donnell 1992; Stokes 1995). For the most part, this criticism reflects the scholarly disappointment with three assumptions concerning elite and mass behavior, not yet submitted to the empirical test. The first assumption is that democratic regimes should warrant a clear-cut correspondence between promises and actions of elected leaders. It follows then, as a second assumption, that citizens pay attention to instrumental aspects of policies. Finally, the third assumption is that voters follow and decide upon economic clues exclusively. Since the recent experience of some countries reveals the manifest irresponsiveness of elected politicians regarding their original economic plans, Latin American regimes are judged not to fit the model of representative democracy but one labeled as "delegative democracy" (O'Donnell 1992; Stokes 1995).

My analysis demonstrates, however, that these assumptions are largely misguided, which raises questions about the diagnosis of leaders' irresponsiveness and unaccountability as the modal pattern of political development in the region. On the one hand, the average Latin American voter is not concerned about promises but results, nor is the merit of reelection of a president solely judged upon economic factors. In fact, leadership considerations founded in the political performance of incumbents or the personal attractiveness of candidates constitute the essential cuegivers of mass publics, along with economic factors, which implies a public tolerance for a change in past pledges or original plans as long as results become pleasing. Although salient, economic incentives do not command voters' preferences in isolation, which means that they do not exhaust the opinion linkage between citizens and leaders. Voters' notions of political representation and public responsiveness are in fact broader.

On the other hand, if the apparent rule was a deficit of accountability, why did six out of ten incumbents fail in seeking reelection, that is, in successfully securing their electoral impunity? If scholars have deemed electoral democracy in Latin America to fall short as a mechanism of effective representation, why did most office-holders, even those who abided by their initial promises, failed to be exonerated at the voting booths? My view is that a systematic pattern of removal of ruling parties from government means that electoral mechanisms of accountability are alive and well. Elections effectively allow voters to sanction incumbents whose past performance they do not approve of and favor those who have served them well. The view that elections are expected to do more than this, such as serve a planning function by allowing citizens to appraise alternative programs, is misguided, as it fails to recognize that electoral campaigns in Latin America are far from educating the public in the region or that the levels of political information of the average Latin American voter remained rather poor.

Electoral choice cannot be viewed only through economic lenses. Even under the exceptional material conditions experienced by the citizens of Latin America in the 1980s and 1990s, extra-economic forces were as relevant, if not more, as economic ones in explaining the voting behavior of Latin Americans in their passage towards mature democracy.

NOTE

1. Furthermore, the empirical evidence makes apparent that elections helped to keep reactions to office-holders and political regimes apart, allowing citizens to "throw the rascals out" without inevitably overthrowing their systems.

Appendix A

Aggregate-Level Analysis—Incumbent Vote Results for Presidential Elections

The elections included for analysis at the aggregate level and their share of valid votes going to the incumbent party or coalition are listed in Table A.1 (More details, see Appendix G). Only electorally competitive contests for president during the 1982–1995 period were included in the analysis. This means that at least two political parties presented credible, not negotiated and opposing tickets for the presidency, there was a minimum of a third of votes won by the opposition party, and the election was not the first time ballots were casted after a non-elected leader was replaced.[1]

Electoral fairness and results free of manipulation are other important features for case selection. In deciding whether to deem an election fair, I have relied on overall assessments of elections by international monitors such as those issued by the Organization of American States (OAS) and Latin American Studies Association (LASA) special task-forces and observation committees, as well as the institutional evaluations by the region's most authoritative agency, Comisión de Asesoramiento y Promoción Electoral de Latinoamérica (CAPEL) (see LASA 1990, 1995; Nohlen 1993). Of course, one cannot be fully certain of the absolute fairness of the electoral processes and their results, since a) there has not been international monitoring for every single contest in which malpractices have been alleged; b) whenever monitoring was made possible, it has been limited to urban areas; c) monitoring could provide only an inconsequential assessment on the skewed possession of resources (e.g., money, access to the media, campaign workers) among the contenders, a factor that has also affected electoral results without resorting to overt manipulation of the vote-count; and d) monitoring could also offer an overall description of the political climate surrounding elections and how much confidence in elections this may have instilled in voters, a fact that could only influence the final outcomes without resorting to fraudulent arrangements.

Table A.1. Descriptive Values of Incumbent Vote-Share

Country (Election Month/Year)	*Incumbent Vote-Share (in %)*
Argentina (5/1989)	32.5
Argentina (5/1995)	49.9
Bolivia (7/1985)	15.3
Bolivia (5/1989)	25.8
Bolivia (6/1993)	20.0
Brazil (11/1989)	5.6
Brazil (10/1994)	54.3
Chile (12/1993)	58.0
Colombia (5/1982)	41.0
Colombia (5/1986)	35.8
Colombia (5/1990)	48.2
Colombia (5/1994)	45.8
Costa Rica (2/1982)	33.6
Costa Rica (2/1986)	52.3
Costa Rica (2/1990)	47.2
Costa Rica (2/1994)	46.6
Domin.Rep.(5/1982)	46.7
Domin.Rep.(5/1986)	39.2
Domin. Rep.(5/1990)	35.5
Domin.Rep.(5/1994)	43.6
Ecuador (6/1984)	13.5
Ecuador (1/1988)	14.7
Ecuador (5/1992)	8.4
El Salvador (3/1989)	36.5
El Salvador (3/1994)	49.3
Guatemala (11/1990)	17.5
Honduras (11/1985)	51.0
Honduras (11/1989)	44.3
Honduras (11/1993)	40.7
Mexico (7/1988)	50.7
Mexico (8/1994)	50.2
Nicaragua (2/1990)	40.8
Panama (5/1994)	29.5
Peru (4/1985)	7.3
Peru (4/1990)	22.6
Peru (4/1995)	64.4
Uruguay (11/1989)	30.3
Uruguay (11/1994)	31.2
Venezuela (12/1983)	33.5
Venezuela (12/1988)	53.0
Venezuela(12/1993)	23.6

Domin.Rep.: Dominican Republic
Sources: Nohlen (1993); *Keesing's Record of World Events* (various years).

NOTE

1. Note that the incorporation of the Mexican and Brazilian elections of 1988 and 1989 respectively may be deemed out of context since the conditions for electoral competitiveness are likely to be questioned. However, a substantial number of observers have agreed upon the highly competitive characteristics of the 1988 contest in México (see Butler and Bustamante 1991; Dominguez and McCann 1995). As for Brazil, the recurrence of subnational contests in the decade before 1989 makes tenable the supposition that competitive electoral practices were already established. Therefore, both of these elections were included in the sample.

Appendix B

Validity of Contextual Characterization for Argentina, Perú, and Uruguay

Overall, a continuum in levels of institutional development and macro-economic stability can be established for these three countries (see Table B.1). Perú is placed at one pole as the case presenting a lower degree of macro-economic continuity and political development prior to the presidential contest. Uruguay occupies the other pole, with higher level of institutional maturation and macro-economic stability. Argentina is in a middle position (see Mainwaring and Scully 1995; Smith et al. 1994).

This classification is further confirmed by the data. As the following table shows, Perú shows higher variability in its rates of economic growth and inflation, as well as the highest annual inflation index. This illustrates the extreme macro-economic volatility that anteceded the electoral experience of April 1995. Also, Perú scores close to the bottom of Mainwaring and Scully's ranking of political institutionalization. Uruguay displays a much lower macro-economic dispersion and scores among the top countries in levels of institutionalization, which entails a context of greater continuity in material well-being and political development prior to the November 1994 contest. Finally, Argentina reveals a volatile economic background with a relatively institutionalized political situation.

Table B.1. Measures of Contextal Conditions by Country

Variable	*Perú*	*Argentina*	*Uruguay*
$GDP_{std.dev.}$ [1]	4.49	3.17	2.43
Δ CPI[2]	1580.5	291.4	73.4
$CPI_{std.dev.}$ [3]	3034.8	527.0	30.3
RANK M&S[4]	4.5	9.0	11.5

Source: Calculations based on CEPAL (1994).

NOTES

1. This represents the standard deviation of the annual rate of change in the gross domestic product (at prices of 1980) between 1990 and 1994.

2. This represents the arithmetic mean in the annual rate of change in the consumer prices index between 1990 and 1994.

3. This represents the standard deviation of the annual rate of change in the consumer prices index between 1990 and 1994.

4. This represents the country's ranking in the classification of levels of partisan institutionalization elaborated by Mainwaring and Scully (1995: 17), where the top possible value is 12, indicating "high" institutionalization, and the bottom is 4, indicating "low" institutionalization.

Appendix C

Caveats about the Research Design

Although this research design resembles a pooled cross-sectional time-series format, its numerous peculiarities still make it amenable to OLS estimation. The caveat is far from minor if one recalls all the implications a pooled cross-sectional time-series format would involve in terms of statistical techniques to be used and problems to be corrected (see Stimson 1985). The basic admonition is that OLS can neither take account of the country variation affecting the dependent variable (with the resulting problems of heteroscedasticity) nor control for the eventual serial correlation of errors over time. However, two characteristics of the sample in use and the way explanations of electoral choice are finally modelled make a case for a consideration of this design as a quasi-pooled cross-sectional time-series and for a legitimate use of OLS.

One, since the maximum number of electoral events per country is four, the study just barely accommodates the standards of a pooled time-series design; moreover, the variation in the sample between countries for which the event at stake is measured only once (e.g., Chile, Guatemala, Nicaragua, Panamá) and those for which is measured four times (e.g., Colombia, Costa Rica, Dominican Republic) further assures that problems related to time-series designs would barely show up. Actually, checking for the possibility of time-driven autocorrelation problems by regressing the residuals of the trimmed model on their lagged values rendered an R-squared value of .018 (significant only at $p = .40$), that is, barely representing any serious trouble for the subsequent analysis. In addition, analyses correlating the residuals of the full and initial trimmed models against time show no significant relationship. Ultimately, problems of autocorrelation are controlled by the inclusion of a lagged version of the dependent variable incidentally modelling the argument of affirmative voting.

A second characteristic of this pooled sample has to do with differences in the sequence, timing, and nature of the observed elections in each country. Whereas the mode is one election every four years, many observations for specific countries are spaced every five or six years, involving a different effect in terms of unmeasured variables such as, for example, general publics' feelings that "it's-time-for-a-change". Besides, some of these contests could be located on an equal footing with those experienced by the advanced democracies of Western Europe and North America, in the sense of being mass-level routines within a highly regularized democratic system (e.g., Costa Rica, Uruguay, Venezuela in 1983 and 1988), while other elections are placed under ill-defined circumstances from the perspective of consolidated democracy, which, in turn, brings distinctive factors into play as determinants of electoral outcomes. These unmeasured effects are likely to pre-announce some misspecification of the model; yet, in this particular context, they also may represent an asset in holding in check any major problem of heteroscedasticity by assuring a pretty much randomized distribution of values.

In practice, I verify the absence of serious problems of unequal variance distribution and correlated errors with predictors through visual inspection of plots of residuals and their standard errors with the actual and predicted variables, as well as with specially created variables assessing population and income level distributions of the countries. Both full and initial trimmed versions of the models show no significant correlation at all.

The trimmed version of the models seeks to provide a parsimonious and realistic specification of the factors determining electoral choice at an aggregate level. This clarification is relevant since another standard critique to OLS estimation in pooled cross-sectional designs is that it does not take into account the pooled structure of the data (see Stimson 1985). This argument makes sense in any muti-national research enterprise in light of the enormous heterogeneity underlying the variability of electoral choice. Naturally, this heterogeneity results from the very fact of dealing with countries which, in spite of regional, cultural or institutional commonalities, still possess their own idiosyncrasies that may ultimately affect the outcomes. A common solution has been to use dummy variables representing each country in the sample (except one used as reference-category) to control for the cross-sectional unit effects, that is, to apply least squares with dummy variables (LSDV) estimation. However, three reasons may make this an inappropriate strategy: 1) some of the observations refer to single events that occurred at the country level (such as in the cases of Chile, Guatemala, Nicaragua and Panamá, each one with a single election fulfilling the conceptual frame proposed, thus making redundant any dummy variable approach); 2) given the general characteristics of the sample, applying LSDV can only exhaust rapidly the degrees of freedom and compromise most inferences; and 3) LSDV may underestimate the global context of macro-economic and macro-political change taken place throughout the 1980s and 1990s by fixing time-invariant variables into the general model, one that, as measurement in levels and rates of change should suggest, attempts to gauge the sensitivity of electorates to fluctuations among and within countries.

All these considerations boil down to a single conclusion: any potential problem concerning the pooled structure of the data not being accounted for should be handled more meaningfully and conveniently by improving the specification of the general model rather than appealing to alternative LSDV. Specifying the model better means including all factors considered directly relevant to a comprehensive explanation of electoral choice, as well as including their interactions with the major features of the institutional and macro-economic contexts. Taking all this into account, the OLS technique is found to meet appropriately the goal of estimating the relative explanatory power of the major arguments about electoral choice.

Appendix D

Aggregate-Level Analysis—Coding Reliability for Explanatory Variables of Electoral Choice

To test coding reliability, all non-economic variables are recoded into five categories. Means and standard deviations for each type are presented. Major economic variables, except for the differenced rate of inflation, are kept with their original values.

Table D.1. Coefficients of Coding Reliability

Variables	*Unstandardized Regression Coefficient*	*Probability of Statistical Significance*	*Standardized Regression Coefficient*
Prior Vote[1]	3.59	.03	.25
Party Strength[2]	3.46	.02	.27
D Political Climate[3]	2.16	.07	.87
GDP Growth	−1.38	.26	−.12
CPI Rate	−0.43	.73	−.04
D Inflation[4]	−3.36	.02	−.27
Candidate Advantage[5]	4.99	.00	.44
Adjusted R^2	.67		
Standard Error	8.73		

NOTES

1. Prior Vote is recoded as (1) "weak prior vote" (20.9 percent or less), (2) "moderate" (between 21 and 33.9 percent), (3) "high" (between 34 and 45.9 percent), (4) "very high" (between 46 and 55.9 percent), and (5) "prior landslide" (56 percent or more). Cut-off points tend to follow the variable's natural breaks in its cumulative distribution. In both cases, a positive sign should be read: as the background in prior

votes obtained by the incumbent is larger, so is its current vote-share. Mean value is 3.58 with a standard deviation of 1.05.

2. Party Strength is recoded as (1) "small partisanship" (15.9 percent or less), (2) "small-to-medium" (between 16 and 24.9 percent), (3) "medium-to-large" (between 25 and 32.9 percent), (4) "large" (between 33 and 45.9 percent), and (5) "very large" (46 percent or more). Cut-off points tend to follow the variable's natural breaks in its cumulative distribution. In both cases, a positive sign should be read: as the amount of structural party-vote obtained by the incumbent is larger, so is its current vote-share.

3. Political Climate Rate of Change is recoded as (1) "large progress" (a negative difference between 2 and 7 points), (2) "small progress" (an amelioration of the amount of one point difference), (3) "no change" (no difference overtime), (4) "small regression" (of the amount of one point difference in a worsening direction), and (5) "large regression" (a positive difference of 2 point scores). Cut-off points tend to follow the variable's natural breaks in its cumulative distribution. In both cases, a negative sign should be read: as the incumbent's performance on issues of political rights and civil liberties shows an improvement overtime, the more votes is able to collect. Its mean value is 2.76, with a standard deviation of 1.26.

4. Inflation Rate of Change is recoded into five categories, collapsing values 3 and 4, and 6 and 7. This yields a mean value of 3.07 and a standard deviation of 1.21.

5. Candidate Advantage is recoded as (1) "great disadvantage" (a negative difference favorable to the challenger of 20 percentage points or higher), (2) "some disadvantage" (between 5 and 19.9 percent below the opposition party's candidate edge), (3) "marginal disadvantage" (a difference between 0 and −4.9 percent), (4) "marginal advantage" (between 0.1 and 4.9 percent in favor of the incumbent), and (5) "some advantage" (5 percent or more). Cut-off points tend to follow the variable's natural breaks in its cumulative distribution. In both cases, a positive sign should be read: as the edge in candidate advantage favors the incumbent party, a higher share of the votes it is expected to collect. Mean value is 2.73, with a standard deviation of 1.36.

Appendix E

Individual-Level Analysis—Survey Question Wordings

This appendix shows the question wordings used for the individual-level analysis, organized on a specific variable basis. First, I trancribed the original language question, then -in parenthesis- it is the translation version. Relevant comments are also included between brackets. Acronyms for countries are: AR = Argentina, PE = Perú, and UR = Uruguay.

VOTING INTENTION

AR = "Para comenzar, y antes de continuar, podría decirme por qué partido o candidato votó Ud. para Presidente el 14 de mayo?" (First of all, could you tell me which party or candidate did you vote for president last May 14?)

PE = "Si quedaran en una segunda vuelta presidencial: Alberto Fujimori y Javier Pérez de Cuéllar, por quién votaría Ud.? (If there were a run-off election for president and Alberto Fujimori and Javier Pérez de Cuéllar were the candidates, whom would you vote for?)

UR = "Si mañana fueran las elecciones para elegir presidente, por qué lema o candidato votaría?" (If presidential elections were held tomorrow, which party or candidate would you vote for?)

EVALUATION OF THE PERSONAL RETROSPECTIVE ECONOMIC SITUATION

AR = "Pasando a temas que tienen que ver con la economía: si comparamos su situación financiera actual y la de su familia con la de hace un año, diría

Ud. que la misma ha: mejorado, empeorado, o permanecido igual?" (Talking about the economy: if you compared your and your family's financial situation with that of a year ago, would you say that it has improved, worsened, or remained the same?) [Categories for "don't know/no answer" were taken only if volunteered and, in the analysis, were collapsed with category "same."]

PE = "Cómo está su situación económica familiar en relación a hace un año: mejor, igual o peor?" (How is your family's economic situation compared to that one year ago: better, worse, or the same?) [Categories for "don't know/no answer" were taken only if volunteered and, in the analysis, were collapsed with category "same."]

UR = "Pensando en su situación económica personal, Ud. diría que en los últimos 6 meses ha cambiado para: mucho mejor, algo mejor, algo peor, mucho peor o ha permanecido igual?" (Thinking of your personal economic situation, would you say that in the last 6 months it has become: a lot better, somewhat better, somewhat worse, a lot worse, or stayed the same?) [The first and last two categories were collapsed as "better" and "worse," respectively; the "don't know/no answer" were taken only if volunteered and, in the analysis, were collapsed with category "same."]

EVALUATION OF THE PERSONAL PROSPECTIVE ECONOMIC SITUATION

AR = "Mirando hacia adelante, cree Ud. que dentro de un año su situación financiera y la de su familia va a ser: mejor, igual, o peor?" (Looking ahead, do you think that in a year your own and family's financial situation will be better, worse, or will remain the same?) [Categories for "don't know/no answer" were taken only if volunteered and, in the analysis, were collapsed with category "same."]

PE = "Cómo cree que estará su situación económica familiar dentro de un año: mejor, igual o peor?" (How do you think your family financial situation is going to be a year from now: better, worse, or the same?) [Categories for "don't know/no answer" were taken only if volunteered and, in the analysis, were collapsed with category "same."]

UR = "Y cómo cree que será su situación económica personal en los próximos 6 meses, diría Ud. que cambiará para: mucho mejor, algo mejor, algo peor, mucho peor o permanecerá igual?" (How do you think your financial situation will be in the next 6 months: a lot better, somewhat better, somewhat worse, a lot worse, or will remain the same?) [The first and last two categories were collapsed as "better" and "worse," respectively; the "don't know/no answer" were taken only if volunteered and, in the analysis, were collapsed with category "same."]

EVALUATION OF THE NATIONAL RETROSPECTIVE ECONOMIC SITUATION

AR = "Comparando la situación económica del país hoy con la de un año atrás, diría Ud. que la misma ha: mejorado, empeorado, o permanecido igual?" (Compared to a year ago, would you say the country's economic situation has: improved, worsened, or remained the same?) [Categories for "don't know/no answer" were taken only if volunteered and, in the analysis, were collapsed with category "same."]

PE = "Cómo está la situación económica del país en relación a hace un año: mejor, igual o peor?" (Compared to a year ago, would you say the country's economic situation has: improved, worsened, or remained the same?) [Categories for "don't know/no answer" were taken only if volunteered and, in the analysis, were collapsed with category "same."]

UR = "Y pensando en la situación económica del país, Ud. diría que en los últimos 6 meses ha cambiado para: mucho mejor, algo mejor, algo peor, mucho peor o ha permanecido igual?" (Thinking of the country's economic situation, would you say that in the last 6 months it has become: a lot better, somewhat better, somewhat worse, a lot worse, or remained the same?) [The first and last two categories were collapsed as "better" and "worse," respectively; the "don't know/no answer" were taken only if volunteered and, in the analysis, were collapsed with category "same."]

EVALUATION OF THE NATIONAL PROSPECTIVE ECONOMIC SITUATION

AR = "Pensando en la situación económica del país dentro de un año, diría Ud. que la misma va a: mejorar, permanecer igual, o empeorar?" (A year from now, do you think the economic situation of the country is going to be: better, worse, or stay the same?) [Categories for "don't know/no answer" were taken only if volunteered and, in the analysis, were collapsed with category "same."]

PE = "Cómo cree que estará la situación económica del país dentro de un año: mejor, igual o peor?" (How do you think the country's economic situation will be in a year: better, worse, or the same?) [Categories for "don't know/no answer" were taken only if volunteered and, in the analysis, were collapsed with category "same."]

UR = "Y cómo cree que será la situación económica del país en los próximos 6 meses, diría Ud. que cambiará para: mucho mejor, algo mejor, algo peor, mucho peor o permanecerá igual?" (How do you think the country's economic situation is going to be in the next 6 months: a lot better, somewhat better, somewhat worse, a lot worse, or will remain the same?) [The first and last two categories were collapsed as "better" and "worse," respectively; the "don't know/ no answer" were taken only if volunteered and, in the analysis, were collapsed with category "same."]

GOVERNMENT-ATTRIBUTED ECONOMIC RESPONSIBILITY[1]

AR = "En cuanto a su respuesta anterior, diría Ud. que la política económica del gobierno tuvo (tendrá): mucho que ver, bastante que ver, poco que ver, o nada que ver?" (In relation to your previous answer, would you say that the economic policy of the government had [will have]: a lot, quite, little, or nothing to do with it?) [The first two categories were collapsed to mean "high responsibility", the final two categories were also collapsed to mean "low responsibility"; categories "don't know/no answer" and answers for those who didn't reply to the original questions on economic situation [that is, "does not apply"] were considered only if volunteered and collapsed as "low responsibility."]

PE = "Al referirse a su [la] situación económica familiar [del país] con relación a hace un año atrás [dentro de un año] Ud. dijo que [LEER RESP.]; Ud. diría que la política económica del gobierno ha sido [va a ser] muy importante, algo importante, poco importante o nada importante para que ello sea así?" (In reference to your [the] personal [country's] economic situation compared to a year ago [a year from now], you said that it has [will be] [READ ANSWER]; would you say that the economic policy of the government has been [will be] very, somewhat, little, or not important at all for that to happen?) [The first two categories were collapsed to mean "high responsibility", the final two categories were also collapsed to mean "low responsibility"; categories "don't know/no answer" and answers for those who didn't reply to the original questions on economic situation [that is, "does not apply"] were considered only if volunteered and collapsed as "low responsibility."]

UR = "Cuán importante cree Ud. que ha sido [será] la política económica del gobierno respecto a su [la] situación económica personal [del país] en relación a los últimos 6 meses [en los próximos 6 meses]: muy importante, algo importante, poco importante, o nada importante?" (How important do you think the government's economic policy has been [will be] in regards to your [the] personal [country's] economic situation in the last [next] 6 months:

very, somewhat, a little, or not important at all?) [The first two categories were collapsed to mean "high responsibility", the final two categories were also collapsed to mean "low responsibility"; categories "don't know/no answer" and answers for those who didn't reply to the original questions on economic situation [that is, "does not apply"] were considered only if volunteered and collapsed as "low responsibility."]

PRESIDENTIAL POPULARITY

AR = "Y cómo evalúa Ud. la forma en que Menem estuvo manejando su tarea general como Presidente? aprueba fuertemente; aprueba, pero con reservas; más bien desaprueba; desaprueba fuertemente?" (How do you approve the way [Carlos] Menem is handling his job as president: strongly approve, approve with reserve, rather disapprove than approve, strongly disapprove?)

PE = "En general, diría Ud. que aprueba o desaprueba la gestión de . . . El presidente Alberto Fujimori?" (Overall, would you say you approve or disapprove the performance of . . . president Fujimori?)

UR = "Qué opinión tiene Ud. de la gestión de Luis Lacalle, diría Ud. que aprueba totalmente la misma, aprueba parcialmente, ni aprueba ni desaprueba, desaprueba parcialmente, o desaprueba totalmente?" (What is your opinion of [president] Lacalle's performance, would you say you strongly approve, approve somewhat, neither approve nor disapprove, disapprove somewhat, or strongly disapprove?)

PARTISAN LEANINGS

AR = "Por tradición política, se considera Ud. a sí mismo como: Peronista, Radical, Socialista, Liberal, Conservador, Nacionalista, Otro, Independiente/Ninguno, No sabe/no contesta?" (By political tradition, do you think of yourself as: Peronist, Radical, Socialist, Liberal, Conservador, Nacionalist, Other, Independent/None, don't know/no answer?) [Category "Peronista" represented leanings for the incumbent party; all other categories were collapsed representing leaning for the opposition.]

PE = "Cómo votó Ud. en el referéndum constitucional de 1993: por sí, por no, no recuerda, no votó?" (How did you vote in the constitutional referendum of 1993: yes, no, don't recall, didn't vote?) [Category "Yes" represented leanings for the incumbent party; all other categories were collapsed representing leaning for the opposition.]

UR = "Por qué partido o lema votó Ud. en las elecciones presidenciales de 1989?" (What party or ticket did you vote for in the presidential elections of 1989?) [References to subgroups, candidates, or the Blanco party represented leanings for the incumbent party; other categories were collapsed representing leaning for the opposition.]

NOTE

1. It applies to both personal and national, retrospective and prospective assessments.

Appendix F

Attribution of Government Responsibility for Economic Conditions in Latin America: Data, Question Wordings, and Sources

Data correspond to the following eleven observations: Argentina, 1988 and 1995; Brazil, 1988, Chile, 1988; Costa Rica, 1981, México, 1994; Perú, 1985 and 1995; Uruguay, 1988 and 1994; and Venezuela, 1988.

The 1988 data comes from the multi-country survey coordinated by Consorcio Polis in mid-1988.[1] In that survey, pollsters asked respondents to assign responsibilities for the country's situation to the government, the opposition, and fellow citizens in a 3-point scale ("a lot," "little," "none"). Fifty-three percent of Argentineans and Chileans, sixty percent of Uruguayans, and seventy-three percent of Brazilians picked the government. The ratios of blame placed upon government versus the opposition, and upon government versus fellow citizens, were, respectively, 1.8, and 1.2, among Argentineans, 2.1, and 3.5, among Brazilians, 3.3, and 2.7, among Uruguayans, and 4.5, and 3.6, among Chileans.

The 1988 Venezuelan data asked individuals to assign responsibility for the current situation to several alternatives: the Venezuelan people (9 percent), politicians (8 percent), AD partisans (5 percent), Copey partisans (3 percent), and the economy (3.5 percent).[2]

The 1994–95 studies of Uruguay and Argentina are partially comparable to the 1988 study, since the former are based upon metropolitan samples (although comprising over 40 percent of the national electorates). In each sample, after questions about the perceptions of economic conditions were introduced, individuals were asked to rate the responsibility of government for that matter in a 4 point scale ("a lot," "some," "little," "none"). Fifty-eight percent of Argentineans and Seventy-nine percent of Uruguayans were concentrated in the first two categories. For a more detailed account of these findings, see Chapter 7: n.1.

In Perú, a 1985 pre-electoral study asked (results in parenthesis): "Do you think the economic crisis has been direct responsibility of the government?

Yes (48 percent), Only partially (37 percent), No (13 percent)."[3] For the 1995 study, 77 percent held the government responsible for the economic situation. See Chapter 7: n.1.

For the case of Costa Rica,[4] the question and results read: "Which is the principal reason for the current economic situation of the country? the Executive power (57 percent), the oil prices (22 percent), the Legislative power (18 percent), the Central Bank (1 percent)."

In México of 1994, the question read (results in parenthesis): "Who do you think it is to blame for the current national situation of the economy? all Mexicans (20 percent), the economic policies of the government (56 percent), Both (15 percent)."[5]

NOTES

1. Consorcio Polis, "Relatório de pesquisa," IDESP, 1988.
2. Data made available by local polling firm Datanalysis, May–June 1988.
3. Editorial, *Debate*, 7, no. 32 (May 1985): 24.
4. Data made available by local survey institute CID-Gallup of Costa Rica, November 1981.
5. Data made available by the Technical Advisory Commission to the Presidency of the Republic of Mexico, August-September 1994.

Appendix G

Sources and References for Elections and Public Opinion Indicators

The Argentinean election of May 1989 had the UCR (Radical Party) as the incumbent party and the PJ (Peronist Party) as the main opposition force. Indicators of partisanship are based on Catterberg and Braun (1989), for confidence in parties, presidential popularity and ideological self-placement see Catterberg (1991). Sources for priority lists are Catterberg (1991) and survey data made available by local polling firm Römer y Asociados. Sources for candidates values are survey data made available by local agency A&C of Argentina (dated of March 1989).

The next election of Argentina under analysis is that of May 1995. Incumbent party was PJ and the newly created Frepaso front was the main opposition. Sources for partisanship are survey data made available by local firm Mansilla, Delich & Asociados. Data on confidence in parties, presidential popularity and ideological self-placement is based on Latinobarómetro, "Latinobarómetro I," 1995 and survey data made available by Römer y Asociados, respectively. The later also based measures of priority lists and candidates evaluations.

The first presidential election of Bolivia examined was held in July 1985, UDP was the incumbent party and MNR was the main opposition party; the next election of May 1989 saw the MNR as incumbent and AND as main opposition. The last election included for Bolivia dates of June 1993 when MIR-AND constituted the incumbent force and MNR embodied the main opposition party. Across all those years, data on partisanship and presidential popularity come from surveys conducted by Encuestas & Estudios. Measures for confidence in parties is based on data collected by ILDIS-Bolivia in 1989 and CIMA, "Barómetro Iberoamericano II," 1993.

Two presidential elections of Brazil were analyzed: that of November 1989 where the alliance PMDB-PFL composed the incumbent force and PT (Workers' Party) represented the largest opposition party, and that of October 1994 that had the alliance of PSDB-PFL as the incumbent group and, again, the PT as main challenger. Data come from various sources: partisanship is based in survey data collected by CEDEC/Datafolha for 1989 and Datafolha alone for 1994. Ideological self-placement for 1989 is also estimated in a second survey by CEDEC dated of March 1990. Confidence in parties for 1989 is based upon a Consorcio Polis study ("Relatório de pesquisa," IDESP 1988) whereas popularity and priority list for that year election come from survey data made available by IBOPE. For the relevant measures surrounding the 1994 election sources are survey data available by CBPA and Datafolha at CESOP-Unicamp.

The Chilean election of December 1993 faced the incumbent Convergencia confronting the right-wing coalition UDI-PRN as main opposition. Data for partisanship, president popularity and priority list is sourced in survey data made available by CEP-Adimark. Confidence in parties, candidate evaluation and ideology are sourced in surveys conducted by CERC and Latinobarómetro, "Latinobarómetro I," 1995.

The elections considered for Colombia total four: always held within a predominant two-party system in the month of May for years of 1982, 1986, 1990 and 1994. At the first contest, voters faced PL (Liberals) as incumbents and PC (Conservatives) as opposition. The next round things changed and the Conservatives were the incumbent force. In 1990 and 1994, the Liberals were the incumbent. Relevant data are sourced in CNC, " Informes CNC," 1982–1994, except for presidential popularity data in 1990 which is based on data made available by consultant agency Bendixen-Law.

In the case of Costa Rica, the Social Christian PUSC and the Liberal PLN alternated as incumbent and main opposition force across the four elections analyzed, always held in the month of February of every fourth year. In 1982 and 1994, PUSC was the incumbent. In 1986 and 1990, PLN was the incumbent. Source for all main variables was the survey data collection of CID/Gallup, except for confidence in parties in 1986-1994 based on the public opinion studies done by USIA and CIMA, "Barómetro Iberoamericano III," 1993.

Also, four elections were included for the Dominican Republic. Elections were held in the month of May of 1982, 1986, 1990 and 1994, with PRD (left-wing party) as incumbent in 1982–1986 and main opposition in 1994, the Populist PR as main opposition in 1982-1986 and incumbent in 1990, and the Social Christian PRSC as the incumbent in 1994. Data gaps are more pronounced for Dominican Republic for the pre-1994 election period. Partisanship in 1994 is sourced in a survey made available by Roper/Rumbo; figures for presidential popularity and priority list are based on a study conducted by Hamilton & Asociados, and confidence in parties is sourced in CIMA, "Barómetro Iberoamericano III," 1993.

Three elections are included for Ecuador. In June 1984, the coalition CFP-DP was the incumbent force confronting the Social Christian PUSC as main opposition. As of the election of January 1988, PUSC was the incumbent and left-wing ID led the opposition pack. The third election held in May 1992 saw ID as the incumbent and the Conservative PUR as main opposition. All data come from CEDATOS database of surveys.

Two elections are analyzed for El Salvador: that of March 1989 and that of March 1994. In the first, centrist PDC held government and right-wing ARENA was the main force in the opposition. In the next election, ARENA was the incumbent and the left-wing FMLN ran as main opponent. The survey database of CID/Gallup supplied the information for most variables except confidence in parties, which is based in USIA survey and CIMA, "Barómetro Iberoamericano III," 1993, respectively. For the public's priority list in 1989, I counted with survey data by the IUDOP Institute at the Catholic University of San Salvador.

Only one election qualified for Guatemala, that of November 1990 holding centrist PDCG as ruling party and center-left MAS as main challenger. Relevant data also come from CID/Gallup survey collection, except for candidates evaluation, which is sourced on a study conducted by US polling firm Belden&Russonello in 1985, and confidence in parties, which is based on a study conducted by local agency Aragon & Asociados.

Three elections are included for Honduras, always held in the month of November. In 1985, so-called Liberal PLH held power and confronted the conservatives of PNH. In 1989, PNH was the incumbent and the PLH its main opponent. In 1993, things changed again, with PLH as the party-in-office. CID/Gallup data collection sources most variables used for analysis except for confidence in parties, which is based in USIA surveys, and presidential popularity and priority list in 1985, which are based on a study conducted by Belden & Russonello consulting firm.

The Mexican presidential elections of July 1988 and August 1994 witnessed the last time PRI was the undisputed ruling party. In the first contest, PRD was the main adversary; whereas in the second, the center-right PAN became so. Indicators of partisanship, popularity and candidates image result from studies collected by IMOP/Gallup, in 1988, and the Technical Advisory Commission to the Presidency of the Republic of Mexico, during 1994, respectively. The former polling firm also supplied data for priority lists in 1988, whereas for 1994 these data came from local agency Ciencia Aplicada.

Confidence in parties was sourced in CIMA, "Barómetro Iberoamericano III," 1993.

Only one presidential election for Nicaragua qualified for inclusion. It was the one held on February 1990 with the left-wing FSLN party in power and the UNO coalition as the opposition front. Relevant data come from CID/Gallup data collection except for confidence in parties and priority list which are sourced in consulting firm SOCMERC.

Also, for Panama, I considered only one election: that of May 1994. The Arnulfista party held office and confronted Populist PRD as main opposition. CID/Gallup databank filled the information for all relevant variables.

Three elections for Peru are included for analysis, always scheduled in the month of April of every fifth year. The first one, in 1985, presented the Conservative AP as the party in office and the Populist APRA as main challenger. Presidential popularity and priority list for this election was sourced in polling firm Bendixen-Law data. The next election of 1990 held APRA as incumbent and the coalition FREDEMO as main adversary. Five years later, President Fujimori's Cambio 90 front disputed with another broad and circumstantial coalition, UPP. All data are sourced in the database of APOYO, a local opinion survey company.

I included two Uruguayan elections, that of November 1989 and 1994 that saw Colorados as the incumbent first and -five years later- saw their opponents Blancos occupying such position. All data come from the data collections of local poll firm Equipos/MORI.

Finally, three elections are considered for Venezuela, always scheduled in the month of December during the period under review. In 1983, the Social Christian COPEY was in office and defied by Populist AD. The Batoba survey available at The Roper Center LASDB collection filled the values for partisanship, priority list, presidential popularity, candidate evaluations, confidence in parties, ideology self-placement, and responsibility attribution for economic performance. In 1988 and 1993, AD was the incumbent whereas the main opposition role was, first, held by COPEY, then by the coalition named Convergencia. Data for relevant variables during these years came from Carrasquero (1995), a University of Zulia survey on candidates image, CIMA, "Barómetro Iberoamericano III," 1993, and consulting firm Harris-Doxa.

Appendix H

Table H.1 Aggregate Measures of Candidate Saliency

Table H.1. Aggregate Measures of Candidate Saliency

	Incumbent Candidate Saliency				*Opposition Candidate Saliency*			
Country (Election Month/Year)	*Party Age*	*Dispute*	*Prestige*	*Final Score*	*Party Age*	*Dispute*	*Prestige*	*Final Score*
Argentina (5/1989)	0	1	0	1	0	.5	0	.5
Argentina (5/1995)	0	1	1	2	1	.5	0	1.5
Bolivia (7/1985)	0	.5	0	.5	0	1	1	2
Bolivia (5/1989)	0	1	.5	1.5	0	1	.5	1.5
Bolivia (6/1993)	0	1	.5	1.5	0	1	.5	1.5
Brazil (11/1989)	0	.5	.5	1	.5	1	0	1.5
Brazil (10/1994)	.5	1	.5	2	.5	1	0	1.5
Chile (12/1993)	0	.5	.5	1	0	0	.5	.5
Colombia (5/1982)	0	.5	1	1.5	0	1	0	1
Colombia (5/1986)	0	1	0	1	0	1	0	1
Colombia (5/1990)	0	.5	0	.5	0	.5	0	.5
Colombia (5/1994)	0	1	0	1	0	.5	.5	1
Costa Rica (2/1982)	0	1	.5	1.5	0	1	0	1
Costa Rica (2/1986)	0	.5	0	.5	0	.5	.5	1
Costa Rica (2/1990)	0	1	0	1	0	1	.5	1.5
Costa Rica (2/1994)	0	1	0	1	0	.5	.5	1
Domin.Rep.(5/1982)	0	.5	0	.5	0	1	1	2
Domin.Rep.(5/1986)	0	.5	0	.5	0	1	1	2
Domin. Rep.(5/1990)	0	1	1	2	0	1	.5	1.5
Domin.Rep.(5/1994)	0	1	1	2	0	1	0	1
Ecuador (6/1984)	0	.5	0	.5	0	1	0	1
Ecuador (1/1988)	0	1	0	1	0	1	0	1
Ecuador (5/1992)	0	1	0	1	1	1	0	2

(continued)

Table H.1. (*continued*)

	Incumbent Candidate				*Opposition Candidate*			
	Saliency				*Saliency*			
Country (Election Month/Year)	*Party Age*	*Dispute*	*Prestige*	*Final Score*	*Party Age*	*Dispute*	*Prestige*	*Final Score*
El Salvador (3/1989)	0	1	0	1	0	1	0	1
El Salvador (3/1994)	0	1	0	1	.5	.5	0	1
Guatemala (11/1990)	0	0	0	0	1	1	0	2
Honduras (11/1985)	0	0	0	0	0	0	0	0
Honduras (11/1989)	0	.5	0	.5	0	.5	0	.5
Honduras (11/1993)	0	.5	0	.5	0	.5	0	.5
Mexico (7/1988)	0	.5	0	.5	1	1	.5	2.5
Mexico (8/1994)	0	.5	0	.5	0	1	0	1
Nicaragua (2/1990)	0	1	1	2	1	1	.5	2.5
Panama (5/1994)	0	.5	.5	1	0	1	0	1
Peru (4/1985)	0	1	0	1	0	1	0	1
Peru (4/1990)	0	0	.5	.5	1	1	0	2
Peru (4/1995)	.5	1	1	2.5	1	1	.5	2.5
Uruguay (11/1989)	0	0	0	0	0	0	0	0
Uruguay (11/1994)	0	0	0	0	0	0	1	1
Venezuela (12/1983)	0	.5	1	1.5	0	.5	0	.5
Venezuela (12/1988)	0	.5	1	1.5	0	.5	0	.5
Venezuela(12/1993)	0	.5	0	.5	1	1	1	3

Domin.Rep.: Dominican Republic
Sources: See Appendix G; Nohlen (1993); *Keesing's Record of World Events* (various years).

References

Acuña, Carlos. "Politics and Economics in the Argentina of the Nineties," in *Democracy, Markets, and Structural Reform in Latin America*, edited by William C. Smith, Carlos H. Acuña, and Eduardo A. Gamarra. New Brunswick: North–South Center/Transaction, 1994: 31–73.

Alducin, Enrique. *Los Valores de los Mexicanos. México: Entre la Tradición y la Modernidad.* México, DF: Banamex, 1991.

Ames, Barry. "Bases of Support for Mexico's Dominant Party." *American Political Science Review*, 64, no. 1 (March 1970): 67–153.

Ames, Barry. "The Reverse Co-Attail Effect: Local Party Organizations in the 1989 Brazilian Presidential Election," *American Political Science Review*, 88, no. 1 (1994): 95–111.

Anderson, Charles. "Towards a Theory of Latin American Politics," in *Politics and Social Change in Latin America*, edited by Howard Wiarda. Boulder: Westview Press, 1992.

Anderson, Leslie. "Surprises and Secrets: Lessons from the 1990 Nicaraguan Election," *Studies in Comparative International Development*, 27, no. 3 (1994): 93–119.

Arroyo, Jesus A., and Stephen Morris. "The Electoral Recovery of the PRI in Guadalajara, Mexico: 1988–1992," *Bulletin of Latin American Research*, 12, no. 1 (1993): 91–102.

Bartels, Larry. "Uninformed Votes: Information Effects in Presidential Elections," *American Journal of Political Science*, 40, no. 1 (1996): 194–230.

Basañez, Miguel. *El Pulso de los Sexenios*. México, DF: Siglo XXI. 1990

Beck, Paul Allen. "Choice, Context, and Consequence: Beaten and Unbeaten Paths toward a Science of Electoral Behavior," in *Political Science: The Science of Politics*, edited by Herbert Weisberg. New York: Agathon Press, 1986: 241–283.

Belluci, Paolo. "Economic Concerns in Italian Electoral Behavior: Toward a Rational Electorate?," in *Economic Conditions and Electoral Outcomes. The United States and Western Europe*, edited by Heinz Eulau and Michael Lewis-Beck. New York: Agathon, 1985: 321–332.

Belluci, Paolo. "Italian Economic Voting: a Deviant Case or Making a Case for a Better Theory?" in *Economics and Politics: The Calculus of Support*, edited by Helmut Norpoth. Ann Arbor: University of Michigan Press, 1991: 63–84.

Bennett, Lance W., and Bart Salisbury. "Rational Choice: the Emerging Paradigms in Electoral Studies," in *Research in Micropolitics*, 2, edited by Samuel Long. Greenwich: JAI Press, 1987: 1–30.

Berelson, Bernard, Paul Lazarsfeld and William McPhee. *Voting: A Study of Opinion Formation in a Presidential Campaign.* Chicago: University of Chicago Press, 1954.

Booth, John, and Mitchell Seligson. "Paths to Democracy and the Political Culture of Costa Rica, Mexico and Nicaragua," in *Political Culture and Democracy in Developing Countries*, edited by Larry Diamond. Boulder: Lynne Rienner, 1994.

Brady, Henry E., and Paul M. Sniderman. "Attitude Attribution: A Group Basis for Political Reasoning." *American Political Science Review* 79, no.4 (1985):1061–1078.

Brockman Machado, Mario. "Ideologia, Socialização Política e Dominação." *Revista Dados*, 17 (1978): 23–58.

Brophy-Baermann, Michelle. "Economics and Elections: The Mexican Case." *Social Science Quarterly*, 75, no. 1 (March 1994): 125–135.

Budge, Ian, and Dennis Farlie. *Explaining and Predicting Elections: Issue Effects and Party Strategies in 23 Democracies.* London: Allen & Unilwin, 1983.

Buendía, Jorge. "Economic Reform and Political Support in Mexico, 1988–1997", in *Public Support for Market Reforms in New Democracies*, edited by Susan Stokes. New York: Cambridge University Press, 2001: 131–159.

Butler, David et al., eds. *Democracy at the Polls: A Comparative Study of Competitive National Elections.* Washington, DC: American Enterprise Institute, 1981.

Butler, Edgar, and Jorge Bustamante, eds. *Sucesión Presidencial. The 1988 Mexican Presidential Election.* Boulder: Westview Press, 1991.

Calvert, Susan, and Peter Calvert. *Argentina. Political Culture and Instability*. Pittsburgh: University of Pittsburgh Press, 1989.

Cameron, Maxwell. *Democracy and Authoritarianism in Peru: Political Coalitions and Social Change.* New York: St Martin's Press, 1994.

Campbell, Angus, Philip E. Converse, Warren E. Miller, and Donald E. Stokes. *The American Voter.* New York: Wiley Press, 1960.

Canache, Damarys, Jeffery J. Mondak, and Annabelle Conroy. "Politics in Multiparty Context: Multiplicative Specifications, Social Influence, and Electoral Choice." *Public Opinion Quarterly* 58, no. 4 (Winter 1994): 509–538.

Canzani, Agustin. "Minorities Democracy. The Uruguayan Elections of 1994," Paper presented at the WAPOR Regional Meeting, Margarita Is., Venezuela, 1995.

Cardoso, Eliana and Ann Helwege, "Below the Line: Poverty in Latin America," *World Development*, 20, no. 1 (1992): 10–37.

Carrasquero, José. "Legitimacy and Popular Support for the Democratic Political System in Venezuela", Ph.D. dissertation. Storrs: University of Connecticut, 1995.

Carrión, Julio. "Partisan Decline and Presidential Popularity. The Politics and Economics of Representation in Peru, 1980–1993," in *Deepening Democracy and Representation in Latin America*, edited by Kurt von Mettenheim and James Malloy. Pittsburgh: University of Pittsburgh Press, 1998: 55–70.

Catterberg, Edgardo, and Maria Braun. "Las Elecciones Presidenciales Argentinas del 14 de Mayo de 1989: la Ruta a la Normalidad." *Desarrollo Económico*, 115 (1989): 361–374.

Catterberg, Edgardo. *Argentina Confronts Politics: Political Culture and Public Opinion in the Argentine Transition to Democracy.* Boulder: Lynne Rienner Publishers, 1991.

CEPAL (Comisión Económica para América Latina). *Preliminary Overview of the Economy of Latin America and the Caribbean*. Santiago de Chile: United Nations, 1989–95.

Chalmers, Douglas. "Parties and Society in Latin America," *Studies in Comparative International Development*, 7 (1973): 102–128.

Clarke, Harold, Marianne Stewart, and Gary Zuk, eds. *Economic Decline and Political Change: Canada, Great Britain, the United States.* Pittsburgh: University of Pittsburgh Press, 1989.

Clarke, Harold, Euel Elliot, William Mishler, Marianne Stewart, Paul Whiteley, and Gary Zuk. *Controversies in Political Economy: Canada, Great Britain, the United States.* Boulder: Westview Press.

Colosio, Luis. "Why the PRI Won the 1991 Elections," in *Political and Economic Liberalization in Mexico*, edited by Riordan Riott. Boulder: Lynne Rienner, 1993: 65–78.

Conaghan, Catherine. "Capitalists, Technocrats, and Politicians: Economic Policy-Making and Democracy in the Central Andes," in *Issues in Democratic Consolidation*, edited by Scott Mainwaring. Notre Dame: University of Notre Dame Press, 1992: 199–243.

Conaghan, Catherine. "'Loose Parties,' 'Floating' Politicians, and Institutional Stress: Presidentialism in Ecuador, 1979–1988," in *The Failure of Presidential Democracy*, edited by Juan Linz and Arturo Valenzuela. Baltimore: The Johns Hopkins University Press, 1994: 256–278.

Conaghan, Catherine. "Polls, Political Discourse, and the Public Sphere: The Spin on Peru's Fuji-golpe," in *Latin America in Comparative Perspective*, edited by Peter H. Smith. Boulder: Westview, 1995: 227–255.

Converse, Philip. "The Nature of Belief Systems in Mass Publics", in *Ideology and Discontent*, edited by David Apter. New York: Free Press, 1964: 206–261.

Converse, Philip. "Public Opinion and Voting Behavior," in *Handbook of Political Science*, edited by Fred Greenstein and Nelson Polsby. San Francisco: Addison-Wesley, 1975: 77–98.

Coppedge, Michael. "Venezuela: Democratic despite Presidentialism," in *The Failure of Presidential Democracy*, edited by Juan Linz and Arturo Valenzuela. Baltimore: The Johns Hopkins University Press, 1994: 322–347.

Crewe, Ivor. "Voters, Parties and Leaders Thirty Years on: Western Electoral Studies and the New Democracies of Eastern Europe," in *Developing Democracy. Comparative Research in Honour of J.F.P. Blondel*, edited by Ian Budge and David McKay. London: Sage, 1994: 56–78.

Dahl, Robert. *Polyarchy.* New Haven: Yale University Press, 1971.

Dalton, Russell. *Citizen Politics in Western Democracies*. New York: Chatham House, 1988.

Dalton, Russell, and Martin Wattenberg "The Not So Simple Act of Voting," in *The State of the Discipline II*, edited by Ada Finifter. Chicago: APSA, 1993: 193–218.

Davis, Charles, and John Speer. "The Psychological Basis of Regime Support among Mexican and Venezuelan Workers: Insttumental or Expressive?". *Comparative Political Studies*, 24, no.3 (October, 1991): 319–343.

Dealy, Glen. *The Latin Americans.* Boulder: Westview, 1991.

Dealy, Glen. "The Tradition of Monistic Democracy in Latin America," in *Politics and Social Change in Latin America: Still a Distinct Tradition?*, edited by Howard Wiarda. Boulder: Westview Press, 1974: 40–69.

Diamond, Larry, Juan Linz, and Seymour M. Lipset, eds. *Democracy in Developing Countries: Latin America.* Boulder: Rienner, 1989.

Dietz, Henry. "Electoral Politics in Peru, 1978–1986." *Journal of Interamerican Studies and World Affairs*, 41, no.2 (1987): 139–163.

Dix, Robert. "Incumbency and Electoral Turnover in Latin America," *Journal of Interamerican Studies and World Affairs*, 26, no.4 (1984): 435–448.

Dix, Robert. "Cleavage Structure and Party Systems in Latin America," *Comparative Politics*, 22, no. 3 (1989): 23–37.

Dix, Robert. "Democratization and the Institutionalization of Latin American Political Parties," *Comparative Political Studies*, 24, no.1 (1992): 488–511.

Domínguez, Jorge, and James McCann. "Whither the PRI? Explaining Voter Defection in the 1988 Mexican Presidential Election," *Electoral Studies,* 11, no.3 (1992): 207–222.

Domínguez, Jorge, and James McCann. "Shaping Mexico's Electoral Arena: The Construction of Partisan Cleavages in the 1988 and 1991 National Elections." *American Political Science Review*, 89, no.1 (1995): 34–48.

Downs, Anthony. *An Economic Theory of Democracy.* New York: Harper & Row, 1957.

Drake, Paul, and Eduardo Silva. *Elections and Democratization in Latin America, 1980–1985.* San Diego: CILAS-CUSMS, UCSD, 1986.

Dugan, William, and Henry Dietz. "Urban Social Classes and Voting Behavior in Lima," Paper presented at the Latin American Studies Association Congress, Washington, DC., (September 1995).

Echegaray, Fabián. "¿Adiós al bipartidismo imperfecto? Elecciones y partidos provinciales en la Argentina," *Nueva Sociedad*, n° 124 (March-April 1993): 46–52.

Edwards, Sebastian. *Crisis and Reform in Latin America. From Despair to Hope.* New York: Oxford University Press, 1995.

Edwards III, George et al. "Explaining Presidential Approval: The Significance of Issue Salience," *American Journal of Political Science*, 39, no.1 (1995): 108–134.

Eisenstadt, Sergei, and Luis Roniger. *Patrons, Clients, and Friends*. Cambridge: Cambridge University Press, 1984.

Enelow, James, and Melvin Hinich. "Ideology, Issues and the Spatial Theory of Elections," *American Political Science Review*, 76, no.3 (1982): 493–501.

Eulau, Heinz and Michael Lewis-Beck, eds. *Economic Conditions and Electoral Outcomes. The United States and Western Europe.* New York: Agathon, 1985.

Fackle, Tim, and Tse-min Lin. "Political Corruption and Presidential Elections, 1929–1992," *Journal of Politics*, 57, no.4 (1995): 971–993.

Fiorina, Morris. *Retrospective Voting in American National Elections.* New Haven: Yale University Press, 1981.

Flisfisch, Angel. "El Surgimiento de una Nueva Ideología Democrática," *Crítica&Utopía*, 8, 1983: 13–35.

Franklin, Mark. "The Decline of Cleavage Politics," in *Electoral Change. Responses to Evolving Social and Attitudinal Structures in Western Countries*, edited by Mark N. Franklin, Thomas T. Mackie, Henry Valen, with Clive Bean. Cambridge: Cambridge University Press, 1992: 383–405.

Gamarra, Eduardo. "Crafting Political Support for Stabilization: Political Pacts and the New Economic Policy in Bolivia," in *Democracy, Markets, and Structural Reform in Latin America*, edited by William C. Smith, Carlos H. Acuña, and Eduardo A. Gamarra. New Brunswick: North-South Center/Transaction 1994: 31–56.

Gamarra, Eduardo. "Market-Oriented Reforms and Democratization in Latin America: Challenges of the 1990s," in *Latin American Political Economy in the Age of Neoliberal Reform*, edited by William C. Smith, Carlos H. Acuña, and Eduardo A. Gamarra. New Brunswick: North-South Center/Transaction, 1994: 1–16.

Gastil, Raymond, coord. *Freedom in the World. The Annual Survey of Political Rights and Civil Liberties.* Westport: Greenwood Press, 1978–1991.

Geddes, Barbara. "The Politics of Economic Liberalization," *Latin American Research Review*, 30, no.2 (1995): 195–214.

Ginsberg, Benjamin, and Alan Stone. *Do Elections Matter?* New York: Sharpe, 1991.

Gonzalez, Luis E. *Political Structures and Democracy in Uruguay*. Notre Dame: Helen Kellogg Institute for International Studies/University of Notre Dame Press, 1992

Guilhon, José de Albuquerque. "Identidade, Oposição e Pragmatismo: Uma Teoria Política do Voto," *Lua Nova*, 26, 1992: 53–79.

Grofman, Bernard. "Models of Voting," in *Research in Micropolitics*, 1, edited by Bernard Grofman. Greenwich: JAI Press. 1987: 2–24.

Harrison, Lawrence. *Underdevelopment is a State of Mind. The Latin American Case*. Lanham: Madison Books, 1985.

Hausmann, Ricardo, and Michael Gavin. "Overcoming Volatility in Latin America," *Development Policy*, 34, (September, 1995): 1–3.

Herman, Edward and Frank Brodhead, *Demonstration Elections. U.S. Staged Elections in the Dominican Republic, Vietnam, and El Salvador*, Cambridge: South End Press, 1984.

Hibbs, Douglas. *The American Political Economy. Macroeconomics and Electoral Politics*. Cambridge: Harvard University Press, 1987.

Hirschman, Albert O. "The Political Economy of Latin American Development: Seven Exercises in Retrospection," *Latin American Research Review*, 22, no. 3, 1987: 7–36.

Huntington, Samuel. *Political Order in Changing Societies*. New Haven: Yale University Press, 1968.

IEERAL, *Estudios*. Fundación Mediterránea, 15, no. 61. 1995.

Inglehart, Ronald. *Culture Shift in Advanced Industrial Society*. Princeton: Princeton University Press, 1990.

Inter-American Development Bank. *Economic and Social Progress in Latin America*. Washington, DC: IADB, 1982–1995.

Inter-American Dialogue. *Annual Report*. Washington, DC: Inter-American Dialogue, 1989.

Jackson, John. "Issues, Party Choices, and Presidential Votes," *American Journal of Political Science*, 19, no.2 (1975): 161–186.

Jacobson, Gary, and Samuel Kernell. *Strategy and Choice in Congressional Elections*. New Haven: Yale University Press, 1981.

Joslyn, Richard. "Candidate Appeals and the Meaning of Elections," in *Do Elections Matter?*, edited by Benjamin Ginsberg and Alan Stone. New York: Sharpe, 1991: 9–31.

Karatnycky, Adrian, coord. *Freedom in the World: The Annual Survey of Political Rights and Civil Liberties.* London: Freedom House, 1992–1995.

Keech, William R. *Economic Politics: The Costs of Democracy*. New York: Cambridge University Press, 1995.

Keesing's Record of World Events. London: Longman, 1992–1994.

Kelley, Jonathan. "Public Images of Foreign and Domestic Political Leaders," *International Social Science Journal*, 146, 1995: 601–614.

Key, V.O. *The Responsible Electorate.* New York: Belnap Press, 1966.

Kieweit, Roderick. *Macroeconomics and Micropolitics.* Chicago: University of Chicago Press, 1983.

Kinder, Donald, and Roderick Kiewiet. "Sociotropic Politics," *British Journal of Political Science*, 11,no.2 (1981): 129–161.

King, Anthony. "What Do Elections Decide?," in *Democracy at the Polls*, edited by David Butler, Howard Penniman, and Austin Ranner, Washington,DC: American Enterprise Institute. 1981: 293–323.

Kirschheimer, Otto. "The Transformation of the Western European Party Systems", in *Political Parties and Political Development*, edited by Joseph LaPalombara and Myron Weiner, Princeton: Princeton University Press, 1966: 177–200.

Kramer, Gerald. "Short-term Fluctuations in U.S. Voting Behavior, 1896–1964," *American Political Science Review,* 65, no.1 (1971): 131–143.

Kramer, Gerald. "The Ecological Fallacy Revisited: Aggregate vs. Individual-Level Findings on Election, and Sociotropic Voting," *American Political Science Review*, 77, no.1 (1983): 92–111.

Ladd, Everett Carl. "The Shifting Party Coalitions—From the 1930s to the 1970s," in *Party Coalitions in the 1980s*, edited by Seymour Martin Lipset, San Francisco: Institute for Contemporary Studies, 1981: 131–135.

Lamounier, Bolívar. "O Voto em São Paulo, 1970–1978," in *Voto de Desconfiança: Eleições e Mudança Política no Brasil, 1970–1978*, organized by Bolívar Lamounier. São Paulo: Vozes-Cebrap, 1980: 15–80.

LASA. *The 1990 Nicaragua Election: Observation Commission Report.* Pittsburgh: Latin American Studies Association, 1990.

LASA. *The 1995 Electoral Process in Peru.* Miami: Latin American Studies Association/North-South Center, University of Miami, 1995.

Lau, Robert, and David O. Sears, eds. *Political Cognition.* Hillsdale: Lawrence Erlbaum Associates, 1986.

Lewis-Beck, Michael. *Economics and Elections: The Major Western Democracies.* Ann Arbor: University of Michigan Press, 1988.

Lewis-Beck, Michael, and Tom Rice. *Forecasting Elections.* Washington, D.C.: CQ Press, 1992.

LoVuolo, Ruben. "The Welfare State in Contemporary Argentina," *Kellogg Institute Working Paper-Democracy and Social Policy Series*, 2 (1995).

Linz, Juan J. "Crisis, Breakdown, and Reequilibration," in *The Breakdown of Democratic Regimes*, edited by Juan Linz and Alfred Stepan. Baltimore: The Johns Hopkins University Press, 1978: 3–111.

Linz, Juan J. "Presidential or Parliamentary Democracy: Does it Make a Difference?," in *The Failure of Presidential Democracy*, edited by Juan Linz and Arturo Valenzuela. Baltimore: The Johns Hopkins University Press, 1994: 230–247.

Lipset, Seymour, and Stein Rokkan. "Cleavages Structures, Party Systems, and Voter Alignments: An Introduction," in *Party Systems and Voter Alignments*, edited by Seymour M. Lipset and Stein Rokkan. New York: The Free Press, 1967: 3–67.

Lupia, Arthur. "Shortcuts Versus Encyclopedias: Information and Voting Behavior in California Insurance Reform Elections." *American Political Science Review*, 88, no.1 (1994):63–76.

Luskin, Robert C. "Explaining Political Sophistication," *Political Behavior*, 12, no. 4, 1990: 331–361

MacKuen, Michael. "Political Drama, Economic Conditions, and the Dynamics of Presidential Popularity," *American Journal of Political Science*, 27, no. (1983): 165–192.

MacKuen, Michael, Robert Erickson, and James Stimson. "Peasants or Bankers? The American Electorate and the U.S. Economy," *American Political Science Review*, 86, no. 3, 1992: 598–611.

Mainwaring, Scott, and Eduardo Viola. "New Social Movements, Political Culture and Democracy: Brazil and Argentina in the 1980s," *Telos*, 61, no.1 (Fall 1984): 17–54.

Mainwaring, Scott. "Democracy in Brazil and the Southern Cone: Achievements and Problems," *Journal of Interamerican Studies and World Affairs*, 37, no.1 (1995): 113–179.

Mainwaring, Scott, and Timothy Scully. *Building Democratic Institutions: Party Systems in Latin America.* Standford: Standford University Press, 1995.

Mancha Navarro, Tomás. *Economía y Votos en España.* Madrid: Instituto de Estudios Económicos, 1995.

Markus, Gregory. "The Impact of Personal and National Economic Conditons on the Presidential Vote: A Pooled Cross-Sectional Analysis," *American Journal of Political Science*, 32, no. 1, (1988): 137–154.

Markus, Gregory, and Philip Converse. "A Dynamic Simultaneous Equation Model of Electoral Choice," *American Political Studies Review*, 73, no.4 (1979): 1055–1070.

Martz, John. "Problems of Conceptualization and Comparability in Latin America," in *Comparing Nations*, edited by Mattei Dogan and Ali Kazancigil. Oxford: Blackwell, 1994: 239–259.

McDonald, Ronald and Mark Ruhl. *Party Politics and Elections in Latin America.* Boulder: Westview, 1989.

Méndez, Gustavo. "Actitudes y Comportamiento de la Opinión Pública," in *Sistema Político y Campañas Electorales* (Caracas: Conciencia 21, 1983): 2–19.

Meneguello, Rachel. "Informação e Esfera Pública," *Opinião Pública*, 1, 1 (1993): 58–61.

Meneguello, Rachel. "Electoral Behaviour in Brazil: The 1994 Presidential Elections." *International Social Science Journal*, 47, no.4 (1995): 627–639.

Miller, Arthur, and Ola Listhaug. "Economic Effects on the Vote in Norway," in *Economic Conditions and Electoral Outcomes: The United States and Western Europe*, edited by Helmut Eulau and Michael Lewis-Beck. New York: Agathon, 1985: 125–143.

Miller, William. "Studying How the Economy Affects Attitudes and Behavior: Problems and Prospects," in *Economic Decline and Political Change*, edited by Harold Clarke, Marianne Stewart, and Gary Zuk, eds. Pittsburgh: University of Pittsburgh Press, 1989: 5–23.

Molinar Horcasitas, Juan and Jeffrey A. Weldon. "Electoral Determinants and Consequences of National Solidarity," in *Transforming State-Society Relations in Mexico: The National Solidarity Strategy*, edited by Wayne A. Cornelius, Ann L. Craig, and Jonathan Fox. La Jolla: Center for U.S.-Mexican Studies, University of California, San Diego. 1994:123–142.

Mora y Araujo, Manuel. "The Nature of the Alfonsín Coalition," in *Elections and Democratization in Latin America, 1980–1985*, edited by Paul Drake and Eduardo Silva (San Diego: CILAS-CUSMS, UCSD, 1986): 109–130.

Moreno, Alejandro, and Keith Yanner. "Predictors of Voter Preferences in Mexico's 1994 Presidential Election," Paper presented at the 1995 Latin American Studies Association, The Sheraton Washington (September 1995).

Morse, Richard. "Claims of Political Tradition," in *Politics and Social Change in Latin America: Still a Distinct Tradition*, edited by Howard Wiarda, Boulder: Westview Press. 1992: 91–119.

Nannestadt, Peter, and Martin Paldam. "The VP-Function: A Survey of the Literature on Vote and Popularity Functions after 25 Years," *Public Choice*, 79, no.3–4 (1994): 213–245.

Nelson, Joan, ed. *Economic Crisis and Policy Choice. The Politics of Adjustment in the Thirld World.* Princeton: Princeton University Press, 1990.

Neuman, W. Russell. *The Paradox of Mass Politics: Knowledge and Opinion in the American Electorate.* Cambridge: Harvard University Press, 1986.

Nohlen, Dieter ed. *Enciclopedia Electoral Latinoamericana y del Caribe.* San José: Instituto Interamericano de Derechos Humanos, 1993.

Norpoth, Helmut, Michael S. Lewis-Beck and Jean D. Lafay, eds. *Economics and Politics: The Calculus of Support.* Ann Arbor: University of Michigan Press, 1991.

O'Donnell, Guillermo, Philippe Schmitter, and Lawrence Whitehead, eds. *Transition from Authoritarian Rule.* Baltimore: John Hopkins University Press, 1986.

O'Donnell, Guillermo. "Delegative Democracy," *Kellogg Institute Working Paper*, 172 (March 1992).

Ozbudun, Ergun, "Turkey, " in *Competitive Elections in Developing Countries,* edited by Myron Weiner and Ergun Ozbudun, Durham: Duke University, 1987: 328–365.

Pacek, Alexander, and Benjamin Radcliff. "The Political Economy of Competitive Elections in the Developing World," *American Journal of Political Science*, 39, no.3 (1995): 745–759.

Page, Benjamin I., and Calvin C. Jones. "Reciprocal Effects of Policy Preferences, Party Loyalties and the Vote," *American Political Science Review* 73, no.4 (1979): 1071–89.

Paldam, Martin. "How Robust is the Vote Function?" in *Economics and Politics: The Calculus of Support*, edited by Helmut Norpoth, Michael S. Lewis-Beck and Jean D. Lafay. Ann Arbor: University of Michigan Press, 1991: 9–31.

Panzer, John, and Ricardo Paredes. "The Role of Economic Issues in Elections. The Case of 1988 Chilean Plebiscite". *Public Choice* 71, no.1–2 (1991): 51–59.

Parodi, Jorge, and Walter Twanama. "Los Pobladores, la Ciudad y la Política: Un Estudio de Actitudes," in *Los Pobres, la Ciudad y la Política*, edited by Jorge Parodi. Lima: CEDYS, 1993: 19–90.

Patterson, Thomas E. *The Mass Media Election: How Americans Choose Their President.* New York: Praeger, 1984.

Payne, Douglas. "Latin America: Ballots, Neo-Strongmen, Narcos and Impunity," in *Freedom in the World: The Annual Survey of Political Rights and Civil Liberties*, coord. by Adrian Karatnycky. London: Freedom House, 1995: 41–55.

Peffley, Mark. "The Voter as Juror: Attributing Responsibility for Economic Conditions," in *Economic Conditions and Electoral Outcomes. The United States and Western Europe*, edited by Eulau Heinz and Michael Lewis-Beck. New York: Agathon, 1985: 275–294.

Petras, James, and Morris Morley. *Latin America in the Time of Cholera: Electoral Politics, Market Economics, and Permanent Crisis.* New York: Routledge, 1992.

Pinto, Celia R.J. "Tendências do Discurso Brasileiro Atual: os Limites dos Discursos das Soluções Milagrosas," in *Cultura Política e Democracia*, organized by Marcello Baquero. Porto Alegre: Editora da Universidade, 1994: 95–118.

Popkin, Samuel. *The Reasoning Voter: Communication and Persuasion in Presidential Campaigns.* Chicago: University of Chicago Press, 1991.

Portantiero, Juan Carlos. "Democracia y la Creación de Rutinas Institucionales," Presentation at the Third World Foundation International Congress, Buenos Aires (May 1985).

Powell, G. Bingham, and Guy Whitten. "A Cross-National Analysis of Economic Voting: Taking Account of the Political Context," *American Journal of Political Science*, 37, no.2 (1993): 394–414.

Quattrone, George, and Amos Tversky. "Contrasting Rational and Psychological Analyses of Political Choice," *American Political Science Review*, 82, no.3 (1988): 719–736.

Rakowski, Cathy, ed. *Contrapunto: The Informal Sector Debate in Latin America*. Albany: SUNY Press, 1994.

Réis, Fábio W. "Identidade, Política e a Teoria da Escolha Racional," *Revista Brasileira de Ciências Sociais*, 3, no. 6: 26–38.

Remmer, Karen. "The Political Impact of Economic Crisis in Latin America in the 1980s." *American Political Science Review*, 85, no.3 (1991): 777–800.

RePass, David. "Issue Saliency and Party Choice," *American Political Science Review* 65, no.2 (1971): 389–400.

Rial, Juan. "The Uruguayan Elections of 1984: A Triumph of the Center," in *Elections and Democratization in Latin America, 1980–1985*, edited by Paul Drake and Eduardo Silva. San Diego: CILAS-CUSMS, UCSD, 1986) 261–283.

Rius, Andrés. "El Gobierno, la Economía, y el Hombre de la Calle," *Suma*, 7 (1992): 17–35.

Rose, Richard, and Thomas Mackie. "Incumbency in Government: Asset or Liability?," in *Western European Party Systems: Continuity and Change*, edited by Hans Daalder and Peter Mair. Beverly Hills: Sage, 1983: 115–137.

Rosenberg, Mark B. "Honduras.", *Latin America and Caribbean Contemporary Record*, VI, 1986–1987: 317–340.

Rosenberg, Mark B. "Can Democracy Survive the Democrats? From Transition to Consolidation in Honduras." in *Elections and Democracy in Central America*, edited by John A. Booth and Mitchell A. Seligson. Chapel Hill: The University of North Carolina Press, 1989: 40–59.

Rosenberg, Shawn, with Patrick McCafferty. "The Image and the Vote. Manipulating Voters' Preferences," *Public Opinion Quarterly*, 51, no.1 (Spring 1987): 31–47.

Schatan, Jacobo, Dieter Paas, and Alvaro Orsatti, comp. *El Sector informal en America Latina: una Seleccion de Perspectivas Analiticas*. Mexico, D.F: Centro de Investigacion y Docencia Economica/Fundación Friedrich Naumann, 1991.

Scully, Timothy, and J. Samuel Valenzuela. "From Democracy to Democracy: Continuities and Changes of Electoral Choices and the Party System in Chile," *Kellogg Institute Working Paper*, 199 (July 1993).

Sears, David. "Self-Interest vs. Symbolic Politics in Policy Attitudes and Presidential Voting," *American Political Science Review*, 74, no.3 (1981): 670–684.

Seligson, Mitchell. "Costa Rica and Jamaica," in *Competitive Elections in Developing Countries*, edited by Myron Weiner and Ergun Özbudun. Raleigh: Duke University Press, 1987: 147–198.

Seligson, Mitchell, and Miguel Gómez B. "Ordinary Elections in Extraordinary Times: The Political Economy of Voting in Costa Rica," in *Elections and Democracy in Central America*, edited by John Booth and Mitchell Seligson. Chapel Hill: The University of North Carolina Press, 1989: 158–184.

Seligson, Mitchell, and John Booth, eds. *Elections and Democracy in Central America. Revisited.* Chapel Hill: The University of North Carolina Press, 1995.

Sigelman, Lee. "Answering the 1,000,000—Person Question: the Measurement and Meaning of Presidential Popularity," *Research in Micropolitics*, 3, edited by Samuel Long. Greenwich: JAI Press, 1990: 209–226.

Simon, Herbert. *Models of Man: Social and Rational.* New York: Wiley, 1957.

Skidmore, Thomas, ed. *Television, Politics, and the Transition to Democracy in Latin America.* Washington, D.C.: Woodrow Wilson Center Press, 1993.

Smith, William, Carlos H. Acuña, and Eduardo A. Gamarra, eds. *Latin American Political Economy in the Age of Neoliberal Reform.* New Brunswick: Transaction, 1994.

Sniderman, Paul, James Glaser, and Robert Griffin, "Information and Electoral Choice," in *Information and Democratic Processes*, edited by John Ferejohn and James Kuklinski. Urbana: University of Illinois Press. 1990: 117–135.

Sniderman, Paul, Richard Brody, and Philliph Tetlock. *Reasoning and Choice. Explorations in Political Psychology.* Cambridge: Cambridge University Press, 1991.

Sniderman, Paul. "The New Look in Public Opinion Research," in *Political Science: The State of the Discipline II*, edited by Ada Finifter. Washington, D.C.: APSA, 1993: 263–297.

Stein, Ernesto, and Jorge Steb. "Political Stabilization Cycles in High Inflation Economies," *Development Policy*, 3 (September 1994): 9–10.

Stigler, Gerald. "General Economic Conditions and National Elections," *American Economic Review*, 63, no.2 (1973): 160–167.

Stimson, James. "Regression in Space and Time: A Statistical Essay," *American Journal of Political Science*, 29, no.4 (1985): 914–947.

Stokes, Susan. "Democracy and the Limits of Popular Sovereignty in South America," in *The Consolidation of Democracy in Latin America*, edited by Joseph Tulchin and Bernice Romero. Boulder: Lynne Rienner, 1995: 59–81.

Stokes, Susan ed. *Public Support for Market Reforms in New Democracies*. New York: Cambridge University Press, 2001.

The Economist Intelligence Unit. *Country Reports* (several countries). London: The Economist, 1987–1995.

Torre, Juan Carlos. "América Latina: El Gobierno de la Democracia en Tiempos Difíciles," *Instituto Di Tella Working Paper*, 13, 1993.

Torres, Arístides. "Fe y Desencanto Democrático en Venezuela," *Nueva Sociedad*, 77 (1985): 28–45.

Trindade, Hélgio, org. *América Latina: Eleições e Governabilidade Democrática.* Porto Alegre: UFRGS, 1991.

Tufte, Edward. *Political Control of the Economy.* Princeton: Princeton University Press, 1978.

Urani, André. "Crescimento e Geração de Emprego e Renda no Brasil," *Lua Nova*, 35 (1995): 5–38.

Valenzuela, Arturo and Pamela Constable. *A Nation of Enemies: Chile Under Pinochet*. New York: Norton, 1991.

Vilas, Carlos. "Entre la Democracia y el Neoliberalismo: Los Caudillos Electorales de la Postmodernidad," in *El Fin de Siglo y los Partidos Políticos en América Latina*, compiled by Silvia Dtrenit and Leonardo Valdés, México D.F.: Instituto Mora, 1995: 323–340.

Von Mettenheim, Kurt. *The Brazilian Voter. Mass Politics in Democratic Transition, 1974–1986*. Pittsburgh: University of Pittsburgh Press, 1995.

Weatherford, Stephen. "Economic Voting and the "Symbolic Politics" Argument: A Reinterpretation and Synthesis," *American Political Science Review*, 77, no.1 (1983): 158–174.

Weffort, Francisco. "Incertezas da Transição na América Latina," in *Dilemas da Consolidação da Democracia,* edited by José G. Albuquerque and José Moisés, Rio de Janeiro: Paz e Terra, 1989.

Weffort, Francisco. "America Astray," *Kellogg Institute Working Paper*, 162, (July 1991).

Wiarda, Howard. "Social Change, Political Development, and the Latin American Tradition" in *Politics and Social Change in Latin America: Still a Distinct Tradition?*, edited by Howard Wiarda. Boulder: Westview Press, 1992: 195–218.

World Development Report 1993. *Investing in Health*. Washington,DC: World Bank, 1993

Zermeño, Sergio. "El Regreso del Líder, Neoliberalismo y Desorden". *Revista Mexicana de Sociología*, 4 (1989): 115–150.

Index

DATE DUE
